Insiders *and*
Outsiders
in Russian Cinema

Insiders *and*
Outsiders
in Russian Cinema

Edited by Stephen M. Norris
and Zara M. Torlone

INDIANA UNIVERSITY PRESS

Bloomington and Indianapolis

In memory of Josephine Woll, admired colleague and friend

This book is a publication of

Indiana University Press
601 North Morton Street
Bloomington, IN 47404-3797 USA

http://iupress.indiana.edu

Telephone orders	800-842-6796
Fax orders	812-855-7931
Orders by e-mail	iuporder@indiana.edu

Library of Congress Cataloging-in-Publication Data

Insiders and outsiders in Russian cinema / edited by Stephen M. Norris
and Zara M. Torlone.
    p.   cm.
  Includes index.
  ISBN 978-0-253-35145-6 (cloth) — ISBN 978-0-253-21982-4 (pbk.)
  1. Aliens in motion pictures. 2. Outsiders in motion pictures. 3. Motion pictures—Russia (Federation)—History. I. Norris, Stephen M.
II. Torlone, Zara M.
  PN1993.5.R9I59 2008
  791.430947–dc22
                                                        2007045910

1 2 3 4 5 13 12 11 10 09 08

Contents

Acknowledgments

The editors gratefully acknowledge the following people for their help with this volume's publication: Karen Dawisha, Director of the Havighurst Center for Russian and Post-Soviet Studies at Miami University; Anne Clemmer, Brian Herrmann, and Daniel Pyle at Indiana University Press; Karen Kodner, our copy editor; and Melissa Cox Norris, who designed the original version of the cover.

Introduction

Insiders and Outsiders in Russian Cinema
Stephen M. Norris

At the 26th Moscow International Film Festival in 2004, Dmitrii Meskhiev's World War II drama *Our Own* (*Svoi*) captured the grand prize. The film explores one of the central issues of wartime—the way in which populations are divided into "ours" and "theirs." Meskhiev does not settle for simple definitions of these terms. He sets his film in a town occupied by the Nazis, a place where the local population must choose between resistance and collaboration, passivity or action, life and death. These choices force the characters in the film to confront the issue of who exactly is "our own." In the case of the village headman (played by Bogdan Stupka) this choice divides his family.

Svoi opens with a Nazi attack on an unnamed Red Army post. Two of the main characters, one a Russian NKVD officer (Sergei Garmash), the other a Jewish commissar (Konstantin Khabenskii), escape the attack by changing out of their uniforms and into peasant clothes. They are captured by the Germans and forced to march in a prisoner column. Because of their change of clothes they are spared the fate of fellow NKVD members and Jews in the USSR, the specific targets of the Nazi war of extermination launched in the east. Clothing in this instance becomes a means by which Soviet citizens can lay claim to different identities, switching not just garments but meanings of "us" and "them." In the case of the two protagonists, these boundaries are crossed in two senses. For those living under occupation, they have become more like Russian villagers and less like Soviet oppressors; while in the eyes of the occupiers they have become less "Jewish" and more "Slavic."

The two fall in with a fellow survivor of the attack, a sniper named Mit'ka (Mikhail Evlanov). As they march in a prisoner column, the young soldier lets them know that his village is nearby. When the column turns a bend in the road, the three escape. Once they reach the village, they meet

Mit'ka's father, the headman, and learn that he spent years in the Gulag after being branded a kulak. Mit'ka, now an escapee, threatens to disrupt the delicate balance that his father had achieved by working with the Nazis and local collaborators in an effort to protect "his" village and his two daughters, both of whom have husbands fighting in the Red Army. The headman quickly ascertains the true identities of his son's comrades, and must decide how to proceed.

The tension that the film depicts revolves around the headman and his choices—who, ultimately, is *svoi*? His son, whose escape leads the Nazi occupiers to ratchet up searches in the village? His daughters, whose husbands' actions also threaten to destroy the peace? His fellow villagers, including Mit'ka's girlfriend Katia (Anna Mikhalkov), who have also learned how to survive under Nazi occupation? The two escapees and Red Army members, who represent the system that sent him to the camps? Or his occupiers, some of whom are local people also upset with Soviet power? Meskhiev's film blurs the lines between "us" and "them," between outsiders and insiders, categories that Soviet culture attempted to define clearly. Moreover, none of the characters represent an officially approved "us" in the Stalin era: POWs, kulaks, and anti-Soviet collaborators are not part of the ideal Soviet society.

Svoi tackles issues that are covered in this volume's essays: the title of the film alone, combined with the decisions characters must make, plays with the idea of who belongs and who does not. The contributions that follow place concepts of "ours" and "theirs," of outsiders and insiders, at the center of Soviet and Russian film history. Scholars of Russian film have largely written about cinema from three perspectives: works that focus on a given era (usually stressing how films relate to politics),[1] monographs that explore a particular director (often critically acclaimed ones such as Sergei Eisenstein or Andrei Tarkovskii, but even more commercially successful ones like Nikita Mikhalkov),[2] or works that focus on genres within Russian cinema.[3] The essays that follow instead approach Russian film from a different angle, one that examines how films and filmmakers over the course of the twentieth century attempted to identify what it meant to be "Soviet" and what it meant to be "Russian."[4] The contributions focus upon two crucial periods in Russian history, two eras where questions of outsiders, others, and identities have been at their most fluid.[5]

Julian Graffy examines early Soviet films, when identifying a sense of "Sovietness" was paramount both to filmmakers and Soviet officials. Film proved to be an important medium through which Soviet citizens could learn about who belonged and who did not. Early Soviet films and their directors offered images of foreign outsiders who could become insiders through acceptance of the Soviet system. Graffy argues in his essay that the process of defining who is "ours" and who is "theirs" has long played an important role in Russian cinema. He explores the ideological role that foreign characters played in early Soviet cinema. In particular, Graffy analyzes how Soviet films established the basis for who could be seen as "ours" in the USSR. Graffy's focus on foreigners and how foreign characters "achieved consciousness" by visiting the Soviet Union reveals that the attempt to clarify who was an outsider and who was not formed a central aspect of Soviet films.

Yuri Tsivian furthers this discussion of foreignness in early Soviet culture by focusing on a little-studied aspect of Russian film cultures: the reediting of films for foreign consumption and for domestic viewing. Soviet authorities in the 1920s, fearful of the influence foreign cinema might have upon domestic audiences, employed film reeditors to make foreign films more ideologically acceptable (and thus make "their cinema" acceptable for "us"). At the same time, the editors themselves, in the words of Sergei Eisenstein (one of the re-editors), played a "wise and wicked game" in their jobs, constantly shifting boundaries between foreign and Soviet, "theirs" and "ours." Ultimately, the game of identifying selves in film, as Tsivian argues, profoundly influenced the development of early Soviet cinema and how identities could be constructed.

Clothing also can play an important ideological function in articulating concepts such as otherness. The NKVD officer and Jewish commissar in *Svoi* shed their clothing in an attempt to change their identities, an act that has roots in Stalinist cinema. Emma Widdis argues that "dress is a sign of belonging" and demonstrates what the two protagonists of *Svoi* knew about Stalinist Russia—that clothing could be an important symbol of identifying "us" and "them." Widdis focuses on the films of Aleksandr Medvedkin, Boris Barnet, Konstantin Iudin, and other early Soviet directors who conveyed a sense of "dressing the part" to help define Sovietness.

Josephine Woll returns to the use of foreigners in Stalinist cinema in her essay "Under the Big Top." Woll focuses on one film—the beloved 1936 musical comedy *Circus*—and how it incorporated ideas of *svoi* (ours) and *chuzhoi* (theirs) into its plot about an American circus performer who finds happiness in Stalin's Russia. Woll argues that films like *Circus* played a vital role in allowing Soviet audiences in the 1930s to see who belonged to the "Soviet family" and who did not.

Joan Neuberger also tackles the use of foreigners in a single film, Sergei Eisenstein's *Ivan the Terrible*. The film contains as many foreign characters as Russian, and foreigners seem to be clearly marked as "drag queens, circus clowns, and slugs." As Neuberger writes, however, Eisenstein used foreign characters to blur the lines between binaries such as "us" and "them." Far from being outsiders, the foreigners in *Ivan the Terrible* (and Mary Dixon in *The Circus*) serve as a means to question stereotypes about outsiders and insiders.

As these essays make clear, Soviet cinema employed foreigners to articulate concepts such as *svoi* and *chuzhoi* to audiences. At the same time, the boundaries between these categories remained slippery ones on the big screen, for foreigners could become "ours" by accepting Soviet ideologies, while Soviet citizens could just as easily become "foreign" by wearing the wrong clothes. Soviet cinema may have attempted to identify "ours" and "theirs," but this binary identification proved to be an elusive one to define, much as it proved difficult to articulate in Soviet society as a whole. As Alexei Yurchak has effectively argued, the terms cannot be reduced to any simplistic definitions, and despite the efforts of Soviet directors to make these distinctions in their films, the definitions they provided never were simple ones.[6]

The time and place of Meskhiev's drama also provides an important tool for delving into the issues of national identity and of who belongs and who does not to a given nation—it is a war film. Wars and the culture they produce serve as one of the most powerful means of articulating amorphous concepts such as "nationhood" and "otherness."[7] The war against Nazi Germany in particular has served as a defining myth of Soviet and even post-Soviet life. Known as the Great Patriotic War, the victory over Nazi Germany became a "holy war" of sorts, and postwar culture glorified the Russian people, their leaders, and their role in repelling the invaders.[8] The subtitle of Meskhiev's film offers a clue into the way in which the film plays with the existing myths about the war—*Holy War, Usual Story* (*Sviashchennaia voina, obychnaia istoriia*). The story told in *Svoi*, however, is far from the "usual" one about the war. While the Germans remain enemies, the film suggests that the "real" enemies are as likely to be "your own" people.

Both Soviet and post-Soviet films feature "enemies" as another means by which "us" and "them" can be articulated. Stalinist cinema, as Peter Kenez writes in his essay, used the category of "enemy" as a lesson for Soviet audiences, one that helped filmgoers picture outsiders. Kenez argues that Soviet films adapted to historical circumstances by focusing on internal enemies in the 1930s, external enemies during the war, and Cold War foes (both internal and external) during late Stalinism. The shifting ways in which "the enemy" could be depicted reinforced not only how adaptable this category could be but also how important it was to Soviet cinematic culture.

Post-Soviet Russia, Oleg Sulkin argues, has many parallels to the Stalinist era in the frequency that enemies appear on the screen. The collapse of the Soviet Union has led to a renewed attempt to define "Russianness" through numerous means, but once again film has provided a complex visual medium through which enemies can be identified and "us" and "them" can be articulated. From Chechens to New Russians, as Sulkin argues, post-Soviet cinema has again provided enemies that can be both internal and external.

The NKVD officer and Jewish commissar, examples of both internal and external enemies in *Svoi*, believe that they have to protect their new identities as villagers at all costs. When a fellow captive and later a villager learn that they are no longer "ours," the two protagonists kill them. This sort of vigilante justice and whether or not it is justified is a central component, as Tony Anemone argues, of the post-Soviet films directed by Aleksei Balabanov. Perhaps no director working in Russia after 1991 has explored the issues of outsiders and insiders more than Balabanov. Through his extraordinarily popular *Brother* series, the 1998 cult hit *Of Freaks and Men*, and 2002's *The War*, Balabanov has consistently used outsiders and vigilante heroes as a means of redefining what it means to be "Russian" after the USSR. Much like the escapees in *Svoi*, Balabanov's heroes (particularly Danila from the *Brother* series) often resort to violence in an effort to preserve what they see as "ours."

Svoi appeared at a time when other Russian filmmakers had begun to reexamine World War II in their films. As Stephen Norris notes in his essay, 2002 proved to be a watershed year in how directors used both past and present wars to delve into issues of nationhood, outsiders and insiders, and mythmaking. Both Andrei Konchalovskii's *House of Fools*, which takes place in the Chechen Wars, and Aleksandr Rogozhkin's *The Cuckoo*, which is set in wartime Lapland, garnered a great deal of attention and prompted wide discussion when they appeared. Both directors used outsiders—inmates in an insane asylum and three castaways who have left World War II, respectively—as a means to test the boundaries between "us" and "them" that wars tend to create. *Svoi* represented one more film that tackles the links among war, identities, and otherness that the films of 2002 inspired.

As this survey, which stretches from early Soviet films about foreigners to Meskhiev's 2004 film about World War II, suggests, Russian cinema has consistently used outsiders to define who is *svoi* and *chuzhoi*. The sociologist and anthropologist John Jervis has argued that the very evolution of modernity has involved conscious strategies of exclusion. A modern sense of identity, as Jervis writes, rests on contrasts: in order to understand who we are, we also have to articulate who we are not. Yet Jervis also notes that the divisions between "us" and "them" are not as clear-cut as they are constructed to be. The development and evolution of a given culture involve what Jervis terms "transgressing the modern," or a blurring of the lines between "us" and "them."[9] Perhaps no cultural form has both represented modernity as well as delved into its exclusionary practices more than cinema. From their inception, films have defined, reinforced, and subverted ideas about national culture. Through their production and popular reception, they have also helped to define what should be considered part of the nation and what is outside of it. *Svoi* represents another attempt to test these boundaries, to transgress the modern conceptions of exclusion.

This process of exclusion, as the authors here all demonstrate, has been central to Russian cinematic history. Russian filmmakers tapped into longstanding cultural processes that defined "us" and "them." Iurii Lotman has famously argued that Russian culture before the eighteenth century revolved around binaries, a "system of collective memory and collective consciousness" that stressed polarities. According to Lotman, Russian medieval culture did not envisage intermediate neutral spheres—only categories such as "holy" and "sinful" or "Russia" versus the "West" mattered. Even Peter the Great, as Lotman argues, furthered this binary culture—Russia now had "old Russia" and "new Russia."[10] At the same time, Peter's changes fueled the search for a modern Russian identity, a task that both used binaries and created new ones. Over the course of the eighteenth century and particularly after Napoleon's invasion of Russia in 1812, Russians began to define themselves as different from "the West." To be "ours" meant not to be like "them," as countless novels, poems, songs, popular prints, and other sources stressed.[11] The introduction of film to Russia represented just one more medium through which binaries about what "Russianness" meant could be negotiated. As Julian Graffy notes in this volume, the very first Russian film, 1908's *Sten'ka Razin*, furthered existing notions about "Russia" as different from "the Orient."

Russian directors have primarily viewed their primary task as one of education, rather than just entertainment, evident even in *Sten'ka Razin*. After the 1917 Revolutions, Soviet culture again attempted to divide the world into binary categories, a process that continued to be articulated for the remainder of the Soviet Union's existence.[12] Soviet films visually depicted outsiders becoming insiders in an effort to define a sense of Sovietness while also providing visual characterizations of enemies. While the task of defining "us" and "them" has remained a central one in Russian cinematic history, defining Sovietness and Russianness has involved sifting through ideas of foreigners, outsiders and insiders, a blend of orientalist and occidentalist ideas, and historical memories of past binary constructions. All of these processes are taken up in the essays that follow.

At the same time, however, the contributors emphasize that the attempt to make clear distinctions between "us" and "them" remains a difficult process, one that Meskhiev explores so well in *Svoi*. Outsiders constantly become insiders, foreigners can be "us," and enemies always change. As a recent volume on Russian national identity articulates, imagining a nation such as "Russia" involves a process that requires constant negotiations, representations, and re-imaginings.[13] As a visual, multisensual medium, film has consistently played a vital role in depicting outsiders and insiders, one of the central components to the process of articulating nationhood. Mette Hjort and Scott Mackenzie have stated that "films do not simply represent or express the stable features of a national culture, but are themselves one of the loci of debates about a nation's governing principles, goals, heritage, and history."[14] The end of *Svoi* expresses these debates quite clearly. The village headman, after his son has killed the local police chief, turns to the NKVD officer and points his gun. The officer, thinking he will be killed, cries out "I'm one of yours, one of yours (*Ia zhe svoi, svoi*)." The headman answers: "no one is going to hurt you," then watches as the officer runs away. However, the headman tells his son to follow the NKVD man, imploring him "to go and defend the motherland." Despite his hatred for the regime (an antipathy that would have made the headman not one of "ours" in the Stalin era), the old man accepts that he does have a homeland and that it does represent something important for him. As his son and the NKVD officer run off, another boundary has been crossed, just as another idea of who can be seen as "ours" has been offered.

NOTES

1. See, for example, the works in the I. B. Tauris Russian Cinema Series, particularly Peter Kenez, *Cinema and Soviet Society from the Revolution to the Death of Stalin* (London: I. B. Tauris, 2001); and Josephine Woll, *Real Images: Soviet Cinema and the Thaw* (London: I. B. Tauris, 2000). Other important works and collections that take similar approaches include Jay Leyda, *Kino: A History of the Russian and Soviet Film* (London: Allen and Unwin, 1973); Denise Youngblood, *The Magic Mirror: Moviemaking in Russia, 1908–1918* (Madison: University of Wisconsin Press, 1999); Denise

Youngblood, *Movies for the Masses: Popular Cinema and Soviet Society in the 1920s* (Cambridge, U.K.: Cambridge University Press, 1992); Richard Taylor, *The Politics of the Soviet Cinema, 1917–1929* (Cambridge, U.K.: Cambridge University Press, 1979); V. I. Fomin, ed., *Kino i vlast: Sovetskoe kino, 1965–1985 gody* (Moscow: N.p., 1996); V. I. Fomin, *Kinematograf ottepeli. Dokumenty i svidetelstva* (Moscow: N.p., 1998); and Anna Lawton, *Kinoglasnost: Soviet Cinema in Our Time* (New York: Cambridge University Press, 1992).

2. Recent examples of this approach include David Bordwell, *The Cinema of Eisenstein* (Cambridge, Mass.: Harvard University Press, 1993); Vida Johnson and D. Petrie, *The Films of Andrei Tarkovskii: A Visual Fugue* (Bloomington: Indiana University Press, 1994); and David MacFadyen, *The Sad Comedy of El'dar Riazanov: An Introduction to Russia's Most Popular Filmmaker* (Montreal: McGill–Queen's University Press, 2003); and the three Kinofiles Filmmakers' Companions published by I. B. Tauris: Birgit Beumers, *Nikita Mikhalkov: Between Nostalgia and Nationalism* (London: I. B. Tauris, 2005); Emma Widdis, *Alexander Medvedkin* (London: I. B. Tauris, 2005); and Jane Taubman, *Kira Muratova* (London: I. B. Tauris, 2005).

3. David Gillespie, *Russian Cinema* (London: Longman, 2003) represents a recent example of this approach. In addition, I. B. Tauris has published short works on individual films, ranging chronologically from *The Battleship Potemkin* (1926) to *Burnt by the Sun* (1995).

4. An inspiration for this approach is Emma Widdis, *Visions of a New Land: Soviet Film from the Revolution to the Second World War* (New Haven, Conn.: Yale University Press, 2003). The collection edited by Birgit Beumers, *Russia on Reels: The Russian Idea in Post-Soviet Cinema* (London: I. B. Tauris, 1999), although focused only on one era, tackles how post-Soviet filmmakers have attempted to construct Russian nationhood in their films.

5. See Sheila Fitzpatrick, *Tear Off the Masks! Identity and Imposture in Twentieth-Century Russia* (Princeton, N.J.: Princeton University Press, 2005), for how Soviet identities and post-Soviet identities have been constructed. For more on the categories of "us" and "them" in Stalin-era Russia, see Sarah Davies, "'Us' Against 'Them': Social Identity in Soviet Russia, 1934–1941," *Russian Review* 56, no. 1 (January 1997): 70–89. Alexei Yurchak reveals how Soviet citizens continued to renegotiate the categories of *svoi* and *chuzhoi* in his recent work, *Everything Was Forever until It Was No More: The Last Soviet Generation* (Princeton, N.J.: Princeton University Press, 2006), particularly 102–25.

6. Yurchak, *Everything Was Forever until It Was No More*, 103.

7. Like Sonya Rose, I generally prefer the term "nationhood" to "national identity," although the two are similar. Rose, echoing Rogers Brubaker, argues that "nationhood" captures the idea that nations are "central and protean . . . categor[ies] of modern political and cultural thought, discourse, and practice." See Sonya Rose, *Which People's War? National Identity and Citizenship in Wartime Britain, 1939–1945* (Oxford: Oxford University Press, 2003), 7. It is a measure of how slippery these terms are that, while preferring the term "nationhood," Rose uses "national identity" in the title of her book. Alon Confino has noted "the failure of theory to encompass the malleability of nationhood," for no definition of the term "fully embraces its ambiguous and often contradictory meanings." Confino, *The Nation as a Local Metaphor: Württemberg, Imperial Germany, and National Memory, 1871–1918* (Chapel Hill: University of North Carolina Press, 1997), 3. Although it is outside of this study's parameters, the debate about

Russian national identity is a heated one. Many historians argue that Russian national identity did not exist before Stalin (David Brandenberger, *National Bolshevism: Stalinist Mass Culture and the Formation of a Modern Russian National Identity, 1931–1956* [Cambridge, Mass.: Harvard University Press, 2002]), that imperial identity subsumed national identity in the Russian case (Geoffrey Hosking, *Russia: People and Empire* [Cambridge, Mass.: Harvard University Press, 1997]), or that Russian national identity has always been weak or fragmented (Vera Tolz, *Russia: Inventing the Nation* [London: Edward Arnold, 2001]). By contrast, other historians argue that a Russian national identity developed from below or the side and separately from imperial identity. Simon Franklin and Emma Widdis state, "Much discussion of Russian identity is driven by the belief . . . that the question has an answer, that Russianness is a 'thing' to be located, described, and explained." Franklin and Widdis, by contrast, argue that "identity is not a 'thing' to be objectively described," but "a field of cultural discourse," while "Russian identity is and has been a topic of continual argument, of conflicting claims, competing images, contradictory criteria." Rather than resolve these contradictions, they advocate an approach that allows for an understanding of the "multiple cultural expressions and constructs" as the identity or identities. See Simon Franklin and Emma Widdis, eds., *National Identity in Russian Culture: An Introduction* (Cambridge, U.K.: Cambridge University Press, 2004). My own work follows this view and thus explains the usage of "national identity" and "nationhood" in this volume: Stephen M. Norris, *A War of Images: Russian Popular Prints, Wartime Culture, and National Identity, 1812–1945* (De Kalb, Ill.: Northern Illinois University, 2006).

8. For more on the war and its place in Soviet culture, see Amir Weiner, "In the Long Shadow of War: The Second World War and the Soviet and Post-Soviet World," *Diplomatic History* 25, no. 3 (Summer 2001): 443–56; and Geoffrey Hosking, "The Second World War and Russian National Consciousness," *Past and Present* 175, no. 1 (May 2002): 162–87.

9. John Jervis, *Transgressing the Modern: Explorations in the Western Experience of Otherness* (Oxford: Blackwell, 1999).

10. Iurii Lotman and Boris Uspenskii, "Binary Models in the Dynamics of Russian Culture (to the End of the Eighteenth Century)," in *The Semiotics of Russian Cultural History*, ed. Alexander D. Nakhimovsky and Alice Stone Nakhimovsky (Ithaca, N.Y.: Cornell University Press, 1985), 30–66.

11. See Hubertus Jahn, "'Us': Russians on Russianness," in Simon Franklin and Emma Widdis, eds., *National Identity in Russian Culture: An Introduction* (Cambridge, U.K.: Cambridge University Press, 2004), 53–73.

12. See, for example, the use of binaries in Soviet poster art explored in Victoria Bonnell, *Iconography of Power: Soviet Political Posters under Lenin and Stalin* (Berkeley: University of California Press, 1997); and how Cold War propaganda constructed a binary world in Richard Stites, "Heaven and Hell: Soviet Propaganda Constructs the World," in Gary Rawnsley, ed., *Cold War Propaganda in the 1950s* (New York: St. Martin's, 1999), 85–104.

13. Franklin and Widdis, *National Identity in Russian Culture*.

14. Mette Hjort and Scott Mackenzie, eds., *Cinema and Nation* (London: Routledge, 2000), 4.

Insiders *and*
Outsiders
in Russian Cinema

The Foreigner's Journey to Consciousness in Early Soviet Cinema

The Case of Protazanov's Tommi

Julian Graffy

Foreigners in Early Russian Film

The kind of "otherness" being examined in this essay is very straightforward—the films I shall examine have a foreign protagonist. It is a commonplace of the study of Russian history, politics, or culture to say that because of a widespread perception of Russian backwardness, Russians have always had a nervous desire to compare themselves and their culture with other countries, particularly those of the rest of Europe (which raises the question whether Russia is part of Europe or not) and the United States. The latter has provided a particular point of reference since both countries share an ambiguous attitude to Europe and both have the same vastness, large population, and huge economic potential based on natural resources. Thus Russia was imagined as a "New America" by the Symbolist poet Aleksandr Blok in his poem of that title of December 1913.[1]

Russian film has also always been eager to draw comparisons between Russian/Soviet life and the life and attitudes of those who live beyond its borders, and in this context we are able to draw upon a very large range of cinematic material consisting both of films set in Russia that feature foreign characters and of films set abroad, including adaptations of Western novels and plays. As Yuri Tsivian argues in his essay in this volume, the history of the carefully controlled importation of foreign films during the Soviet era also yields useful evidence. It both tells us how those responsible for running the Soviet film industry and specifically for the choice of films to import used this mechanism to construct an ideologically driven picture of Western life in the minds of Soviet viewers, and also how, perversely, those Soviet viewers managed to "read between the lines" and use this material to give themselves some sense of what life outside the Soviet Union was actually like.

Film came to Russia in 1896, only months after the Lumière Brothers' films were shown in Paris, but it was a decade before there was native Russian production of acted films. Since all these first films were foreign and most of the subjects and the characters in them were foreign, film itself was considered to be a "foreign" phenomenon. In this context it is not surprising that the first Russian producers wanted their studios to make films about Russian subjects and Russian history. What is conventionally called the first Russian film, Vladimir Romashkov's *Sten'ka Razin*, released on November 16, 1908, took as its subject the life of the Don Cossack who led a peasant revolt in 1670, capturing several towns along the Volga before he was defeated and taken to Moscow to be broken on the wheel.

Sten'ka has remained a central hero of the Russian popular imagination, so that it is appropriate that he should be the subject of the first Russian film. What is interesting, however, is that the film does not show him and his men revolting. Instead it shows their "forest revels," their epic drinking bouts, which evoke another key aspect of the Russian self-image. Sten'ka is also shown reveling with a captive Persian princess. Though they themselves are hardly model upstarts, the rebels blame the princess for diverting their leader from the true path, and plot against her. Thus the first foreigner to be depicted in a Russian film is constructed as the quintessential "perfidious jade" of European Orientalism. Race, gender, religion, dress, behavior, all mark her out as "Other," and her fate is sealed: in the film's final sequence she is thrown into the Volga. The mother of Russian rivers envelops the threat to Russian manhood.

Overall, however, the prerevolutionary industry's eyes remained firmly directed on Russian characters and Russian themes. Sometimes foreign works were taken as source material but reimagined in a Russian setting, a practice followed by Evgenii Bauer in his films *Grezy* (*Daydreams*, 1915), taken from the 1892 novel *Bruges la Morte* by the Belgian Symbolist writer, Georges Rodenbach, and *Zhizn' za zhizn'* (*A Life for a Life*, 1916), which is based on the hugely popular novel *Serge Panine* by Georges Ohnet. It is also perhaps instructive that in Bauer's *Silent Witnesses* (*Nemye svideteli*, 1914), the characters with foreign names, Ellen and Baron von Rehren, are represented as cynical and treacherous hedonists and adulterers.

Despite the introverted gaze of Russian directors, Western films continued to be widely shown in Russia throughout the silent era, both before and after the Revolution, and they remained extremely popular with audiences.[2] The influx of foreign films provided a stream of images of Western characters and Western life, and fostered cults of Western stars. The Russian industry had been thrown into chaos by the 1917 Revolution, and it did not reemerge on any scale until 1924. Contrary to its prerevolutionary practice, it immediately started giving its audiences pictures of foreigners, perhaps in conscious or unconscious contrast to the images provided by the repertoire of popular French, German, and American films. Specifically it provided a subset of films whose plots told the story of a visit by a foreigner to the USSR and examined his or her reaction to this experience. Indeed, the Soviet industry's representation of foreigners becomes centered on their reactions to the Soviet system.

Coming to Consciousness

The phenomenon identified by Katerina Clark as "coming to consciousness," widespread in the fiction and the films of the period, followed a model set by such pre–Socialist Realist works as Maxim Gorky's novel *Mother* (*Mat'*, 1907) and involved an encounter between a character who is well intentioned but not ideologically "conscious" and a mentor figure who can direct the character's energy in a politically conscious direction.[3] In the case of *Mother* the peasant heroine learns from the words and the behavior of her politically conscious son, Pavel, and his friends.

The model was widely used in film, for example in works about the collectivization of the Russian village, including Sergei Eisenstein's *The Old and the New* (*Staroe i novoe*, 1929), Aleksandr Dovzhenko's *Earth* (*Zemlia*, 1930), and Aleksandr Medvedkin's *Happiness* (*Schast'e*, 1935), but it is also present in the Civil War drama *Chapaev*, directed by the Vasil'ev "brothers" in 1934, in which the commissar, Furmanov, leads the commander, Chapaev, to a political understanding of the nature of the struggle he is involved in, and therefore to consciousness. Boris Shumiatskii, the head of the Soviet film industry, regarded this film as a model that Soviet cinema should follow.

Foreigners in Russian Film: Mr. West

In April 1924 Lev Kuleshov's *The Extraordinary Adventures of Mr. West in the Land of the Bolsheviks* (*Neobychainye prikliucheniia Mistera Vesta v strane bol'shevikov*) opened in the Soviet Union. The hero, Mr. West, whose very name announces the director's polemical intent, is the President of the New York YMCA, and is motivated to visit Moscow, as an intertitle tells us, by "Yankee curiosity." This film is very well known, and I do not intend to linger on it, but it is worth noting that both the character and his treatment in the film's plot set the model that later films would follow throughout the

Figure 1.1. The Foreigner with Potential: Mr. West.
From Lev Kuleshov, *The Extraordinary Adventures of Mr.*
West in the Land of the Bolsheviks (1924).

Soviet period. Mr. West's experience, and that of the foreigners who follow in his footsteps, of coming to accept the rightness of the Soviet system, is a particular subset of the coming to consciousness trope identified by Katerina Clark. In the films of this type the first stage is to identify the protagonist as a foreigner, and in Kuleshov's film this is done in a spectacularly obvious way, with Mr. West carrying a flag and wearing stars-and-stripes socks, but it is also crucial that the figure about to experience change is identified as a positive character, a character with potential—Mr. West is shown to be kind and well intentioned (see fig. 1.1).

Next, his reactions to Soviet reality are tested. Gradually he comes to consciousness and understanding, and learns a political and personal lesson, making a choice that marks his acceptance of the Soviet Bolshevik way of life. At the end of the film Mr. West sends his wife the following radio message: "Dear Madge: I send you greetings from Soviet Russia. Burn those New York magazines and hang a portrait of Lenin in the study. Long live the Bolsheviks! Yours, John."

So in *The Extraordinary Adventures of Mr. West in the Land of the Bolsheviks* the cinematic model of coming to understanding, acceptance, and consciousness has been established. In fact, arguments still rage about Kuleshov's representation of Mr. West, of the Bolsheviks, and of the underworld gang he gets involved with, for Mr. West is shown as gullible and naive, innocent and malleable. This is what makes him suitable "human material" and causes both the gang and the Bolsheviks to try to manipulate him. But Kuleshov's (almost certainly ambiguous) intentions are in a sense irrelevant here.[4] *Mr. West* has set a model for other filmmakers to follow.

Eight months after *Mr. West*, another misguided American appeared in a Soviet film, in the form of the rotund businessman, Oliver McBright, in Iurii Zheliabuzhskii's *The Cigarette Girl from Mossel'proma* (*Papirosnitsa ot Mossel'proma*), released in December 1924. Perhaps modeled on the caricatures of capitalists familiar to us from the cartoons of the revolutionary period and echoed in Sergei Eisenstein's film *Strike* (*Stachka*), which would open the following year, McBright is first seen teetering unsteadily down from his private plane on a mission to sell Russian women his ready-to-wear collection. Following in the footsteps of Mr. West, he packs his many heavy cases into a carriage, but they are far too bulky, and, of course, when the carriage drives off it loses a wheel. McBright has not come to Russia to learn, but to exploit the fallibility of Soviet women, and his scheme is not crowned with success.

Following the Model: Visitors from East and West

The model of the visiting outsider, from East or West, who comes to the Soviet Union, sees that it is good, and in most cases takes or sends the lesson back home, is widespread in the first years of the Soviet film industry. A political example of the genre, involving an encounter of a character from the East, is provided by Vsevolod Pudovkin's film *Storm over Asia* (*The Descendant of Chingiz Khan* [*Potomok Chingus Khana*]), released in November 1929. Set in the east of the Soviet Union during the Civil War, it tells the story of a Mongol trapper, Bair, who encounters a group of Red partisans. When the leader of the partisans dies from wounds he has received, he passes on a message to his group that they must be faithful to the legacy given to them by Moscow. This scene of ideological baton passing adds another dimension to the ritual of becoming Soviet, with stress laid on language and on a particular ideologically powerful word. When Bair is arrested and interrogated by officers of the British Intervention Forces, he proves that he has learned his lesson by his smiling acceptance of the

Figure 1.2. Bair Proves His Bolshevism.
From Vsevolod Pudovkin's *Storm over Asia* (1929).

epithets "Red" and "Partisan" and his warm reaction to the word "Moscow" (see fig. 1.2). This knowledge is powerful enough to save his life and to stop him succumbing to the blandishments of the British, and at the end of the film he leads a rebellion against their power.

Vsevolod Ivanov's Story "Armored Train 14-69"

Iakov Protazanov's 1931 film *Tommi* was based on an episode in Vsevolod Ivanov's 1921 story "Armored Train 14-69" (*Bronepoezd 14-69*), which appeared in the January–February 1922 issue of the journal *Krasnaia Nov'* and was published in book form later that year.[5] Ivanov later wrote a highly successful stage version and the story was reissued twenty-seven times before the fortieth anniversary of the revolution and translated into a number of languages. Ivanov recalls the writing of the story in his memoir "The History of My Books" (*Istoriia moikh knig*).[6] After arriving in Petrograd from Omsk at the start of 1921, he became close to Proletkul't and joined the Serapion brothers, a group of writers who sought to separate the arts from political constraints.[7] In spring 1921 he gave a lecture to the workers on an armored train, which caused him to remember a piece he had read in a Siberian Red Army paper about lightly armed partisans seizing an armored train from the Whites and the heroic self-sacrifice of the Chinese partisan and former Tsarist coolie Sin Bin-U, who had given his life for the Revolution by lying down on the tracks to stop the train. When the armored train he was visiting was sent to the Far East, Ivanov transferred the action to that area.

"Armored Train 14-69" is set in 1920 and centers on the experiences of three men, Nezelasov, Peklevanov, and Vershinin. Captain, later Colonel, Nezelasov is a White officer who dreams of being Bonaparte. Sent to bring the armored train, which is carrying a lot of ammunition, out of the taiga and into the port where he is stationed, so that the local garrison can use the ammunition to fire their guns and put down the incipient rebellion, Nezelasov is beset by fears of cowardice and eventually killed by a group of partisans led by Vershinin. Peklevanov, the second major character, is a revolutionary who took part in the 1905 Revolution. At the start of the story he escapes from imprisonment by the Whites. He lies low in the city and organizes rebellion, in association with the partisan leader Vershinin, but he, too, is eventually shot by a member of the Japanese intervention forces. At the start of the story Vershinin is still attempting to let the Civil War pass him by, but when they learn that their two young sons have been killed by a White punishment brigade both he and his wife join the partisans. It is Vershinin, who at great cost and with only lightly armed peasant troops, captures the train from Nezelasov and his men and successfully drives it to the town where it is used to complete the defeat of the local Whites.

There are a number of foreign characters in the story, allied with both sides in the conflict. So the battle between Red and White, and thus between "us" and "them," is not confined to the Russian characters but is echoed in the behavior of their foreign allies. The forces of the Intervention are represented as predominantly American and Japanese, though there are also passing references to Czech troops, to "*khrantsuzy*" (French) in the town, to well-dressed Canadian troops, to an Italian, or possibly Portuguese ship in the port, and to an English general, General Knox, who is concerned that his children's nanny has gone missing.

Both the Americans and the Japanese are constantly reported as about to send reinforcements, though their troops turn out be less impressive than their reputation would suggest and by the end of the story both countries have proclaimed themselves neutral. The Americans are associated with technical efficiency—the cannon that the two sides are fighting over is described as American and of first-class quality—and with materialism, and therefore with the White cause. When one of the ships they send to the port is found to contain manufactured goods instead of ammunition this delights the White sympathizers. Captain Nezelasov's foolish mother expresses her desire to leave by ship for America with the words, "We are fed up of war, we want to relax in America!" Reprimanded for this statement she insists that everyone wants to go to America, it's just that some people are ready to say so openly. The American indifference to the human misery of the story is also suggested by the figure of a correspondent wearing "a service jacket with shining green buttons and striped stockings" who asks in fractured Russian, "A etta? . . . A etta? . . . Sh . . . sh-to (What is that)?" To stress the incongruity of this figure he appears again at the end of the story, "clean and smooth," "smooth, slippery and elusive as a fish in water," to the irritation of the little Russian soldier who sees him, and who, in the story's last sentence, wants to remember not him but "all the amazing and lofty things that had happened during those days."

While the American troops remain in the shadows, the Japanese, whose territorial ambitions in this area of the Russian Empire were fresh in the minds of the local population, are represented as more of a visible presence in the town, and it is one of their spies who eventually kills Peklevanov.[8] Vershinin describes them as worse than tigers, and we learn that they have burned the Civil War hero Sergei Lazo to death. Vershinin's assistant, Vas'ka Okorok, is afraid that the Entente will contaminate the Russian language, introducing "a tower of Babel" into the area. "I'll speak Russian to you and you'll reply in Japanese," he tells Vershinin, one of the many signs of anxiety about language in a story in which the ability to understand Russian, and more specifically the new Soviet form of the language that includes a number of terms referring to the international class struggle, is of crucial importance.

But the two main, and most individualized, foreign characters in the story are associated with the cause of the partisans. The local Chinese peasant, Sin Bin-U, had been forced by the Tsarist army to dig trenches. On his return he had found his hut destroyed and his wife and children missing, while he himself was accused of rebellion and almost killed by Nezelasov. Appalled by this inhumanity and treated with kindness by the Red workers, he had secretly gone over to the partisans.[9] While scraping together a living as a seller of sunflower seeds he spied on the activities of the Whites. Though this character is linguistically stereotyped—his Russian is marked by a confusion of the letters "r" and "l"—the plot of the story turns him into a hero. When it becomes clear that the Armored Train must be stopped, so that the partisans can capture the ammunition it is carrying, both he and Vas'ka Okorok lie down on the line. But when fear eventually forces Vas'ka to get up and walks away, Sin Bin-U shoots himself, thus offering his life for the cause and in turn becoming "Soviet."

The other key foreign character in the story is one of two unnamed American soldiers traveling in a cart in the story's central chapter, programmatically entitled "A Man from Alien Lands" (*Chelovek chuzhikh zemel'*). The older of the two men exclaims: "All is on fire, all! Why are we here?" (The words are in English in the text.) It is of course significant that whereas the leaders of the Entente know that the true reason for the intervention is to support the interests of their Capitalist White allies, this enlisted man *does not know why he is here.* And before his younger comrade can enlighten him, he is captured by Vershinin's wife Nastas'ia, who, after the murder of her sons, has also joined the partisans. Cowering in his light flannel uniform, the young soldier is beaten and taken to Vershinin. When the men announce that "*merikantsa pymali* (we've caught a Merican)," there are many calls to finish him off. But Vas'ka Okorok, who, we have learnt earlier, had previously been spreading Red propaganda among the White troops, and who has the gift of oratory,[10] insists that first an attempt must be made to "propagandize (*upropagandirovat'*)" him.[11] Of course the American understands nothing, as Vas'ka tells him to go back home and explain the true situation to his fellow citizens, while Vershinin adds that his people, like the Russians, plough the land, unlike the Japanese, who grow rice, and Sin Bin-U (a man from an alien land who *does* understand) adds for good measure that "we do not need your order (*tvoia poliadok nam ne nada*)!"

Alas, all the American can do is to look around helplessly and say: "I don't understand," leading the peasants to sympathize "It's not his fault. He doesn't understand Russian, poor thing." But Vas'ka insists that he must understand and that all they need to do is to find the right word . . . if only they had a book with a picture. When Vershinin despairingly declares that there are no such words, Vas'ka suddenly insists that there are and slowly, syllable by syllable, pronounces the word "Lenin." His whole body shaking, the American recognizes the word and joyously replies "That is a boy!"[12] After this, a peasant woman arrives with an icon showing the scene in Genesis 22 in which Abraham prepares to sacrifice his son Isaac. This picture is also used for ideological propaganda, since Abraham is interpreted as representing the bourgeoisie, Isaac the suffering proletariat, and God, looking down from the clouds as the interventionist forces, "the Americans, the English, the Japanese, all that scum of imperialism (*vsia eta svoloch' imperializma*)."[13] These words from the international language of class struggle, "bourgeois," "proletariat," "imperialism," are familiar to the American, and he suddenly adds, in a mixture of English and fractured Russian, "Proletariat, Rabotchi . . . ia . . . rabotchi . . . Auto . . . I am a worker from Detroit auto-works," adding "Imperializm? Imperializm doloi (Imperialism? Down with Imperialism)!"[14]

The language of international solidarity has put at rest Vas'ka's fears of a linguistic tower of Babel.[15] In delight he explains to the other peasants that this is a worker who has been forcibly conscripted by the bourgeoisie. Sin Bin-U adds that the lesson of internationalism is that there should be not a Russian, Chinese, or American republic but a single Red Republic. Vershinin decrees that the man be fed and released and Vas'ka insists that everyone can have the truth explained to them, "you just have to have a heart." And that is the last we hear of the American. This is but a minor episode in Ivanov's story, though it will form the core of Protazanov's film.

Iakov Protazanov's Film *Tommi*

After his return from emigration, Iakov Protazanov made a number of films concerned with the path to Revolutionary consciousness, the Civil War, and the struggle between supporters and opponents of the Revolution. His first Soviet film, *Aelita* (1924), plays this theme out by doubling the characters of two Moscow engineers, Los', who eventually accepts the new status quo, and Spiridonov, whose inability to do so causes him to emigrate. Protazanov underlines the clash of fates by having both characters played by the same actor, Nikolai Tsereteli. In *His Call* (*Ego prizyv*), made the following year to mark the anniversary of Lenin's death, the daughter of a worker who has been shot during the Civil War joins the Bolshevik Party. Two films of 1927, both, like *Tommi*, from literary sources, continue the theme. In *The Man from the Restaurant* (*Chelovek iz restorana*), taken from a story by Ivan Shmelev set in 1916–1917, the middle-aged waiter hero slaps the face of a factory owner who has attempted to seduce his daughter. And in *The Forty First* (*Sorok pervyi*), taken from the story by Boris Lavrenev, the Red sniper Mariutka overcomes her love for the White lieutenant Govorukha-Otrok. Putting revolutionary duty before personal emotion she shoots him when he attempts to escape captivity. Thus the turn to a Civil War theme was not new either for Protazanov, or for Russian cinema as a whole.[16] But it was Protazanov's first sound film, and the first time he could address this ideologically important theme with the added persuasive power of the spoken word.

Among the many consequences of the coming of sound to Soviet cinema in the early 1930s was the possibility of developing the ideological message that films could convey. It is no coincidence that the first Soviet sound feature was Nikolai Ekk's film *Ticket to Life* (*Putevka v zhizn'*), released on June 1, 1931, which is set in a children's labor commune and tells the story of their reclamation as worthy Soviet citizens. Exactly five months later, on November 1, 1931, Protazanov's *Tommi* was released in time to mark the fourteenth anniversary of the Revolution.

Tommi dramatizes a single episode of Vsevolod Ivanov's original, the episode of the propagandizing of the foreign soldier from the chapter "A Man from Alien Lands" discussed above. It clearly cannot be considered an adequate representation of the whole of Ivanov's source material, a fact that caused great irritation to Ivanov, who described the film as "a waste of money, time, and talent."[17] It was also savagely attacked by the critic Grigorii Groze, who accused Protazanov of surgically removing most of the original, of rendering its political content sterile, of making a potentially counter-revolutionary film that would disorientate the worker viewer, and of misrepresenting the role of the partisans in the Civil War.[18] Viewed on its own terms, however, *Tommi* provides an exemplary case study for the representation of the foreigner in early Soviet cinema, all the more interesting for its pioneering use of sound.

Like Pudovkin's *Storm over Asia* before it, *Tommi* tells the story of an encounter between a band of Red partisans and an outsider who comes to accept the rightness of their cause. The film alters Ivanov's original to make the soldier a member of the British Intervention Force, the "Tommy" of the title (the use of this name to suggest a typical British soldier is explained at the beginning of the film in an intertitle) and of his coming to proletarian consciousness.[19]

Tommi opens with scenes of a forest under thick snow. This snowy landscape will recur throughout the film, not only as its setting, but also as a metaphor both for Russia and for the arduousness of the task the partisan heroes have to achieve. The men are engaged in dragging a captured cannon through the snow in order to use it to capture the Whites' armored train, which contains the shells they need to support the rebellion that is about to break out in the town. In the film's first episode one of the men is crushed under the cart on which the cannon is being carried, a motif of heroic sacrifice that is common in films that follow this model.[20] Vas'ka, known in the film as Vas'ka "Ozornoi" (Vas'ka "Mischief"), the character who will later play a crucial part in persuading the British soldier of the wrongness of the Intervention, is told to take his place. The men occupy an abandoned church and from its watchtower they see that their path is blocked by a British base, another example of the symbolic use of landscape. The British, identifiable by their smart uniforms, which are unlike the rough clothes of the partisans, and also by the fact that they seem very keen on drill, block the path across "hunchback bridge (*gorbatyi most*)." When one of the Red soldiers knocks against the bell in the bell tower, he is heard by the English sentry, who thus knows that the Reds are about.

Following the model set by Mr. West, the next sequence identifies the British soldiers and, in this case, also shows their own subconscious sense that their presence here is inappropriate, expressed through a yearning for home. The Union Jack is seen in close-up, flying over the base, as incontrovertible an identifier as Mr. West's stars-and-stripes socks. The British troops begin to sing "It's a Long Way to Tipperary," one of the favorite British songs of World War I. Written in 1912, it was introduced to the Front in 1914 by the Second Battalion Connaught Rangers, who had been stationed in Tipperary between 1908 and 1910. A million copies of the song were sold in 1914 alone.[21] The British soldiers sit pensively listening to the song, and then join in. Like the Union Jack, it works as a signifier of their otherness, and the words, particularly the refrain "Goodbye, Piccadilly! Farewell, Leicester Square! It's a long, long way to Tipperary, but my heart's right there," provide evidence of their latent awareness that they have no reason to be in Far Eastern Russia, intervening in another country's war.[22] But their reverie is brutally interrupted by an order barked by an officer, "Quick! Quick! Get up!"

The Chinese trader, Sin Bin-U, sells sunflower seeds to a White officer. His Russian is even more nonstandard than in Ivanov's original, and he is played in an exaggeratedly and disturbingly comic way by the Russian actor Mikhail Kedrov, though it is clear that he is being represented as a positive figure, one who has already recognized the rightness of the Red cause. He has noticed that there are many English around and he asks about them, and about the English commander who will be in charge of the Russian officers. The White officer asks for cocaine, and when Sin Bin-U tells him that there is none, he calls him "Chinese mug" (*morda kitaiskaia*) and kicks his basket over, thus confirming Sin Bin-U's decision to defect to the Reds.

Znobov reads the partisans an order from the Revolutionary Partisan Headquarters to deliver the captured cannon and ammunition to the town in time to support the projected uprising. He refers to the wall of imperialism and interventionists that stands before them. When one man wonders how they can manage to do so with "merikantsy" all around, another retorts that it is "absurd" for partisans to be afraid of the English. Instead, he insists that they have to resist the capitalists, interventionists, and bourgeois who want to steal their land, their factories, and their forests. As in Gorky's novel *Mother*, the source of this structural model, the rhetoric deployed is that of class and internationalism, combined with a strong commitment to the Russian land. They determine to respect the order they have been given by making their way through the virgin land of the woods and across a bridge over the river.

In the next scene British officers, who look remarkably similar to the ones in *Storm over Asia*, speak in a mixture of English and poor Russian about the British army being in charge, while an Orthodox priest, who has already been shown giving them information, looks on. Neither of these elements is in the original. "Armored Train 14-69" has no characters representing the Orthodox Church, but the priest introduced by Protazanov is repeatedly shown as an ally of the Whites and a craven flatterer of the English officers. The role of the officers of the Interventionist forces is also greatly increased by Protazanov, who thus, following Lenin, stresses the distinction between the Interventionist officers, whose motives are entirely suspect, and the simple soldiers, who can be brought to enlightenment.

After a further shot of the Union Jack and the British sentry, Sin Bin-U follows a group of English soldiers to the bridge that the partisans will need to cross. The English soldiers look inept and forlorn. Donning skis, which by contrast indicate how at home he is in this environment, Sin Bin-U goes off to report to the partisans. The unnamed soldier who will become the Tommi of the film's title is left to guard the bridge. He sits smoking his pipe and looking pensively into the water, while "Tipperary" appears again on the sound track. A flashback of memories of his life back home, working in a steel foundry, establishes his worker credentials. A bowler-hatted boss visits the foundry, where there are notices encouraging the workers to inform on absent colleagues. When Tommi objects he is abused by a foreman and then hit by a piece of heavy machinery. Both the iconography and the plot of this sequence recall the representation of the prerevolutionary Russian factory in Sergei Eisenstein's film *Strike*, providing further evidence that in *Tommi* Protazanov wanted to stress international worker solidarity rather than nation. This sequence serves, as do similar scenes in other films and novels of the period, to show that the soldier possesses the positive qualities that will make it possible for him to find the true path and pass the series of tests that will bring him to understanding.

At the very moment in which, in his reverie, he is hit by the machinery, Tommi is captured by Sin Bin-U and the partisans, blindfolded, and taken off to the main partisan group. "Brothers, we have caught a Merican (*Brattsy, merikantsa pymali*)," they shout, stressing yet again that for them all foreigners are the same. He is abused by the partisans as a devil and a bourgeois lackey. Sin Bin-U reports to Vershinin (whose role is considerably less important than in the original story) on the many Englishmen and the White officer who lie in their path.[23] A woman calls Tommi "satan" and there is another flashback to the arson and killings inflicted upon villagers by the Whites, followed by calls for Tommi to be killed. But Vas'ka Ozornoi meets Tommi's gaze and realizes that there is "human material" that can be saved here. It is notable that the two men are physically similar, and Vas'ka will perform the role of mentor. He calls, "Let me speak. Wait before you kill him (*Dai slovo skazat'. Pogodi ubivat'*)." Vas'ka's alternative plan is for Tommi to be "propagandized." In a speech that strikingly combines the lexis of international class solidarity with peasant slang he says: "In my opinion we should propagandize the whore. Let him sniff out the Bolshevik truth and then he will tell his own people back home. If he doesn't understand our Bolshevik soul, then we have to finish him off (*Nado, po-moemu, up-ropagandirovat' etu kurvu. Dai bol'shevistskuiu pravdu poniukhat' da svoim potom rasskazhet. Ezheli ne poimet on nashei rabochei dushi, togda znachit obiazany my ego koknut'*)."[24]

The men are certain that he will not understand and are amused at the prospect of hearing Vas'ka speak "American," but Vas'ka is determined that Tommi will learn "Bolshevik truth" and eager to persuade him that it is wrong for the British working class to fight against Russian workers and peasants. The introduction of the sound film had, of course, destroyed the internationalism of cinema, but in the following sequence Protazanov uses the soldier's inability to understand Russian in the service of the film's narrative in a moving and sometimes comic way.

"Lad, listen, we are all peasants and workers," says Vas'ka, "We are all workers, do you understand, workers (*Paren', slushai!* . . . *my vse, krest'iane, da rabochie* . . . *My—trudiashchiesia, ponimaesh', trudiashchiesia*)."[25] But despite his best efforts Tommi has failed to follow this, perplexedly announcing, in English, "I don't understand!" and provoking a response from the partisans of, "He doesn't understand Russian, the poor fellow!" As in the Ivanov story, Vas'ka thinks that perhaps a picture would do the trick and Sin Bin-U goes off in search of one. The men are determined to waste no more time and to finish Tommi off, but Vas'ka insists: "No, he will understand. If only I could . . . find the word . . . a real word . . . Lad . . . you explain to your people there in detail that it is not a good idea to destroy our land." But for a second time Tommi announces: "I don't understand!"

Figure 1.3. Comrades: Sin Bin-U and Tommi.
From Iakov Protazanov's *Tommi* (1930).

The pressure to kill him mounts and the men begin to disperse, leaving the two young men together, occupying the whole frame in a picture of shared despondency. But still Vas'ka is insistent, pedaling the word "understanding" that is shorthand for the acquisition of proletarian consciousness, "No, he'll understand . . . he has to understand (*Net, on poimet . . . on dolzhen poniat'*)."[26] Suddenly he realizes that he has, indeed, found the word that will bring understanding. So he begins for a third time: "*Slushai, paren', slushai . . . poimi . . . poimi, poimi. Lenin! Lenin! Lenin!*" Tommi repeats the magic word, three times, eventually understanding its solemn import, and excitedly adds, "Hurrah!" The sacred word has had its desired effect (see fig. 1.3). A more sophisticated version of the same trope, more sophisticated since the listeners are Russian speakers, is used by Isaak Babel in the story "My First Goose" from his *Red Cavalry* (*Konarmiia*) cycle, in which the narrator Liutov is asked what is in the papers. He quotes the words of Lenin in *Pravda* to the assembled Cossacks, adding that "I read and exulted, exultantly spying out the mysterious curve of Lenin's straight line." Here, too, Lenin's words work their magic, provoking the Cossack Surovkov to exclaim, "The truth tickles every nostril."[27]

Tommi's realization is directly followed by an intertitle quoting Lenin's words—"We conquered the entente because we removed from them the workers and peasants dressed in soldiers' uniforms"—words that exactly echo both the plot of the film and Lenin's words of 1919 quoted earlier. The men are delighted, and at this point Sin Bin-U returns with the icon of Abraham preparing to sacrifice Isaac, which the peasant woman had produced in Ivanov's story.[28] With Sin Bin-U's help, Vas'ka interprets the picture, making the same references to the proletariat, the "scum of Imperialism" and "the Soviet republic" that he had made in the story. Once again, the "international" words are accessible to Tommi, and at this point he moves from mere understanding to affirmation, announcing, somewhat ungrammatically in a mix of languages—he has miraculously learned a bit of Russian—that "I am proletariat. *Imperializma . . . doloi!*" for which he is kissed and embraced by Vas'ka. Tommi, unlike Mr. West, had made his trip to Russia *before* there was any hint of his coming to consciousness, and his first experience of the country was that of an (unwitting) occupier. Now he chooses to change his identity, placing class over nationality by associating himself definitively with his fellow workers. The early Soviet years were a period of radical reshaping of identity, as eloquently described by Sheila Fitzpatrick.[29] The sequence ends with a triangular shot of Vas'ka, Sin Bin-U, and Tommi, worker representatives of three great nations. Repeating the word *tovarishch* (comrade), Vas'ka and Sin Bin-U shake Tommi's hand.

Throughout his film, Protazanov had shown more interest than Ivanov in representing both the positive and the negative foreigners in some detail. So this conversion sequence, the film's emotional center, is followed by a further scene involving the English commander, who is now seen drinking champagne with Russian officers and the priest.[30] In comically bad Russian—though we learn that he had lived in Russia for many years before the Revolution and had industrial interests—the English commander drinks to Russian hospitality and English civilization: "*Dzhentl'men. Ia p'et za velikii russkii gostepriims . . . i angliiskii sivilizats* (Gentlemen, I drink to the great Russian hospitality . . . and English civilization)." This scene of indulgence by the international officer class is intercut with another of the partisans heroically dragging the cannon across the bridge. Yet another shot of the Union Jack punctuates the sequence. In the final scene of the film, Tommi completes his conversion experience. Watching the heroic exertions of the band of peasants he tears off and throws away his army cap band, like the Union Jack before it an emblem of his previous allegiance, and joins Vas'ka and Sin Bin-U as they drag the cannon through the snow in another tableau of international solidarity. A peasant shouts, "Chapaev is with us," to which Tommi replies, "All right," and the men continue on their way, singing a song of Chapaev's exploits in the Urals.[31] The last image is of ice-break and thaw, in symbolic contrast with the images of deep snow with which the film had opened.[32]

The film ends with another quotation, this time from Kliment Voroshilov, who in 1931 was Commissar for War and the Navy: "That is how it was . . . and if once more . . . our class enemies attack the country in which socialism is being built . . . the worker and peasant Red Army will cover our borders with its breast and throw the enemy far back beyond them." Thus *Tommi*, though set in the revolutionary past, proclaimed its relevance to the new concerns about the threats to the Soviet Union's borders, to both east and west, concerns that permeated both the political discourse and the feature films of the 1930s.[33] While drawing upon the structure provided by *Mr. West*, both in terms of the sympathetic characterization of the Westerner and in terms of the plot motif of a journey to Russia, Protazanov radically increases the political significance of the representation of the foreigner and his experience.

Later Treatments of the Theme

The plot structure applied in *Tommi* was used repeatedly in films throughout the Soviet period, though space here permits only a brief outline of the fate of the theme. In Boris Shpis and Rokhl Milman's film *The Return of Nathan Becker* (*Vozvrashchenie Neitana Bekera, Nosn Beker Fort Aheym*), released a year later, at the end of 1932, the returnee is a Jew whose family had emigrated to the United States before the Revolution and who comes back to the Soviet Union to help build Magnitogorsk. The story of Vsevolod Pudovkin's *The Deserter* (*Dezertir*), released in September 1933, begins in the Hamburg docks. The hero, Karl Renn, is too fearful and inconstant to continue to support a strike by dockers and gets himself included on a workers' delegation to the USSR. But he, too, learns his lesson through observing the life of Soviet workers, realizes that he has been evading responsibility, and, in a new twist to the master plot, returns to Germany and the conflict, in which, in the film's final sequence, he pays the ultimate sacrifice (see Peter Kenez's essay in this volume for more on this film).

Perhaps the most important example of the genre is presented in Grigorii Alexandrov's 1936 film *The Circus* (*Tsirk*), which is the subject of the essay in this volume by Josephine Woll. Once again, the plot is constructed around the path to understanding by the sympathetic foreigner. Here, too, there is comic play upon the inability of that foreigner to understand Russian (and, for Western audiences, comic play on hearing Russian actors speak "English"), and much stress is laid upon the Russian verb *ponimat'*, "to understand." Another important contribution to the "Eastern" version of the master-plot is provided in Aleksandr Zarkhi and Iosif Kheifits's 1940 film *His Name Is Sukhe-Bator* (*Ego zovut Sukhe-Bator*), in which the eponymous Mongol hero leads a rebellion against foreign occupiers in the autumn of 1919, in alliance with Soviet forces.

In later decades the model was applied in the analysis of the behavior of such groups as the fellow traveling journalists discussed in the work of David Caute,[34] and Russian émigrés coming back in search of their roots. In 1979, when the country had begun to open up to the outside world, Georgii Daneliia made fun of the foreign visitor in *Autumn Marathon* (*Osennii marafon*), the tale of the Russian intellectual Andrei Buzykin. Already worn down by the demands of wife, mistress, and work, he is quite incapable of coping with the energy exuded by his jogging Danish colleague, Bill Hansen. By 1990, the idea of Westerners coming to the Soviet Union in search of political enlightenment was almost ludicrous, yet Nikita Mikhalkov could still find mileage in the trope in his film of that year *Hitchhiking* (*Avtostop*), in which a world-weary Italian drives through Europe to snowy Russia, where he gives a lift to a heavily pregnant woman. Realizing that it is too late to get the woman to hospital, he joins her husband in helping her to give birth in the snow. Stunned by the couple's stoicism and interpreting it as a manifestation of the Russian soul, he decides to effect a reconciliation with his own family and telephones his estranged son.

The Theme Reversed

In the late and post-Soviet cinema, as Oleg Sulkin argues later in this volume, the trope is reversed. One mechanism of reversal is to take the Russian hero abroad. In *Urga. Territory of Love* (*Urga. Territoriia liubvi*), a film made in 1991 by the same director, Nikita Mikhalkov, the Russian truck-driver hero, unable to find work in the Soviet Union, is forced to become a guest worker in Mongolia. Here he witnesses a new alliance between East and West, effectively expressed in a symbolic scene in an Ulan Bator discotheque, an alliance that excludes the Russians and their currency of tawdry Lenin badges. A second way of reversing the trope is to bring an outsider to Russia but make what he finds there less than edifying. This is the model used in Aleksandr Rogozhkin's hugely popular comedy *Peculiarities of the Russian Hunt* (*Osobennosti natsional'noi okhoty*, 1995), in which a young Finn joins a Russian hunting party only to find that almost the only activity engaged in on the trip is heavy Russian drinking.

Régis Wargnier's *East-West* (*Vostok-Zapad*), made in 1999, is set in 1946.

Though the film has a French director and its two female stars are French, it is otherwise made by Russians. It tells the story of a French woman who follows her Russian husband back to the USSR at the end of World War II, only to find that she has made a journey to hell. The film concludes with the self-sacrifice of the hero in getting his wife and child out of this torment. But in yet another reversal of the model, made by a Russian director who in his recent films has pandered to wounded Russian patriotism, Aleksei Balabanov, in his *Brother 2* (*Brat 2*, 2000), sends his hero, Danila, to the United States. The New York he finds is totally Russian, while Chicago is inhabited almost entirely by venal black pimps and gangsters. In the film's final sequence Danila saves Dasha, a bald, exploited Russian prostitute, and takes her home to Russia to the sound of the famous Nautilus Pompilius song "Goodbye America." In Balabanov's 2002 film, *War* (*Voina*), the weedy English hero John has to learn a lesson in male toughness from his Russian friends (both of these films are discussed by Anthony Anemone in his essay in this volume on Balabanov's vigilante heroes).

Postscript

That the basic model, of Russian directors structuring a film around the visit of a foreigner to Russia and his reactions to the experience, is still capable of yielding fruitful insights into Western perceptions of Russia and into Russian reactions to those perceptions, is, of course, apparent from the broad discussion provoked by Aleksandr Sokurov's 2002 film *Russian Ark* (*Russkii kovcheg*). The cinematic debate about Russia's otherness, and about perceptions of Russia by those whom Russians perceive as "other," is far from over.

NOTES

1. Aleksandr Blok, "Novaia Amerika," in *Sobranie sochinenii v 8 tomakh* (Moscow-Leningrad: Gosudarstvennoe izdatel'stro khudozhestvennoi literatukh, 1960–1965), vol. 3, 268–70.

2. See Denise Youngblood, *Movies for the Masses: Popular Cinema and Soviet Society in the 1920s* (Cambridge, U.K.: Cambridge University Press, 1992).

3. See especially Katerina Clark, *The Soviet Novel: History as Ritual* (Chicago: University of Chicago Press, 1981), 15–16, 21–22.

4. For cogent analyses of the political ambiguity of "Mr. West," see R. M. Iangirov, "K istorii 'Mistera Vesta . . . ,'" *Shestye tynianovskie chteniia. Tezisy dokladov i materialy dlia obsuzhdeniia* (Riga and Moscow: Izdanie osushchestvleno na srodstva redkolleggi, 1992), 217–22; and Vlada Petric, "A Subtextual Reading of Kuleshov's Satire *The Extraordinary Adventures of Mr. West in the Land of the Bolsheviks (1924),*"

in Andrew Horton, ed., *Inside Soviet Film Satire: Laughter with a Lash* (Cambridge, U.K.: Cambridge University Press, 1993), 65–74.

5. References to this story will be made to Vsevolod Ivanov, in *Sobranie sochinenii v 8 tomakh* (Moscow: Gosudarstvennoe izdatel'stro khudozhestvennoi literatukh, 1958–1960), vol. 1, *Partizanskie povesti*, 547–709 (henceforth, Ivanov, *Sobranie sochinenii*, vol. 1).

6. The chapter of "Istoriia moikh knig" devoted to "Bronepoezd 14-69" was first published in the journal *Molodaia gvardiia* (1957): 1. It is quoted here from Ivanov, *Sobranie sochinenii*, vol. 1, 45–51.

7. For more on the Serapion Brothers, see Martha Weitzel Hickey, "Recovering the Author's Part: The Serapion Brothers in Petrograd," *Russian Review* 58, no. 1 (1999): 103–23.

8. For a discussion of the story's representation of the Japanese, see Karen Petrone, "Masculinity and Heroism in Imperial and Soviet Military-Patriotic Cultures," in Barbara Evans Clements, Rebecca Friedman, and Dan Healey, eds., *Russian Masculinities in History and Culture* (Basingstoke and New York: Palgrave, 2002), 172–93 (esp. 179–80).

9. The same plot motif is used to explain the defection of the White colonel's batman Potapov in Dmitrii Furmanov's Civil War novel *Chapaev*, which itself would be filmed in 1934.

10. For an account of the qualities required from the new proletarian orator, see Michael S. Gorham, *Speaking in Soviet Tongues: Language Culture and the Politics of Voice in Revolutionary Russia* (De Kalb, Ill.: Northern Illinois University Press, 2003), 100–101, 121–24. For the Party's stress of the role of "agitatsiia" (agitation), see A. M. Selishchev, *Iazyk revoliutsionnoi epokhi. Iz nabliudenii nad russkim iazykom* (Moscow: Rabotnik prosveshcheniia, 1928), quoted from the reprint of this edition (Moscow: Editorial URSS, 2003), 101.

11. That attempts were indeed made to propagandize the American interventionist troops is apparent from information provided by M. Minokin in the notes to the edition of "Bronepoezd 14-69" quoted above. In the summer of 1919 a leaflet was disseminated under the title "American Workers," inciting them to join with the Russian Bolsheviks in attacking "their mortal enemy, the bourgeoisie," and on another occasion five captured Americans were "propagandised," by partisans, "using only international words," and then released. See Ivanov, *Sobranie sochinenii*, vol. 1, 716. In this they were following Lenin's 1919 instructions to tell foreign captives that the Bolsheviks were fighting "not only for Soviet Russia, we are fighting for the power of the workers of the entire world" (quoted in ibid., 717).

12. The passages of English dialogue are quoted exactly as they appear in the text. Their clumsiness is, of course, a source of some amusement to English readers. This phrase is footnoted in Russian as "Vot eto paren'!"

13. For the use of the word *svoloch'* in revolutionary discourse, see Selishchev, *Iazyk revoliutsionnoi epokhi*, 71–72.

14. For the currency of "foreign words," including "proletarian," "propaganda," and "imperialism" in the discourse of the new revolutionary intelligentsia, see Selishchev, *Iazyk revoliutsionnoi epokhi*, 28.

15. For a recent assessment of the language used in the episode of the capture of the American and a stimulating general analysis of the language of the Soviet revolution, see Daniel E. Collins, "The Tower of Babel Undone in a Soviet Pentecost: A

Linguistic Myth of the First Five-Year Plan," *Slavic and East European Journal* 42 (1998): 423–43, 430.

16. A silent film version of Fadeev's Civil War story "Razgrom" (The Rout), which also represents the Japanese as enemies, directed by Nikolai Beresnev, was released on September 10, 1931. For an analysis of Fadeev's representation of the Japanese enemy, see Petrone, "Masculinity and Heroism," 179.

17. Ivanov's reaction was printed in *Literaturnaia gazeta*, December 3, 1931, and is quoted from A. Crespi and S. de Vidovich, eds., *Prima dei codici. Il cinema sovietico prima del realismo socialista 1929–1935* (Venice: Edizioni La Biennale di Venezia, 1990), 177.

18. Gr. Groze, "Bronepoezd, pushchennyi pod otkos," *Sovetskoe iskusstvo*, November 20, 1931, quoted in Crespi and de Vidovich, *Prima dei codici*, 177.

19. On the use of the name "Tommy Atkins" to suggest a typical British soldier in World War I, see, for example, http://www.wordiq.com/definition/Tommy_Atkins (accessed September 2, 2004). For a new study of World War I that plays on the continuing use of this name, see Richard Holmes, *Tommy: The British Soldier on the Western Front* (London: HarperCollins, 2004).

20. In the film this episode of heroic martyrdom replaces that of Sin Bin-U in the story. In the film Sin Bin-U survives to continue the struggle.

21. For information on the history of the song, and the words, see http://www.iol .ie/~tipplibs/Long.htm (accessed September 2, 2004).

22. Once again, the pronunciation of the English words by Russian actors offers an unintended amusement to English-speaking audiences, just as it will do later in the passages of English in Grigorii Alexandrov's 1936 film *Tsirk*. The Russian actors playing English soldiers sing of leaving "Lyster Square." The same song is also sung in another film of 1931, Semen Timoshenko's *Snaiper. Iskusstvo ubivat'* (Sniper: The Art of Killing), released two months after *Tommi*, on January 2, 1932. It is likely that the English journalist Malcolm Muggeridge is referring to one of these films in his memoirs when he speaks of being taken by Prince Mirskii to a party in Moscow in the early 1930s and meeting an Englishman who has just returned from an assignment on a Soviet film "to teach the extras playing the part of the British troops to sing 'Tipperary,' which had really been quite difficult; they had to learn the words phonetically, and he himself had been pretty shaky on the tune. He was deadly serious about his curious assignment." Malcolm Muggeridge, *Chronicles of Wasted Time*, vol. 1, *The Green Stick* (London: Collins, 1972), 239.

23. The reversal of importance of the roles of Vershinin, the quiet thinker, and Vas'ka, the lively orator, is symptomatic of the move from prose to the sound film, with its greater capacity for drawing attention to rhetorical language.

24. The character of Vas'ka in the film, while not making explicit reference to it, draws upon the past experience of the character as an "agitator," as described in Ivanov's story. On the privileging of the charismatic spoken, oratorical word in the period immediately after the revolution, see Gorham, *Speaking in Soviet Tongues*, 11–14. On the mixture of rough peasant speech and political terminology in the "new language" of revolution, see Selishchev, *Iazyk revoliutsionnoi epokhi*, 68–71. On the language of the Red Army soldier, see I. N. Shpil'rein, D. I. Reitinbarg, and G. O. Netsaii, *Iazyk krasnoarmeitsa* (Moscow-Leningrad: Gosizdat, 1928). For the evidence this book provides about the difficulties soldiers had with the new Soviet vocabulary, see Gorham, *Speaking in Soviet Tongues*, 28.

25. On the use of the word *paren'* as a form of address by the new Party and So-

viet class, instead of the formal *molodoi chelovek*, see Selishchev, *Iazyk revoliutsionnoi epokhi*, 70–71.

26. The stress the film places on the need to come to understanding echoes the story's concern with the value of the acquisition of discipline and also of knowledge, represented for example in Vershinin's constant testing of his own knowledge of the multiplication tables.

27. Isaak Babel, "Moi pervyi gus'," dated 1920 and first published in the newspaper *Izvestiia Odesskogo gubispolkoma*, May 1923. Quoted here from Isaak Babel, *Detstvo i drugie rasskazy* (Jerusalem: Biblioteka-Aliia, 1979), 132.

28. The use of religious models and religious imagery was a commonplace in early Soviet films about the Revolution, including Eisenstein's *Strike* (1924) and *Battleship Potemkin* (*Bronenosets Potemkin*, 1925) and Aleksandr Dovzhenko's *Earth* (1930), sometimes combined with an explicitly antireligious message. Protazanov's previous film, *The Feast of St. Iorgen* (*Prazdnik sviatogo Iorgena*, 1930) had made fun of religious charlatans. *Tommi* combined a negatively presented priest with the appropriation of the religious values of sacrifice and conversion to the Red cause. The use of religious values and imagery in "antireligious" plots is only superficially a paradox. Peasant and worker audiences, while often illiterate, were familiar with Bible stories, and the elements of model moral behavior and redemptive self-sacrifice were a commonplace in the narrative that had been constructed about the revolutionary process.

29. Sheila Fitzpatrick, "Making a Self for the Times: Impersonation and Imposture in 20th-Century Russia," *Kritika* 2, no. 3 (2001):469–87. The article opens with the assertion that "Reinvention is what revolutions are about" and goes on to invoke Stephen Kotkin's concept of "speaking Bolshevik," invoked in his *Magnetic Mountain: Stalinism as a Civilization* (Berkeley: University of California Press, 1995). "Speaking Bolshevik" is what Vas'ka has already learned to do, and what he now teaches Tommi.

30. The cut from worker sacrifice to capitalist excess, precisely exemplified by drinking champagne, is made on two occasions in Eisenstein's *Strike*.

31. Chapaev's cinematic glory was yet to come, in the Vasil'ev brothers' film of 1934, but Dmitrii Furmanov's prose celebration of his exploits had already made him a legendary hero of the Civil War.

32. The symbolic ending of a film with an image of thawing snow or a newly free-flowing river was used repeatedly by Vsevolod Pudovkin in his films of the 1920s.

33. For a fascinating analysis of the cinematic representation of the Japanese threat to the Soviet Union's eastern borders see Irina Mel'nikova, "Iaponskaia tema v sovetskikh 'oboronnykh' fil'makh 30-kh godov," *Japanese Slavic and East European Studies* 23 (2002): 57–82.

34. David Caute, *The Fellow Travellers: A Postscript to the Enlightenment* (London: Weidenfeld and Nicolson, 1973); and David Caute, *The Dancer Defects: The Struggle for Cultural Supremacy during the Cold War* (Oxford: Oxford University Press, 2003).

The Wise and Wicked Game

Reediting, Foreignness, and
Soviet Film Culture of the Twenties

Yuri Tsivian

For Boitler

The term "reediting" (*peremontazh*) as used in the Soviet film industry of the twenties means: the reworking of a film to suit it to a country other than that of its origin. Aside from the reediting in the proper sense of the word, this term also embraced such operations as retitling, altering the main title, changing character names, and adding new scenes to preexisting footage. Usually, reediting is associated with censorship, and is regarded as part of the political history of film. In this essay, I want to look at it through the lens of film style and culture. I will discuss two activities: the reworking of foreign films for Soviet screens and the reworking of Soviet films for export. Apparently similar, these practices served different sections of the film industry (reediting for export was part of production—or, rather, postproduction—performed, as a rule, at the studio where the prototype print had been made, whereas incoming films were reedited by their distributors).[1] Each practice was motivated by its own policy and, as I want to show, by its own aesthetic logic. I will begin with a discussion of reediting for export, pass to the reediting of imported films, and, finally, discuss some implications of reediting for Soviet film culture of the twenties concentrating on the reaction of Formalist theorists and LEF (Left Front) theorists. Ultimately, the process of reediting afforded early Soviet filmmakers and editors an opportunity to test ideas of foreignness and to articulate (as well as play with) the ways in which Soviet identities should be portrayed.

Reediting for the Foreign Market

While the reediting of foreign films (as I will show later) caused a number of press discussions that can be used as historical sources, no information

Figure 2.1. Wrong Endings? Sukhanov Smiles before Death.
From Grigorii Kozintsev and Leonid Trauberg's S.V.D.
(*Soiuz velikogo dela, Union of the Great Cause,* 1927).

(naturally!) on home productions as being reedited for export is available in Soviet papers. To get an idea of what the practice looked like, studio archives and foreign release prints of Soviet films are about all the evidence available for study.

A set of documents from the Leningrad film factories may serve as an example of exporters' activities. It is an exchange of departmental memos between the Export-Import Division and the Art and Script Bureau (*stsenarno-khudozhestvennoe biuro*) of the Sovkino regarding the final sequence of Grigorii Kozintsev and Leonid Trauberg's film S.V.D. (*Soiuz velikogo dela, Union of the Great Cause,* Sovkino Leningrad, 1927) (see fig. 2.1). The film is a "romantic melodrama against the background of history" (as the filmmakers defined it),[2] scripted by Iulian Oksman and Iuri Tynianov. In the film, a young army officer, Sukhanov, involved in the Decembrist rebellion of 1825, is betrayed, captured, escapes with a traveling circus, and is killed by an officer of the Tsar's punitive squad.[3] The Export-Import Division was not happy with the endings: in the 1920s, it was a common belief (derived, among other sources, from distribution practices of the teens) that the death of a hero made foreign sales problematic. As it follows from these letters, the Export-Import Division religiously held on to this belief. In the Soviet print, the film ends with a series of shots, the last of which creates an effective visual "rhyme" between the end of the film and the death of its hero:

1. High-angle medium shot. Interior of the church. The punitive squad officer shoots.
2. Medium close-up. The same location. Sukhanov walks toward camera, pauses as he gets the bullet in his back, smiles faintly, exits past camera.
3. High-angle long shot. Wounded, Sukhanov walks toward the exit.
   Long shot. Exterior, the church door. Sukhanov appears in the door, crosses the frame, and exits to the right.
4. Long shot. Exterior landscape with the church in the distance. Some running figures [the soldiers?] cross the space.
5. Low-angle long shot. Exterior, another landscape. The silhouette of Sukhanov crosses the space walking toward camera with unsteady steps. Exits to the right.
6. High-angle long shot. Another landscape, with the river. Sukhanov enters, falls on the ground by the water under a lone birch tree.
7. High-angle long shot. The same church door as in shot 3. The General's wife, Vishnevskaia, in love with Sukhanov, appears in the door, looking for him.
8. Close-up. Sukhanov's face, looking off-frame, smiles faintly, goes out of frame as his head falls on the ground.
9. High-angle long shot. By the river. Vishnevskaia runs and bends over Sukhanov's body.
10. Landscape shot with the river.
11. Medium close-up. Sukhanov's head thrown back by the water.
12. Long shot. Silhouette of the church.
13. Close-up. Sukhanov's head.
14. Close-up. Vishnevskaia looks at him, takes a shawl off her shoulders.
15. Close-up. Sukhanov's head; slowly, the shawl is drawn over his face till its dark fabric fills the frame. Although there is no dissolve after this shot, the title "The End" that follows it looks as if it surfaced on the shawl.

After the studio preview, Kozintsev and Trauberg received a letter from the Export-Import Division dated June 29, 1927, requesting a retake of this rather extended death sequence (it lasts, from the moment of the gunshot, for two minutes at 24 frames per second). This is what the exporters suggest:

> Taking into account the demands of the foreign market, we request that [the second ending] is made in the following version:
> "General's wife finds the hero in a faint (not dead) on a bank of the river."
> The next scene: "a park (nearby one can see a villa, and farther off a lake or even better a sea), the hero is sitting in an armchair having a bandage indicating that he is wounded."
> Nearby, in the same park, a table is served; general's wife is taking care of the convalescent hero. Title. "The end."
> In order not to miss the sales season we request that the retake takes place urgently.
> Head of Export-Import Division (Kaufman)[4]

At first, Kozintsev and Trauberg refused. Here follows a time gap in correspondence probably caused by the fact that the "sales season" (whatever it was) was missed anyway. The (undocumented) pressure must have been resumed after the film opened in Russia: about six months after the receipt of the above request, the Art and Script Bureau finally sent their counter-proposal with a new twist of the story (although the letter is not signed, I believe that the idea belongs to Iuri Tynianov, who was employed at that time at the bureau as script consultant).[5] The proposed ending looks like a compromise between the sad and the happy: the villain is punished, the hero is saved, but the bullet hits the woman:

19/XII/27

"S.V.D."
(Export version of the ending)

1. In the church, the officer in charge of the punitive squad is replaced by Medoks [the main villain of the story, traitor and gambler]. Medoks shoots at Sukhanov, but Vishnevskaia shields him with her body. Sukhanov rushes toward Vishnevskaia. Vishnevskaia's shoulder is lightly wounded. Sukhanov lifts her and leaves the church as the soldiers part to let them pass.
2. In the forest near the church, a circus van with artists is waiting for them.
3. In the van, fugitive soldiers are hiding.
4. Sukhanov, with Vishnevskaia on his arms, runs toward the van.
5. Sukhanov brings Vishnevskaia into the van.
6. The coachman gives the horse a rein. The van moves.

7. On the church floor Medoks is shown dying. A pack of cards falls out of his torn uniform.

8. In the van. Sukhanov is bending over Vishnevskaia who is lying on a heap of circus rags. Her face—a smile.

9. The snow is raised by the wind. Icy tree branches are rocking. The snow whirls stronger. The van moves slowly through the snowstorm.

10. Sukhanov looks into Vishnevskaia's eyes. Vishnevskaia—Sukhanov.

11. In the church, Medoks is lying on the floor, dead, a fan of playing cards spilled next to him. The ring with the letters "S.V.D." has fallen off his motionless hand.

12. A sentry is asleep at the frontier pole. In the distance the van is seen disappearing in the snowstorm. Whirling snow fills the screen.[6]

Compare shot 12 of the new ending with the last shot (15) of the original one: in the original a dark shawl is drawn over the hero's face, effacing the dead hero's image. This shot was conceived as a subtle, self-conscious effect—visually, the shawl is used as a sort of diegetic "wipe"—and not only conceived, but distinguished as "amazing" in a critical review: "the shawl covers the face of the killed rebel as if it were a camera diaphragm."[7] I can imagine how frustrated Kozintsev and Trauberg must have been by Kaufman's letter. In November the ending is praised in a critical review, and in December they are requested to submit an export ending that leaves no room for this exquisite find! This must be what this snow shot was about: taking advantage of the December weather, the filmmakers wanted the snow to suggest an elegant narrative ellipsis (the scene in which Sukhanov is shot was set in the summer) and compensate for the lost closure effect. Instead of the dark shawl used to suggest a "wipe," the filmmakers now plan to use the falling snow to simulate a slow "fade" to white.

The reaction followed in three days. Careful not to offend the authors, Kaufman nevertheless rejects the circus van variant:

> Far from opting against your second version of the S.V.D. ending in essence, we still consider it necessary to make it such as we agreed at a personal meeting with the director of the film and comrade Grinfeld.[8]

Comrade N. Y. Grinfeld mentioned in the letter was at that time the head of the studio; it is not clear which of the two film directors was present at the power meeting that Kaufman alludes to; no records of this meeting exist, but from a memo sent on the next day it follows that some specific conditions of British distribution had been discussed:

> I repeat that we consider it necessary to make the ending of *S.V.D.* such as we agreed with the director of the picture . . . because then the picture will be admissible for England as well.[9]

On January 16, 1928, the alternative ending was finally ready. Alongside with the "happy outcome issue," its studio preview minutes contain a reference that makes one think of religious censorship as one of the reasons why the head of the studio insisted on retaking the ending:

> The second version of the ending for the film *S.V.D.* was commissioned by the Export-Import Division who insisted that the "happy ending" of the picture and elimination of the "gunshot in the church" was a necessary pre-condition for the penetration of the film into some Western countries. The recommendations of the Export Division have been fulfilled.[10]

This "gunshot in the church" business seems to explain matters. A church is a dicey site for an execution, and the scene could encounter objections on the part of clerical censors, particularly in England where censorship was particularly sensitive to sacrilege.[11] If this was indeed the reason, it becomes clear why such things were decided at confidential meetings like the one held at the studio director's office in Leningrad. In a country professing atheist ideology as Soviet Russia did in the twenties, the fact of changing a film to suit clerical censorship must have looked embarrassing. Yet, in the perspective of the film industry, this was a perfectly sound solution: in contrast to the reeditors of imported films, studio-based exporters were not dealing in ideologies, but exporting entertainment.

There are some questions I hesitate to answer at this time. I wonder if the decisions taken by Export-Import Divisions were based on any kind of market research or rather on received ideas or maybe on personal taste developed while watching Western films? Did reedited versions really improve sales? Did the exporters suppress the original versions or, rather, offer both endings to their potential purchasers? A more thorough research into infrastructures of international distribution would help, but also a comparative analysis of home release and foreign release prints. The only print of *S.V.D.* I have been able to see so far is a hybrid copy: because the home release version of the film is only partially preserved at Gosfilmofond, some footage (about two reels) from a French-language print found in Belgium is added to make the Russian archival print complete. The added footage bears some marks of reediting. For example, in French intertitles General Vishnevskii (evidently, a difficult name for a Francophone filmgoer) changes his name to "General Neff" (he crops off the first and third syllables and spells the remaining syllable so that it looks "Russian"), but it is unlikely that the general's name was changed already at the Sovkino studio. It is hard to spot any other changes other than by viewing both prints back to back on a double-gauge viewing machine. In the Belgium print, as Kristin Thompson tells me, the ending is not preserved, yet we get a pretty good idea of what the ending debate came down to from a shot list of the export version preserved at the Film Folder Division of the State Film Archive in Moscow.[12] As it turns out, the filmmakers' counter-proposal with the lady wounded and the final shot "fading out" to white as the falling snow fills up the screen was never shot. No one is harmed (Kaufman wins!), and the whole scene takes place inside the circus van, probably because they were short of funds (or snow) to go out to shoot on location. In the circus van, the fugitive Sukhanov falls asleep, his head leaning against the shoulder of his beloved, who is asleep, too; a sympathetic gypsy man, the proprietor of the circus, carefully draws a blanket over the faces of the sleeping couple. So, the quasi-diegetic closure is there after all, but I do not believe it worked quite as effectively as it does in the Russian version: to make it really work, you need someone dying under the cover.

Another debate (coming to us from an earlier time) between producers and exporters shows that efforts to bring Soviet films closer to what was called "the psychology of the Western viewer" were not confined to happy endings or preventive censorship—sometimes general questions of style and narrative were at issue. This time the subject was *Palace and Fortress* (*Dvorets i krepost'*, directed by Aleksandr Ivanovskii, 1924; production company Sevzapkino); the controversy arose around the way the film was cut. To enhance the contrast cued by the film's title, a large section of the film intercut scenes set in a prison cell of the Petropavlovsk fortress with others set in the court of the Tsar—a novelty for a Soviet film of the time, noticed by reviewers and theorized in an article by Viktor Shklovskii.[13] When the film reached the headquarters of the Soviet Trade Delegation (*Torgpredstvo*) in Berlin, the head of its Art Section Maria Andreeva (a former Moscow Art Theatre star and the civil wife of Maxim Gorky) requested that it should be reedited to suit the taste of German spectators: "So that the American montage is replaced with sequential montage, that is, first [you must] show all the scene in the palace pasted together, then all the scenes in the fortress."[14] The request was followed by a proposal to hire "an experienced German director" (Conrad Veidt was proposed as a possible reeditor!) to do the work properly. The Sevzapkino representative in Berlin resented the idea; his letter to the studio reported: "I could not agree with the interests of the Sevzapkino being sacrificed in such a way, and to such a violation of basic rights of the director and the author."[15] To remain on good terms with the Trade Delegation in Berlin, the Sevzapkino authorities replied in a rather elusive manner: "We agree that a good director should be approached to edit 'Palace and Fortress' in accordance with the taste of foreign audiences, but on the condition that [such reediting] does not violate the artistic and historical integrity that was our major concern as the picture was being produced."[16]

This controversy today seems to be a minor matter of film style, but it makes more sense if we remember that in 1924 crosscutting was still perceived as a specifically "American" technique believed by many to be ill-suited for "European" viewers primed for longer takes and uninterrupted narratives. Around this time we find similar arguments circulated in press debates about the future of Soviet cinema, with partisans of the "German" way insisting on the priority of the image, and the "Americanizers" stressing the importance of montage.[17] Ironically, in Germany we find the same kind of anxiety about their exports, the only distinction being that here producers feared that German films might look too slow: Eric Renschler and Mark Silberman mentioned Fritz Lang's *Spionen* as an example of a film whose export version was cut faster than the one released at home; the same goes for *Metropolis*, with the exception that when the home version of this film proved to be a box-office failure, UFA made a decision to recut the home print according to the "American style."[18]

Reediting for the Home Market

The attempt to reedit for Russia's home audiences began even before this market opened for foreign films. In April 1918, for want of new pictures (only a few had been produced and imported during the Civil War), the newly founded Moscow Cinema Committee (*Moskovskii kinokomitet*) decided to requisition old positive prints from private film factories and recut those found suited for rerelease. Lev Kuleshov was among the first professional filmmakers engaged in the reediting of prerevolutionary films, and it was on the basis of his experience as a reeditor that the famous "Kuleshov experiments" were devised.[19]

The reedit of *To the Strong—Glory* (*Sil'nym slava*) stands out as a most radical example from this early period. Released by the Moscow Kinokomitet in February 1919, it was presented as "capital reediting [*kapitalnyi peremontazh*]" of Vladimir Gardin's 1916 war melodrama *Glory to the Strong . . . Death to the Weak*, which featured two brothers, the owners of the successful Kremlev business, in love with Varia, an artist's model.[20] Anatolii

Kremlev is weak, gambles and drinks, and finally wins Varia's attention; unable to bear it, the strong brother Vasilii joins the army, becomes a hero, is wounded, soon recovers, and, as the contemporary synopsis concludes, "together with Varia—now a sister of mercy—sets off again to serve the great cause. Glory to the strong! Anatolii realizes how futile his life is and commits suicide. Death to the weak!"[21] The reedited version (an "agit-film" directed by Nikolai Malikov and [re-]scripted by V. Dobrovolskii) reduced the original 1,603 meters to 700 meters and, of course, overhauled the story. Although the reedit does not survive, we know that, instead of the family drama between the two capitalist brothers, *Sil'nym slava* became a Sovietized film about a "clash between a worker and a bourgeois."[22] I wonder what they did to Varia.

In December 1922, the Central State Cine-Photo Enterprise (Goskino) was founded with an eye, among other tasks, to monopolize distribution—this plan never came true—and help reopen the home market for Western films.[23] This change happened so fast and to such proportions that on February 9, 1923, the Council of People's Commissars (Sovnarkom) instituted the Head Committee for the Control over Cinema Repertoire (Glavrepertkom)—the organ responsible for keeping the influx of foreign films under control. From that date on, all film organizations that arranged their own imports had to submit foreign films to Glavrepertkom for exhibition permits (*pasport kontrolia*). To make sure that the films they planned to import passed the censors, distribution agencies started looking for people who would make them ideologically acceptable. At first, the same person who was hired to translate intertitles would also be required to adjust them ideologically and maybe cut or add a few here and there. Before 1924 no quality standards existed, the translators/reeditors were paid by job done, and the main thing they cared about was that the job was done fast. In the general opinion voiced through film reviews, this resulted in a "complete mutilation of pictures."[24] After a year of such rule-of-thumb practice, some distributors felt that, to assure the censors and appease the critics, the work of reediting must be professionalized, or, to use a phrase from the period, "raised to the new level of quality." An unsigned article in *Zrelishcha* (The Spectacle) reflects this drive to transform the image of the reeditor from that of a tinkerer to that of an expert:

> Montage Bureau
>
> Almost all films going through our distribution agencies get remade, or, so to say, "sovieticized." In most cases, not only titles are changed or written anew, but often the content of the picture needs to be radically reworked.

This peculiar kind of film production has generated a new type of production worker. And, as it usually happens when there is great demand
of labor, the profession develops in two directions. On the one hand
(and above all) hack-work prevails, on the other, there evolves serious
and demanding qualification. . . . And now, as we learned that a group of
young film production workers have organized themselves into a workshop engaged in reediting old and new films, we can only welcome their
initiative. It will, no doubt, unmask some passionate pot-boilers, and give
more screen room to films edited with intelligence and talent. The reform
comes timely. To cut out a scene, to add an intertitle, to change the title
of a picture is one thing—we learned to do it in the very beginning of the
so-called "regeneration" period of the cinema in the S.S.F.R. when all
we had to show were old films. But times change. Aside from having old
films, we now get new ones. Censorship has grown up, and takes more
seriously the task of censoring the works coming to us from the bourgeois
film kitchens. The work of reediting has become so complicated that the
question of qualification is raised. Now only politically educated workers
can reedit a film. And to make it visually acceptable they have to master
the technique of montage.[25]

The Montage Bureau (*biuro montazha*) that the above article promoted
was instituted at Goskino no later than March 1924, with its employees
getting regular salaries rather than piecework wages. Other major film
organizations followed suit—the Leningrad Directorate Sevzapkino, for
example, installed a reediting bureau in their Moscow office. As a final
stage, in 1925, the new all-union company Sovkino launched a campaign
for centralized distribution, the smaller bureau merged into a large Sovkino
reediting bureau (called, unofficially, *motalka*—"editing table") on the
premises of the former Goskino Montage Bureau in Malaia Gnezdnikovs-
kaia Street in Moscow.[26]

How many of the imported films were reedited at all? Nearly all of
them. Sergei Vasil'ev, who worked as an editor for Sevzapkino and Sovkino,
mentions Paul Leni's *Wachsfigurenkabinett* (shown in 1926 and 1928) and
D. W. Griffith's *The Love Flower* (released in 1926 in the USSR) as "experi-
mentally" released intact, and proudly concludes that, at least in the case
of Griffith's picture, the experiment (staged to prove that the reediting was
indispensable) failed. Critics refused to believe that *The Love Flower* was
genuine and blamed "reeditors" for spoiling "the great master's work,"[27]
specifically, through "adding" inept and bombastic intertitles: "Speaking
of intertitles, our Soviet spectators require precision and clarity in the first
place. They abhor any kind of abstraction, sentimentality, elegance (as
one worker [*rabkor*] wrote in his letter to the editor). They want common
sense, normal lifelike colloquial speech and, above all, they want the plot

to be cleared of moral and psychological coatings."[28] I am not sure to what extent this theory reflects the taste of the "Soviet spectator" (a rhetorical figure, anyway), but it does say something about the reeditors' ideas of what a good movie should look like.

Aside from intertitles, what else did the reeditor's work consist of? To begin with, happy endings would be removed as suggesting that one can be happy under capitalism. In some cases (Vasil'ev mentions the names of Cruze, Lubitsch, Chaplin, Von Stroheim) such an operation was presented as liberating: "American endings" were generally believed to be forced upon artists by the capitalist film industry.[29] Erich von Stroheim's *Merry-Go-Round* (in the USSR from 1924), Cecil B. DeMille's *Godless Girl* (in 1930 and 1934 as *To Remain Silent*), and Chaplin's *The Woman of Paris* (from 1925) were mentioned among the films believed to have benefited from losing the original endings.[30]

Sometimes, as in the case of F. W. Murnau's 1924 *The Last Laugh*, a happy ending would, indeed, come off like a lizard's tail. More often, however, either in order to motivate the tragic outcome, or to present its events in a minor key, the whole story had to be turned inside out. As Viktor Shklovskii, who spent some time working in the Goskino Bureau, tells in his book *The Editing Table* (*Motalka*), "Fat and virtuous people were turned into villains as a general rule, but they had to have perpetrated some deeds and they never did. Then we gave them plots; later they needed crimes and they had to die for them. In some worst cases of reediting work, smoke would be cut in—say, there was a disaster happening in a house—and then the reeditor would try to convince us that everything had perished in smoke."[31] Thus, in order for foreign films to appear in the USSR, foreign characters had to be made more "foreign" (and less "Soviet").

At other times, a character's nationality would be changed, as in the case of Cecil B. DeMille's *Male and Female*, whose Russian version, re-named *Fragments of a Shipwreck*, was more than once criticized for being too heavily reedited. I have not seen this version (I doubt if it exists), but the reeditor's idea is easy to reconstruct from a critical article "God Deliver Me from [Fools]," written in 1925 by the theater director, Sergei Radlov. Originally, DeMille's film is about Crichton, a butler to Lord Loam, secretly in love with the lord's daughter, Lady Mary. After Lord Loam's yacht is shipwrecked, his family and servants become stranded on a deserted island where the butler, who is used to manual labor, takes the reins of leadership and wins the love of Lady Mary and deference on the part of the lord. The Soviet reeditor decided to rework this social-Darwinist fable into something like a topical agit-film by turning the two British servant characters into Russian blue-blooded émigrés, and Lord Loam into an American millionaire.[32] As a result, Radlov claims, the characters' cultural, social, and ethnic identities clash with whatever the Russian intertitles are trying to make them pass for:

> The first thing that I saw (I quote from memory—how could I know that the titles were going to be so remarkable): "The October Revolution scattered the fragments of the old world all over the globe." Then we are shown a very imposing young man wearing a lackey's tail coat, with a typical anglo-saxon face followed by the title "Prince Romodanov" [reminiscent of the Romanovs' dynasty name] and the explanation that Russian émigré aristocracy is now waiting upon American millionaires, the same good-for-nothings as themselves. To support this deep idea, a pretty teen-aged girl is shown, with naive wide open eyes on a merry plump face and with the manners of a village ninny, and here comes the title: "Exhausted by all she had to go through in Constantinople [a major transshipping point of Russian emigration], princess NN was happy to get the job of a chamber-maid." Whereupon we are shown how this suffering princess devours a piece of jam pie with serene and healthy appetite, and are told that the poor woman cannot satisfy her hunger after having starved in Constantinople. . . . We are shown our anglo-saxon lackey energetically opening some book. The title assures us that the book is the notorious "Pineapples in Champaigne" by Igor Severianin, despite the fact that written across the back of the book we see "Poems" written in English.[33]

Another source casts some light on who might have been the author of Russian titles for *Male and Female*. In the twenties, these titles became so notorious that as late as 1946 Georgii Vasil'ev still remembered how the print came into his hands about twenty years before. In his autobiography *How I Became a Film Director*, Vasil'ev motivates the necessity of reediting by the fact that in the years when he was employed at the Reediting Bureau some films would arrive from the exporting country already retitled so as to meet the requirements of Soviet censors (a practice mirroring that of refitting Soviet films for export—compare the case of *S.V.D.*). Vasil'ev recalls:

> One day, we received from abroad a number of different films provided with [lists of] "ready-made" Russian intertitles, in each of which the main negative character was introduced with the title: "Count Romodanovsky, the white émigré officer, was as unfit for physical labour as a rooster is for laying eggs." And the same title for another picture, and so on, betraying not only the poor grammar but also the paucity of imagination of the unknown re-editor.[34]

Undoubtedly, *Male and Female*, with "Count Romodanov" in the center, must have come out of this package. "As it follows from a departmental memo entitled 'Our tasks in the field of selection and purchase of foreign films' circulated in the Reediting Bureau in 1925, the bureau regarded such "unknown re-editors" operating abroad as their worst enemies, whose sloppy performance not only spoilt films but also defaced the image of the profession in the public's view." Specifically, the memo discusses (and condemns) the cases when films were reedited at the premises of Soviet Trade Delegations abroad or purchased from production companies with Russian titles already in place.[35] As one reads this memo, before your mind's eyes passes an image of an impoverished Russian émigré count paid by the hour to translate intertitles for Famous Players Lasky Corporation and, to use his own words, as unfit for the job as a rooster is for laying eggs. Here is another example of his product cited in Vasil'ev's autobiography:

> Sometimes you came across such "time-serving" titles (some of these even came printed on celluloid) as: "The marquis repulses me, his mother repulses me, and his castle, too, is repulsive" (while everything else about the heroine suggested that she was not that much repulsed by any of these things).[36]

This was what the reeditors called "hack-work" (*khaltura*). What was considered good work, then? Early in 1924, Sergei Eisenstein and Esther Shub worked on compressing two episodes of *Dr. Mabuse, Der Spieler* into one feature-length film for its repeated release under the title *The Gilded Rot* (for the first time, unabridged and named *Doktor Mabuzo*, Lang's film had been released in 1922). Eisenstein characterized the art of reediting as "wise and wicked,"[37] and (in a passage omitted from Leyda's English translation) he added: "when it really reached the status of 'art' rather than tinkery hack-work—what infinitude of wit went into it!"[38] Wit is the key word here. That less than a month before going into production with *Strike* Eisenstein found time to spend in the Goskino bureau not only tells that he was interested in Lang's secrets of filmmaking (this, too) but also reveals something about the reputation of the place in the circle of Moscow cineastes. Some fairly jolly fellows worked there—we only know the names of those who later became filmmakers: Eisenstein and Georgii Vasil'ev (Sergei, the other of the two "brothers," as I mentioned earlier, worked at that time as a reeditor for the Sevzapkino). Others—a person whom Eisenstein referred to as Birrois, and Benjamin Boitler,[39] whom the fellow-editors recognized as the wittiest of them all—have passed into oblivion. They were connoisseurs: no one in the film industry (or outside it) knew Western cinema better than the reeditors. They were experts: few filmmakers compared to them in mastering the technique of editing (you feel it in Sergei Vasil'ev's writings and lectures of the twenties). They were arrogant: they believed they could *improve* Griffith! And, despite being badged by film critics, they were proud of their profession. When in 1926 Ilia Trauberg's article "Why Are You Not Pleased?" appeared in the *Red Evening Newspaper* complaining that reeditors were standing in the way of studying Western film and ending with a slogan, "The [re-]editor as such must die!,"[40] Sergei Vasil'ev had this to answer:

> Has Ilia Trauberg forgotten that it is for nine years already that the pro-
> letarian revolution has opened its scissors in order to re-edit one sixth of
> the world as it sees fit, and that maybe the time is approaching when the
> other five sixths will be put on the re-editing table?[41]

In these years, the Goskino (later Sovkino) bureau of montage formed a kind of professional elite club, where reeditors played "wise and wicked" often for the sake of the game. As it follows from Vasil'ev's writings, the game consisted of riddles and answers. After having spent some time at the editing table eye to eye with a film, reeditors would invite film directors, camera-men, and "other film specialists" to a preview arranged in the bureau for a guessing game: "Even an experienced re-editor watching the work done by his fellow-editor often cannot tell what scenes had been changed in the picture. . . . And I don't know yet of any case when [someone who was not a reeditor] would guess correctly, and this despite the fact that some 'great figures' often come to our previews."[42] I am not sure how seriously these people were preoccupied with political considerations, but, by all evidence, witty formal solutions were worth their weight in gold. In his 1927 book *The Editing Table*, Shklovskii described one of the wittiest ones—and dared to attribute it to a wrong editor: "I think one of Vasil'ev's inventions is a masterpiece of cinematic thinking. He needed a man to die but he did not die. He chose a moment when the proposed victim was yawning, printed the same frame over and over again, and the movement stopped. The man froze with his mouth open: it remained to add the title: 'death from heart attack.' This device was so unexpected that no one protested."[43] It is unclear whom of the two Vasil'evs Shklovskii had in mind, but Sergei Vasil'ev reacted immediately with a refutation published in the Moscow newspaper *Kino:* "In order to restore justice I hereby declare that I never performed such a trick, and that the authorship of this trick belongs to comrade Boitler."[44]

Boitler must have been a genius of reediting. In an article about film language written years after the event, Eisenstein remembered another of his tricks concerning the reediting of Dimitri Buchowetzki's *Danton* (1921) (see fig. 2.2):

Figure 2.2. The More Soviet Hero: Robespierre.
From Dimitri Buchowetzki's *Danton* (1921).

I cannot resist the pleasure of citing here one montage *tour de force*
. . . executed by Boitler. One film bought from Germany was *Danton*,
with Emil Jannings. As released on our screens [in 1924 under the title
Guillotine], this scene was shown: Camille Desmoulins is condemned to
the guillotine. Greatly agitated, Danton rushes to Robespierre, who turns
aside and slowly wipes away a tear. The sub-title said, approximately, "In
the name of freedom I had to sacrifice a friend. . . ." Fine.

But who could have guessed that in the German original, Danton,
represented as an idler, a petticoat-chaser, a splendid chap and the only
positive figure in the midst of evil characters, that this Danton ran to the
evil Robespierre and . . . spat in his face? And that it was this spit that
Robespierre wiped from his face with a handkerchief? And that the title
indicated Robespierre's hatred of Danton, a hate that in the end of the film
motivates the condemnation of Jannings-Danton to the guillotine?!

Two tiny cuts eliminated a short piece of film from the moment when
Danton spits to the moment when the spit reaches its aim. And the insult
is turned into a tear of remorse. [45]

By playing the game of reediting, Boitler made Robespierre more Soviet and Danton more foreign, an acceptable change from the ideological
standpoint. From time to time, reeditors were approached with requests
to "save" films ruined by studio directors—another meaning of the term
peremontazh. The two Vasil'evs finally got into directing through reediting
others' failures; Viktor Shklovskii was proud of his reputation of being the
best hand in saving hopeless films, studios competed for his help, and his
writings are full of examples of these last minute rescues.

Reediting and Film Culture

Primarily, the art of reediting appealed to those interested in what David
Bordwell calls "*techne*-centered" aesthetics,[46] namely, to the group of Left
Front (LEF) practitioners and that of adherents of Formalist methods in
the theory of literature (Shklovskii was active in both).[47] Two LEF-related
film ideas (neither of which materialized) illustrate the infectiousness of the
games played in reediting bureaus. In 1926 (the year in which the tempera-
ture of press debate about reediting reached its peak) the LEF film critic
Viktor Pertsov published an article, "Film as Review" (*Filma-retsenziia*),
which suggested that, alongside with fiction films, films about fiction films
should be produced at film factories, a visual tool of educating average
cinemagoers. Portions of Pertsov's article sound almost like a proposal:

> The shots of such film will be similar to quotations, analogies, em-
> phases or examples of regularities. Each intertitle of a film like that will
> work as a thesis. By intercutting some most representative fragments, this
> film-as-review will be able to compare different styles of direction and add
> filmic commentaries to them. . . .
> Such film-as-review can be sometimes scholarly, but sometimes work
> as comedy or parody. For example, a critical review of Vladimir Gardin's
> *Cross and Mauser* [1925] published in one of the issues of the newspaper
> *Kino* [November 17, 1925] says that although [the actress] Nina Li tries
> to walk like Mary Pickford, the legs she has to use are still her own. This
> phrase can be used as an excellent scenario situation. In our film-as-review
> it will be manifested by intercutting corresponding quotation-shots from
> a Mary Pickford film and *Cross and Mauser*.
> Often by way of reediting a film you can turn it into an acerbic review
> of itself. Isolated from the rest of the action, a chain of Douglas Fairbanks'
> jumps (specifically, in *Robin Hood*) can serve as the best method of criticiz-
> ing stunts for stunts' sake.
> Can we count on visual means if we want to characterize the social
> and ideological content of a film? At first sight, it seems difficult to express
> abstract ideas by means of visuals. But this, too, can be achieved through
> the montage of similar or dissimilar material from different films.[48]

And so on. The other (somewhat more inspiring) project comes from the pen of Lilia Brik, active in LEF through her connection with Osip Brik and Vladimir Mayakovsky. At the time, Brik was occasionally involved in scriptwriting, acting, and directing. Her first film script (as well as her first film part earlier), *The Glass Eye*, was a film about filming; her second script is lost, but she remembers it in her memoirs: "Soon after [having finished *The Glass Eye*] I wrote a screenplay with a parodic title *Love and Duty*. The entire story of the film would go into the first reel. The other [four] reels would acquire a completely new meaning as a result of re-editing alone: . . . nothing to do with the original plot. Re-editing alone, not a single shot would be added!"[49] The style of the proposed film would change from one reel to another: sensational drama (*boevik*)—a film for teenaged audiences—Soviet reediting—American comedy. In the epilogue, tin cans with film would be shown rolling back to the film factory to be washed off—"the suicide of film."[50]

A number of similar projects are found in studio archives, but only one of them ever saw the screen: the educational film *The ABC of Film Editing* (*Azbuka kinomontazha*), put together in 1926 by Georgii Vasil'ev and Sergei Vasil'ev (before they became known as "the Vasil'ev brothers"), then still working as reeditors for Sovkino. The fact that the film has the same title as Sergei Vasil'ev's book *Azbuka kinomontazha*, published in 1929 as *The Film Montage*, indicates that the author planned both to be used in class. At least once, the film was projected for a seminar course on editing that Sergei Vasil'ev taught at GTK (the Film Institute in Moscow). In 1928, Vasil'ev did use his film during the first class meeting; the film does not survive, but judging by the shorthand records of the instructor's comment after its screening, at least in its final section, the *ABC of Film Editing* demonstrated some tricks of the trade: "From what you have just seen you can conclude that the meaning of any scene can be radically altered, and that the meaning of any piece of film depends on what other pieces of film it is juxtaposed with."[51]

Finally, I want to dwell upon the role of reediting for the "*techne*-centered" theory of art. The title of Viktor Shklovskii's book *The Editing Table* shows the importance of reediting for the Formalist theory of film (and not of film alone: like Shklovskii's two other books with film-related titles, *The Third Factory* and *Day Labor*, *The Editing Table* presented cinema as a quintessential art "baring" the inner mechanism of culture in general). An accomplished car driver and mechanic (he even claimed that some central points of the Formalist doctrine were born as he fixed car engines when serving in the armored car regiment), Shklovskii understood art as a special way of assembling things, and enjoyed watching the whole change

Figure 2.3. Von Stroheim's Karamzin/Romanovskii.
From Erich von Stroheim's *Foolish Wives* (1922).

its meaning as he rearranged its parts on his editing table. For a theorist, this process confirmed what Kuleshov (pioneer reeditor and a maniac driver himself) had earlier shown about cinema and what Tynianov had found about the language of poetry in 1923, namely, that "meanings" are generated through juxtaposition and foregrounding:

> The variety of human movements is not that large. The variety of facial expressions is even smaller. [Changes brought into] intertitles and plot construction can completely re-cue our perception of the film hero.[52]

Shklovskii concludes his article "The Work of Re-Editing" with this perceptive statement on the discrepancy between the position of the maker (in this case, the reeditor) and the viewer of the film:

> The fact is that for the professional [reeditor] the man in the shot does not laugh or cry or mourn, he only opens and shuts his eyes and his mouth in a specific way. He is raw material. The meaning of a word depends on the phrase I place it in. If I place the word properly in another phrase it

will acquire a different meaning, while the viewer [believes] that he is searching for some kind of true, original meaning of the word, [or] a lexical meaning of [actors'] emotions.[53]

Reeditors, in Shklovskii's view, possessed the power to mold identities, and therefore to define what was foreign and what was not.

Other reeditors had the task of turning what had previous been "Russian" into something foreign. Some years earlier, writing about Erich von Stroheim's 1922 film *Foolish Wives* (a film that he was not particularly fond of), another Formalist, Boris Tomashevskii, used the notion of reediting as a pretext for an elegant theoretical paradox aimed at supporting the Formalist concept of the hero in fiction (*geroi literaturnogo proizvedeniia*). The central character of von Stroheim's film (in Russia from 1924) is the Russian émigré officer Vladislav Serge Karamzin (see fig. 2.3). Judging by the Russian distribution title—*The Scion of a Noble Family* (*Otprysk blagorodnogo roda*)—its Soviet reeditor had decided that, for propaganda purposes, this circumstance was playing into his hands. In the original, the count was hateful enough, and, rather than retouching von Stroheim's character, the Russian reeditor simply changed his name to count Sergei Romanovskii (reminiscent of Romanov, Romodanov, Romodanovskii). Paradoxically, Tomashevskii argues, this lack of reediting spoiled the original artistic intent of the director. Because fictional characters are textual functions rather than "real people," their "personal traits," including "nationality," only make sense within a certain set of shared conventions:

> In the epoch of Peter the Great when the "Russian" first penetrated Western literature, this figure represented the type of a "Barbarian in civilized guise [*tip tsivilizuiushchegosia varvara*]." Soon this type became mechanized, lost liveliness, turned into a stereotype. From Voltaire and Stendhal who actively exploited it, this type trickled down to subdominant genres [*mladshie riady*] of literature: cheap novel [*bul'varnyi roman*], comical novelette and musical comedy [operetta]. The function of the "Russian nobleman [*barin*]" became as definite as that of such vaudeville characters as the "Polish pan," the "Siamese princeling," etc. All these figures are pseudo-national variations of the international Prince Esperanto [*kniaz' Volapuk*]. The literature that cultivates such conventional types was not interested in ethnographic precision. No vaudeville director will ever ask an Orientalist what Siamese kings look like. The "branchy cranberries" [*razvesistaia kliukva*, a Russian idiom meaning "sham details of Russian life used in Western literature in order to suggest local color"] is not, as we tend to believe, a naive blunder resulting from European ignorance, but a traditional stereotype, a convention that has not and does not want to have anything to do with the reality of Russian life. "Count Sergei Romanovsky" of the American film [Tomashevskii was not aware of the fact

that in von Stroheim's original the villain's name had been Karamzin] is exactly such a "branchy cranberry" character. The Americans made him wear a caftan *stylized* as a Russian uniform, surrounded him with the grotesque "smoky samovar," "caviar," etc.,—and, at the same time, with objects pertaining to *catholic* religion. They did it because they needed a grotesque type of international swindler, not a "modern Russian white guard." Because the film factory that could afford to build an entire town in its studio, would not spare ten dollars for exact information about Russian uniforms and other details of Russian reality, if they felt it was what they needed. [The reediting bureau of the distribution company] Kino-Sever decided to nationalize this conventional "prince Esperanto," and it was their grave mistake. This film could not possibly have any [anti-émigré] propaganda value in America or Germany because in these countries its hero is perceived exclusively as the familiar type of an exotic, grotesque "Barbarian in civilized guise." Russian translators should have substituted the white guard with something like a "Bulgarian" or Dalmatian officer in order to preserve, *mutatis mutandis*, the function of the type for Russian audiences. This type only exists as the "exotic foreigner," and it remains a foreigner for all nations. He is a foreigner for Russia, too. By keeping his Russian name for their translation, the Kino-Sever re-editors made the type grow heavy. A conventional literary mask was turned into a realistic image responsible for its own naturalism. But since this film does not accept responsibility for being true to life, and "branchy cranberry" is all it counts on, instead of serving as propaganda, its sham Russianness only amuses the spectators.[54]

Of course, Tomashevskii's argument was no more than an intellectual exercise in Formalist poetics (I do not think he would seriously consider cutting out the samovar and caviar in order to transform von Stroheim's character into a Bulgarian). Apart from being poeticians, Formalist scholars were also part of film audiences, and, as Viktor Shklovskii wrote, "the audiences see through and resent the re-editing of films."[55] Reediting fascinated them as a technology of making meaning, but they were not impressed by the results. For no obvious reason (or was it Boitler's hand again?), in the Russian version of Pabst's *Die Freudlose Gasse* (released in 1925; the Russian version survives at the State Film Archive in Moscow), Asta Nielsen does not kill her lover. In October 1926, in a newspaper interview about the issue of reediting (such interviews were part of the press campaign against the arbitrary rule of reeditors in foreign film distribution launched by Ilia Trauberg in the article referred to earlier), Iuri Tynianov evoked this rather pointless trick in order to put reeditors in their place—which, as the interview suggests, was no higher than cleaning other people's bad work:

Re-editing [skills] developed from the habit of dealing with low quality product. One can rework a very bad tragedy into a bad drama and a decent "scenic" picture. But one cannot convert a bad tragedy into a good one by way of simply re-editing it.

The habit of saving bad films shows even poorer results when the re-editor touches a good picture. The work of the director, actors, and the cameraman cannot be completely buried—some elements remain, and the good picture becomes a good but spoilt picture. In *Freudlose Gasse*, instead of the heroine, her former fiancée was turned into a murderer. The re-editor was, probably, proud of his work. But on the screen the hands of the murderer remained those of a woman. An intertitle explaining that these hands belonged to a man would hardly help! This is a case of "artistic re-editing," because you can scarcely find any ideological motivation for it. But in well-made pictures ideology is present at once in multiple elements of plot and style, and no scissors or paste can help anyone to get rid of it.[56]

Tynianov's argument can be interpreted both as a reply of an irritated film viewer and a theoretical statement coming from the pen of an expert in textology—the science of establishing the genuine version of an author's text. One is torn between Tynianov's position according to which there may be only one consequence of reediting a good film, that is, spoiling it, and that of the modern film historian Paolo Cherchi Usai, who claims that, given the number of versions of every silent films preserved in every country of the world, all we can do is to admit that "the 'original' version of a film is a multiple object fragmented into a number of different entities equal to the number of surviving copies."[57] Cherchi Usai's point is innovative because it invites us to perceive film history as a process rather than as a gallery of art objects. Yet, as any new powerful theory, this position puts us in front of new questions, one of them being: once we admit that there is more than one version to every film, do we also have to put up with a bit of Boitler in every film by Griffith or Pabst? Eisenstein was right: the game of reediting could be both wise and wicked. It became wicked when a good film fell into the hands of either too stupid or too witty a reeditor. But one can see its wisdom in a larger perspective: for a whole generation of Soviet filmmakers the art of reediting served as a school of editing proper, as Joan Neuberger's article on Eisenstein's use of foreign characters demonstrates. When we see a man strangling another man with the help of Asta Nielsen's hands we can simply dismiss the whole thing as a senseless joke, yet should we ignore Eisenstein's reedited version of *Doctor Mabuse, the Gambler* even if Lang's film was reduced to six reels, its title changed to *Gilded Rot*, its famous protagonist turned into a petty adventurer under the trivial name of Mr. Brown, and the whole issue of hypnotism erased from the film's story?[58] Mutilation? Perhaps, but less so if we think of it in terms of how much the new version reminds us of Eisenstein's own *Strike* made the same year. Why should Eisenstein, who by 1924 was already a famous theater director and whose first film was ready to go into production, spend days in the editing room recutting a German movie? A ready answer might be: to learn from Lang. Perhaps, but isn't it a strange way of learning as a result of which nothing of Lang's style can be traced in Eisenstein's films (or Lang's own film, for that matter)? Possibly, a more adequate answer would be: to learn from Boitler, in other words, to master the art of "mutilating" films by changing characters' identities, taking apart coherent narratives, and reassembling them in most eccentric ways—in a word, to learn the lesson of deconstruction so manifest in many of the best Soviet films of the twenties.

NOTES

1. In vertically integrated organizations like the Leningrad Sovkino the reediting of both export-bound and imported films could be affiliated with the same institutions, which fact should not mislead us into presenting them as similar activities. In the case to be discussed shortly, any changes made either in outgoing or incoming prints had to be approved by the head of the Export-Import Division of the Sovkino, Yevgenii Kaufman. Yet it seems that this subordination was technical rather than operational. Kaufman was mainly in charge of postproduction reediting, while the decisions taken by the Reediting Bureau (a division dealing with foreign pictures) were coordinated directly with the Glavrepertkom (the Main Repertoire Committee, or, to put it bluntly, the Soviet Board of Censors).

2. LGALI (Leningrad State Archive of Literature and Art), f. (fond), 257, op. 16, d., 20, 1.112.

3. On Tynianov's and Oksman's scenario see: Yuri Lotman and Yuri Tsivian, "SVD: Melodrama and History" (in Russian), in *Tynianovskie chteniia* (Proceedings of Tynianov Conference), ed. Marietta Chudakoia and Evgenii Toddes (Riga: Nauka, 1985), 46–77.

4. LGALI (Leningrad State Archive of Literature and Art), f. (fond), 257, op. 16, d., 20, 1.112. According to the Sovkino Personnel Division Record preserved at another archive, the head of the Export-Import Division, Yevgenii Dmitrievich Kaufman (born 1886), was formerly a professor at the University of Tambov (RGALI [Russian State Archive of Literature and Art], f. [fond], 2496, op. 2, d., 10).

5. On Tynianov's work at the Sovkino studio see Evgenii Toddes and Yuri Tsivian, "Tynianov and Film" (in Russian), *Iskusstvo kino* (The Art of Cinema) 7 (1986): 88–98.

6. LGALI (Leningrad State Archive of Literature and Art), f. (fond), 257, op. 16, d., 20, 1.120.

7. Ippolit Sokolov, "S.V.D.," *Kino-front*, nos. 9–10 (1927): 22.

8. LGALI (Leningrad State Archive of Literature and Art), f. (fond), 257, op. 16, d., 20, 1.121.

9. LGALI (Leningrad State Archive of Literature and Art), f. (fond), 257, op. 16, d., 20, 1.122.

10. LGALI (Leningrad State Archive of Literature and Art), f. (fond), 257, op. 16, d., 20, 1.123.

11. I thank Kristin Thompson for this information.

12. Film Dossier (*filmovoe delo*) was a folder containing a shot list, censorship license, and other documents required to come with every print in order for it to be legally exhibited in film theaters. Gosfilmofond (the State Film Archive near Moscow) stores a collection of such dossiers catalogued by film titles.

13. Viktor Shklovskii, "Palace and Fortress and the Cinematograph" (in Russian), *Zrelishcha* (Spectacle), no. 76 (1924): 14. The article makes a distinction between "parallel editing" and crosscutting of alternating events.

14. Quoted after L. Zevakina, "From the Formative Years of Soviet Distribution Abroad (Materials Pertaining to the Activity of Leningrad Cinema Organizations)" (in Russian), in *Voprosy istorii i teorii kino* (Question of Film History and Theory) (Leningrad: Nauka, 1975), 80.

15. Ibid. It is not clear from Zevakina's article whether the letter resisted the idea of reediting in general or the fact that foreign filmmakers would be employed to perform it. I have not consulted the archival sources myself yet.

16. Ibid., 81. As Zevakina's article attests, after *Palace and Fortress* was previewed on the premises of the Trade Delegation in the presence of some German distributors, it proved to be so successful that there was no further need to discuss the issue.

17. See Yuri Tsivian, "Caligari in Russia: German Expressionism and Soviet Film Culture," in Thomas W. Gaethens, ed., *Kuenstlerischer Austauch/Artistic Exchange: Akten des XXVIII. Internationalen Kongresses fuer Kunstgeschichte, Berlin, 15.–20. Juli 1992* (Berlin: Akademie Verlag, 1992–1994), 153–64.

18. These observations came up during the discussion of this paper at a 1995 conference, "Nation, National Identity, and the International Cinema," held at La Bretesche, France, organized jointly by the University of Wisconsin and the Bochard Foundation.

19. As Kuleshov's 1921 proposal states, the experiments aimed at formulating not only the methods of film production, but also those of reediting (see Kuleshov's proposal in "The Rediscovery of a Kuleshov Experiment: A Dossier," compiled by Ekaterina Kholchlova, Kristin Thompson, and Yuri Tsivian, *Film History* 8, no. 3 [1996]: 357–67).

20. Only two reels out of six survive from the 1916 film.

21. For the complete text of the synopsis and filmography see: Yuri Tsivian (research), Paolo Cherchi Usai, Lorenzo Codelli, Carlo Montanaro, and David Robinson, eds., *Silent Witnesses: Russian Films, 1908–1919* (London: British Film Institute and Edizioni dell'Immagine, 1989), 362.

22. *Kino i vremia (Byulleten, vypusk 3)* (Cinema and Time), bulletin no. 3 (Moscow: Gosfilmofond, 1963), 173.

23. See Richard Taylor, *The Politics of the Soviet Cinema 1917–1929* (Cambridge, UK: Cambridge University Press, 1979), 72.

24. Sergei Vasil'ev, "What the Argument Is About" (in Russian), in Vasil'ev Brothers, *Collected Works in Three Volumes*, vol. 1 (Moscow: Iskusstvo, 1981), 140. In this 1926 essay responding to the press polemics about reediting that took place in October 1926, Vasil'ev gives a short survey of reediting practices as they developed from 1923 to 1925.

25. *Zrelishcha* (The Spectacle), no. 77 (1924): 13.

26. The way in which the reeditor's work was organized can be reconstructed from documents preserved in Sovkino archives. The reeditor received a test copy of a film, previewed it, defined the coefficient of necessary reediting, reported it to the head of the Bureau, reedited the test copy and compiled its shot list (title list), then s/he did paper work required for the presentation before the Board of Censors (*Glavrepertkom*) including: filmographic data, figures for the initial and the cutout footages, four copies of the title list. Then s/he applied for an appointment at the Board of Censors, where s/he had to be present in the viewing room while the members of the Board of Censors were watching the film, reading new intertitles aloud, and explaining the changes made in the film. If the reeditor disagreed with the censors, s/he reported his/her disagreement to the head of the bureau, after which s/he gave the list of titles to the typesetter, proofread them, and sent the title cards to the laboratory to be shot and developed. Once the titles were back from the lab, the reeditor spliced them into the test copy, previewed it, and sent the result to be stored. The whole reediting process was supposed to be entered into a special journal. If, despite the efforts of the reeditor, the Board of Censors decided to ban the film, the reeditor was supposed either to reassemble the copy in its initial order or, if this appeared impossible to do, to spin the take-outs together in one reel and pack it separately from the main set of reels, ensuring that the print returned to the producer with no footage missing. The reeditor had rights to control the way his/her film was exhibited in film theaters, and to change on the spot whatever s/he considered necessary to change. (RGALI [Russian State Archive of Literature and Art]), f. [fond], 2496, op. 1, d., 5).

27. Vasil'ev Brothers, *Collected Works in Three Volumes*, vol. 1, 143; see also 229.

28. Ibid., 144.

29. Ibid., 145.

30. *Kino i vremia (Byulleten, vypusk 1)* (Cinema and Time), bulletin no. 1 (Moscow: Gosfilmofond, 1960), 210.

31. Richard Taylor and Ian Christie, *The Film Factory: Russian and Soviet Cinema in Documents 1896–1939* (London: Routledge and Kegan Paul, 1988), 168; I made changes in the translation of this excerpt to bring it closer to the original.

32. The plot is based on the British play *The Admirable Crichton* by Sir James M. Barrie; see *The American Film Institute Catalog: Feature Films, 1911–1920*, vol. F1, 568–69.

33. Sergei Radlov, *Desit' let u teatre* (Leningrad: Priboi, 1929), 227–29.

34. Vasil'ev Brothers, *Collected Works*, vol. 1, 110.

35. RGALI (Russian State Archive of Literature and Art), f. (fond), 2496, op. 1, d., 17.

36. Vasil'ev Brothers, *Collected Works*, vol. 1, 111.

37. Sergei Eisenstein, *Film Form*, ed. Jay Leyda (New York: Harcourt, Brace, 1949), 10.

38. Sergei Eisenstein, *Izbrannye proizvedenija v shesti tomakh* (Moscow: Iskusstvo, 1963), vol. 5, 69.

39. As it follows from Sovkino Personnel Division records, Eduards Birois (a Latvian name), born 1891, formerly a journalist from Pskov, was a patient worker with a broad range of interests, but often too slow to meet his deadlines (RGALI [Russian State Archive of Literature and Art]), f. (fond), 2496, op. 2, d., 10. The record does not mention Benjamin Boitler.

40. *Red Evening Newspaper*, October 6, 1926, no. 325, 1239.

41. Vasil'ev Brothers, *Collected Works*, vol. 1, 157.

42. Ibid., 147–48.

43. Taylor and Christie, *The Film Factory*, 169. I made changes in the translation of this excerpt to bring it closer to the original.

44. "Sergei Vail'ev," *Kino*, no. 16, 1927.

45. Eisenstein, *Film Form*, 11. I made changes in the translation of this excerpt to bring it closer to the original.

46. David Bordwell, *The Cinema of Eisenstein* (London and Cambridge, Mass.: Harvard University Press, 1993), 35–39.

47. Founded in 1923, the Left Front for the Arts (LEF) attempted to revive the connections between politics and art. Led by Vladimir Mayakovsky, its members included such cultural luminaries as Osip Brik, Sergei Eisenstein, Dziga Vertov, Vsevolod Meyerhold, Viktor Shklovskii, and Aleksandr Rodchenko.

48. B. Pertsov, "Filma-retsenziia" (in Russian), *Sovetskii ekran* (Soviet Screen), no. 13 (1926): 3.

49. L. Yu. Brik, "The Last Months," in *Vladimir Maiakovskii, Memoirs and Essays*, ed. Bengdt Jangfeldt and Nils Ake Nillson (Stockholm: Almquist and Wiksell International, 1975), 13–14.

50. Ibid.

51. Vasil'ev Brothers, *Collected Works*, vol. 1, 241.

52. Taylor and Christie, *The Film Factory*, 169. I made changes in the translation of this excerpt to bring it closer to the original.

53. Ibid. I made changes in the translation of this excerpt to bring it closer to the original.

54. Boris Tomashevskii, "Foolish Wives" (in Russian), *Zhizn' iskusstva* (Life of Art), no. 10 (1924): 16.

55. Taylor and Christie, *The Film Factory*, 168; I made changes in the translation of this excerpt to bring it closer to the original.

56. "Yuri Tynianov on Re-editing," *Krasnaia gazeta (vechernii vypusk)*, *Red Newspaper*, evening edition, October 22, 1926, no. 249, 1253.

57. Paolo Cherchi Usai, *Burning Passions: An Introduction to the Study of Silent Cinema* (London: BFI Publishing, 1994), 84.

58. *Gilded Rot* does not survive as a film, but its cutting lists signed by Esther Shub and Eisenstein are preserved in Shub's archive (RGALI [Russian State Archive of Literature and Art], f. (fond), 3035, op. 1, d., 2).

3.

Dressing the Part

Clothing Otherness in Soviet Cinema before 1953

Emma Widdis

Almost two decades after the revolution, in his classic film of 1935 *Schast'e* (*Happiness*), the idiosyncratic director Aleksandr Medvedkin pictured acceptance into the new Soviet world as the literal and metaphorical shedding of old clothes. His hero, Khmyr', has—after a long battle with himself and others—finally become a happy and productive member of his collective farm. In the final scenes of the film, he and his wife Anna take a trip to the city where he visits a department store and is re-clothed—transformed from peasant into Soviet man (see figs. 3.1 and 3.2).

Figure 3.1. Khmyr' as Backwards Peasant.
From Aleksandr Medvedkin's *Happiness* (1935).

Figure 3.2. Clothes Make the Soviet Man.
From Aleksandr Medvedkin's *Happiness* (1935).

The symbolic significance of this scene is clear. Khmyr' enters the modern world: he discards his old peasant attire of felt shoes and smock, and with it, implicitly, his old self, and emerges as a shaven, besuited Soviet citizen. In Medvedkin's typically playful style, however, Khmyr"s entry into the Soviet world is by no means simple: the former peasant is shown comically battling with the apparatus of the emerging Soviet consumerism, caught in the revolving doors into the department store, and intimidated by superior salesmen. And his old clothes are not so easily shed: for all his (increasingly desperate) efforts to abandon them inconspicuously in rubbish bins, it seems for a while that he is fated to carry the evidence of his former self with him into the future. Ultimately, however, the message is that Khmyr' purchases the signs of Sovietness. Clothes carry meaning; dress is a sign of belonging. And the distinctions are symbolically graphic. In the film's final scenes, back in the countryside, he is finally able to discard his old clothes, only to see his enemies, impoverished by their self-imposed exclusion from the collective, seize greedily upon them. Those outside the collective remain semiotically bound by the old symbolic order; Khmyr"s escape into the new symbolic order signals his acceptance into the new world.

Medvedkin's use of the symbolic vocabulary of clothing and belonging here was not accidental. It was part of an ongoing debate about the nature and form of Soviet clothing during the late 1920s and into the 1930s. In June 1928, a headline in the newspaper *Komsomolskaia pravda* posed a crucial question: "How should we dress?"[1] What, it asked, was correct Soviet dress; what was the ideologically appropriate fashion for the new age? Such questions were increasingly widespread. In the same year, the periodical magazine *Krasnaia panorama* (*Red Panorama*) began to issue a supplementary magazine, *Iskusstvo odevat'sia* (*The Art of Dressing*). Its first issue contained a forward by Anatolii Lunacharskii, in which he acknowledged that "a certain amount of smartness and fashion [*moda*] is by no means unsuited to the proletariat."[2] Five years later, in 1933, *Komsomolskaia pravda* began to publish a regular column under the heading "We want to dress well."[3]

What did all this mean? Did it herald the beginning of a new attitude to Soviet fashion? How was Sovietness to be encoded in clothes? And what, if so, was *un*-Soviet dress? The evidence — even the very existence — of such debates leads us to question the so-called prohibition of fashion in Soviet Russia.[4] The standard narrative of Soviet fashion, at least in the West, is one of its absence, of the gray sameness that is supposed to have distinguished the Soviet street: in the words of one historian of dress, "It is drab, dull, old, and simple."[5] Communism, it is suggested, eliminated fashion.

Fashioning the Collective

One of the earliest attempts to theorize the role and significance of fashion in modern society was made by Georg Simmel in 1914. According to Simmel, fashion in Western societies provides a uniquely synthetic answer to two apparently contradictory ambitions: it allows for "fusion with our social group and the accentuation of the individual." "Fashion," Simmel suggested, "is the imitation of a given pattern and thus satisfies the need for social adaptation. It leads the individual onto the path that everyone travels . . . . At the same time, and to no less a degree, it satisfies the need for distinction, the tendency toward differentiation, change, and individual contrast."[6] For Simmel, writing just three years before the Bolshevik revolution claimed to usher in a new kind of social order, these two aims were essential to the very existence of fashion as concept and reality: "If one of the two social tendencies essential to the establishment of fashion, namely, the need for integration on the one hand and the need for separation on the other, should be absent, then the formation of fashions will not occur and its realm will end."[7]

The implications of this statement for Soviet society—and for Soviet fashion—are manifold and contradictory. According to Simmel, the collectivist imperative of Soviet Russia should render fashion irrelevant and impossible. Theoretically, the drive for integration would supersede the need for individual differentiation, and the "realm" of fashion would come to an end. In practice, of course, as these debates on "dressing well" suggest, the picture was far more ambiguous. Dress and fashion were in fact as complex and negotiated in Soviet Russia as elsewhere.

Why then did fashion and clothing retain such significance in postrevolutionary Russia? Perhaps Simmel himself pinpointed the essential feature of dress and clothing in relation to the Soviet project when he suggested that, in the West, fashion performed "the double function of holding a given social circle together and at the same time closing it off to others."[8] In Soviet Russia, dress and clothing functioned as symbols of belonging, defining participation in the collective project, and exclusion from it. A specifically Soviet form of dress, therefore, was an ideological imperative, a means first of distinguishing the Soviet world from the West, and second, within that Soviet world, of distinguishing the good and the bad, the loyal citizen from the saboteur or class enemy. My focus in this essay is on this second category. I will not look at oppositions between Russia and elsewhere, or even at graphic distinctions between insiders and outsiders, but on the subtle signs of belonging that linked or separated different categories of so-called insiders.

I will provide a brief survey of the emerging language and symbolism of clothing during the 1920s and 1930s, before focusing on a number of key films from the late 1930s and 1940s. Specifically, I will suggest that the binary distinctions of Soviet and un-Soviet dress blur considerably in films of the late 1930s and 1940s. The clear-cut oppositions of belonging and nonbelonging begin to break down; in their place, in a new language of dress, a comprehensive and all-encompassing vision of Sovietness begins to emerge. In the formation of an ideology of Soviet dress, cinema had a crucial role to play. First, it could shape tastes, offering models of style and beauty for audiences to emulate. In addition, in a more complex sense, I will suggest that filmmakers used the symbolism of clothing as a prism through which to talk about the role of cinema itself, to articulate an ideologically palatable ideal of glamour and "entertainment" that was central to the survival of their own art.

Dressing Proletariat

Of course, this preoccupation with the ideological meaning of clothing was not invented by the Soviets—no more than clothing stores and "fashion" appeared out of nowhere in 1917. By 1911, there were seventy-three "fashion shops (*modnye magaziny*)" in Moscow alone, and 267 stores stocking ready-to-wear clothing. One hundred fashion journals were in circulation between 1800 and 1917. As Christine Ruane has shown, the growth of department stores and fashion *ateliers* in the urban centers of Imperial Russia was accompanied by intense discussion of national identity.[9] As the modes of consumption that proliferated in Russia's metropolitan centers in the second half of the nineteenth century were largely based on Western prototypes, and the principal fashion influences came from Paris in particular, fashion was largely viewed as a foreign import. What, then, was Russian fashion? What was a specifically Russian form of shopping?

In the Soviet context, however, such consumerist preoccupations should surely have become obsolete. In the immediately postrevolutionary years, pragmatic and ideological imperatives alike seemed to demand a rejection of the bourgeois preoccupations of fashion. According to the leading Soviet historian of costume, Tat'iana Strizhenova: "For almost a decade after the revolution, 'fashion' was synonymous with impermissible luxury, frivolity."[10] "Let us tackle those who imitate the dandies of the Petrovka [a fashionable Moscow street] with their 'latest models from abroad,'" *Komsomolskaia pravda* declared. "Let us create new styles of hygienic, purpose-designed, beautiful clothes, made of good material, styles that will be a general guide to all young people."[11]

A number of factors affected questions of dress in early Soviet Russia. First, there was the unavoidable reality of shortages. In simple terms, clothing was difficult to get hold of: according to Nadezhda Mandel'shtam, "All of us, women, mothers, secretaries, we all looked liked scarecrows."[12] Alongside this, and certainly related to it, avant-garde designers such as Nadezhda Lamanova, Varvara Stepanova, Aleksandra Ekster, and Liubov' Popova sought new modes of clothing appropriate to the revolutionary utopia. In the words of Lamanova, "Artists must take the initiative, working to create from plain fabrics simple but beautiful garments befitting the new mode of working life."[13]

From the beginning, Soviet avant-garde designers (many of whom were linked to the "Workshop of Contemporary Dress" established on the initiative of Lamanova in Moscow in 1919) were well aware of the ideological power of dress. As part of the material culture of everyday life, it must be changed in line with the wholesale "transformation of everyday life" that was the revolutionary imperative. In fashion, the dominant aesthetic was one of functionalism: Soviet clothing would be distinguished from that of the West by its rejection of ornament; its form would be determined solely by practicality, by the needs of its wearer and his or her tasks. At its most extreme, the prototype of the *prozodezhda* (production clothing), which was to provide a kind of "uniform" of Soviet citizenship, realized this ideal. Loose-fitting and based on geometric shapes, it would allow the human body full freedom of movement, and, in its uniformity, overcome the vagaries of fashion, gender, and individualism, dressing all men and women alike: "Today's Fashion Is the Worker's Overall" ran the headline of a manifesto article by Varvara Stepanova.[14]

This, then, was a self-conscious attempt to escape from the tyranny of Fashion, Western-style. As Ekaterina Degot points out, however, there is a crucial ambivalence here. The Soviet avant-garde defined itself according to its focus on the "new."[15] Yet it criticized Western fashion for the very same thing: fashion was consistently defined negatively according to its emphasis on novelty for novelty's sake, its perpetual change, its rejection of the functional and utilitarian, its impracticality, and—above all—its individualism. The Soviet product, by contrast, would be collective and practical; its newness would be revolutionary and modern, not subject to the fluctuations of taste.

In practice, however, avant-garde fashion never achieved the wholesale transformation of everyday life to which it aspired, and had little real impact on the clothing of ordinary men and women in Soviet Russia of the 1920s. Most of these designs never went beyond the sketch; others appeared only in costumes for theater (and, to a lesser extent, for film). In Vsevolod Meierkhol'd's 1922 production of *The Magnanimous Cuckold* (*Velikodushnyi rogonosets*), for example, the actors wore Liubov' Popova's blue-gray geometric smocks, a prototype design for the *prozodezhda*. Ironically, Soviet avant-garde fashion design remained in the realm of art, rather than that of production. The pages of the fashion magazine *Atel'e* (Atelier), launched by Lamanova and her colleagues in 1923 (with Anna Akhmatova on its editorial board), were filled with articles by artists and writers such as Boris Kustodiev and Marietta Shaginian, and the magazine lasted only one year, eventually pronounced too "elite."[16]

In a sense, the appropriation of fashion to the world of high art was initially strategic, a means of diminishing its consumerist, capitalist associations, and appropriating it to the revolutionary avant-garde cause. It did not, however, solve the pressing problem of creating real Soviet dress. In real terms, meanwhile, ordinary men and women, of whatever class or political persuasion, were faced with a real fashion dilemma: how to configure their appearance to match the demands of the day? How to appear to belong? At a conference of the Communist Youth League during the 1920s, such urgent questions provided the subject of heated debate: "What should a Komsomol member wear, and can you tell a class enemy by his clothes?" one agenda asked.[17] For a while, the Komsomol adopted a uniform known as the *Iungshturm* as a symbol of membership.

More broadly, "fitting in" became a kind of fashion statement. In the new game of belonging (where the stakes were increasingly high), appearing Proletarian was, in fashion-speak, the look of the season. Writing to his wife Stepanova during a trip to Paris, for example, Aleksandr Rodchenko showed acute awareness of the new demands: "I'm proletarizing my dress in the Western style," he wrote, "I even want to buy a blue blouse [a reference to the revolutionary theater group, the Blue Blouse] and corduroy trousers."[18] During the early 1920s, in times of shortages, the most easily available, ideologically appropriate clothing for women consisted of a black skirt and white blouse, often with a red scarf, echoing the aesthetics (and political credentials) of the French Revolution.[19] For men, the leather jacket (immortalized by Pil'niak in his images of leather-clad revolutionaries in the novel of 1919, *The Naked Year* [*Golyi god*]), was a symbol of the military-revolutionary aesthetic. In practice, however, alongside these drives to standardize the Soviet aesthetic, prerevolutionary fashion remained the sought-after mode for the wealthy and the aspirational ideal for young women of all classes.[20] French magazines were available in Soviet Russia throughout the NEP years, and a number of new fashion magazines appeared during the 1920s. Foreign film stars such as Mary Pickford, appearing in the many Western films distributed in Soviet Russia at this time, acted as models for stylish feminine beauty and stylish dress.[21]

Overall, then, cultural texts of the 1920s reveal a schizophrenic relationship with fashion. In cinema, costume exhibited the hybrid nature of Soviet dress: from the avant-garde costumes designed by Aleksandra Ekster for Iakov Protazanov's 1924 *Aelita,* to the studied neutrality of Sergei Eisenstein's *typage* and the "ordinary" street clothes of the heroes and heroines of Boris Barnet's "everyday" (*bytovye*) comedies, Soviet cinema of this period offers a remarkable snapshot of the hybrid nature of early Soviet dress. One message is relatively consistent, however: an admiration of bourgeois fashion appears as a signal of ideological regression. In Barnet's *A Girl with a Hatbox* (*Devushka s korobkoi,* 1927), for example, "bourgeois" fashion makes its appearance in the form of the hat shop where the reprehensible "Madame Irene" sells her wares, and in Madame Irene herself, whose stylized languor and luxurious Parisian-style clothes (she appears first in a silk kimono) act as signs of her corrupt individualism. In Iurii Zheliabuzhskii's 1924 comedy, *The Cigarette Girl from Mossel'proma* (*Papirosnitsa ot Mossel'proma*), the overweight American businessman Oliver McBright visits Moscow hoping to import his ready-to-wear collection. The eponymous cigarette girl, Zina, is lured from her humble profession into the twin worlds of glamour: acting and modeling. Her white dress (its drop-waist and ruffled skirt already clearly influenced by the fashions of the time) is swapped for the luxury and brilliance of McBright's ready-to-wear dresses (usually, and certainly symbolically, in dark colors, and embellished with jewels and fur). At the end of the film, however, she rejects the false lure of that world. Similarly, in Protazanov's *Aelita* (1924), the engineer Loos is fascinated by Ekster's extraordinary stylized costumes for the Martian princess whom he spies through his super-powered telescope; his wife Natasha, meanwhile, is nearly seduced by a rich entrepreneur who offers her silk stockings and fashionable clothes. Both, in the end, realize the error of their ways.

Thus, in the cinema of the 1920s, fashion appeared as an element of the past, an ideological regression to be overcome in the march toward the future. In the same way, as Oksana Bulgakova has pointed out, film beauties were often depicted as "relics of a past beauty, as something exotic which somehow remained in this new life."[22] What was needed, however, was a new vision of Soviet beauty—and of Soviet style. As "Vlad" Korolevich put it in his short book of 1928, cinema needed to feature "real" women—in real clothes: "Do you have a wife, a sister, or simply a woman you love? She doesn't wear the dress of a *paysanne*, or leather trousers, or a lace peignoir. She carries a briefcase only when she's going to work. You've never seen her on screen. And you want to see her. The woman of today."[23] This woman's style, Korolevich implied, was something new: neither that of the peasant, nor the leather trousers of the revolutionary combatant, nor the petty-bourgeois lace of the *meshchanka*. It was "Soviet fashion"; and it needed to be described, pictured—and created.

Soviet Style

In early Soviet Russia, then, fashion did not disappear. And in the early 1930s, it began to appear more consistently as part of the discourse of Soviet everyday life. The reality of a short supply of consumer goods in this period was counterbalanced by public emphasis on growth of consumer choice.

"Moscow is dressing well!" ran a celebratory headline in the *Trud* (*Labor*) newspaper in 1934.[24] In the same year, the *Tsentralnyi dom modelei* (Central House of Fashion) opened in Moscow, and an elite clothes shop opened in Dom 12, Nevskii Prospekt in Leningrad. Quality clothing was often a reward for the overfulfillment of production targets: the Stakhanovite man and woman emerged as the supermodels of the era; awards ceremonies were the Soviet equivalent of the Oscars, with these "ordinary" men and women often clothed in the latest styles.[25] Of course, such style, and such quality clothing, were supposed to filter down to other social levels. Also in 1934, a specific clothes "atelier" opened at an electrical factory in Moscow to "serve the workers of the factory," and an article in Pravda emphasized the demanding consumer that the factory worker had become.[26] Social stratification was very much part of the Soviet system of consumption, however. The first "Fashion Ateliers" began as independent units attached to department stores, offering custom-made clothing for the wealthy: customers would be invited to look through foreign fashion magazines and select styles to be copied. By the second half of the decade, several of these ateliers had begun to produce their own higher-grade, ready-to-wear lines. According to Natalia Lebina, the "standard outfit" of a well-dressed man or woman during the 1930s consisted of a Boston suit or dress of crepe de Chine with a woolen overcoat and leather shoes. In practice, however, this was certainly an ideal rather than a reality, at least for the majority of the population — and cinema had a key role to play in presenting that ideal.

From about 1933 on, a new rhetoric of "beauty," and even of luxury, attached itself to the discourse on clothing. It was carefully negotiated, for the stakes were high and the issues sensitive. In 1934, for example, the journal *Nashi dostizheniia* (*Our Achievements*), started by Maxim Gorky in the early 1930s as a means of social incorporation, telling the stories of the contributions of the so-called little people to the project of Socialist construction) published a special issue dedicated to questions of consumption. Its articles exhibit a complex, self-reflexive relationship to so-called Western models of consumption and ideals of beauty. In one, "A Beautiful Thing,"[27] V. Lebedev proclaimed that "freedom from fashion is one of the greatest victories of Soviet construction." "Let's say it straight out," he wrote: "Fashion, which is a result of bourgeois civilization, is powerless in our country. . . . We approach fashion critically; it is transformed in relation to our consumer."[28]

Alongside this praise of a supposedly fashion-free world, however, Lebedev called for "variation" in Soviet style, and for a socialistically appropriate form of "beauty." There must be a distinctly Soviet form of clothing.

The drive toward conformity symbolized by the Komsomol's *Iungshturm* uniform was subtly rejected in discussions of fashion in the early 1930s.[29] As improved mechanization enabled the development of factory-made clothing, and the infamous *sovetskii standart* (mass-produced items) appeared, the emphasis of Soviet discussions of fashion shifted away from a drive toward the uniform, and toward a call for variety. In parallel, the poor quality of much of the new mass-produced clothing brought increasing emphasis on the "right" of the ordinary man or woman to clothing of a good standard. In *Nashi dostizheniia*, for example, a short story entitled "A Life of Luxury" told of one Kostia Zaitsev, member of a prosperous provincial collective who, on an outing to the city, buys silk pajamas with an atlas decoration.[30] He is called into his local management office and accused of "breaking away from the masses (*otryv ot massy*)." Ultimately, however, it is not Zaitsev that the story criticizes, but the small-minded managers who view his interest in good quality products as an *un*-Soviet attitude. The story ends with Zaitsev having not just the pajamas, but also a couple of excellent suits and a good watch. "Nowadays people want not just boots, but good boots," the narrator concludes.[31]

The New Consumer

This emphasis on quality was evident in many discussions of consumption in the second half of the 1930s. The ability to discern became a marker of Soviet achievement: "The new consumer is demanding," another article in *Nashi dostizheniia* proclaimed: "We're building the Dnepr power station, the Belomor canal, so surely we can make a nice suit?"[32] In film, Konstantin Iudin's 1939 film, *A Girl with Character* (*Devushka s kharakterom*), directly treated this rhetoric of the discerning consumer. The film's heroine, Katia Ivanovna, inadvertently arriving in Moscow from Siberia, finds work in a fur shop in one of the new Soviet department stores. In one intriguing scene, she is initiated into the secrets of Soviet-style sales patter, as her employer teaches his recruits how to sell furs "to the Soviet consumer"—supposedly a quite different breed from her "capitalist" counterpart. This scene, at once comic and serious, reflects the new reality of Soviet consumption, and captures the key slogan of the day: "We treat fashion critically."

Thus discernment became the key category that differentiated Soviet fashion from its bourgeois equivalent in the West. The ability to distinguish a good quality product from poor, and a concurrent obsession with the need for quality products, was not just a pragmatic response to the reality of poor-quality goods. It became a form of fashion in itself—or at least, a displacement of traditionally fashion-related categories such as choice and style into different fields. In Soviet terms, the stylish consumer became the discriminating consumer. Shopping was configured as a kind of empowerment: the Soviet consumer was, whether by choice or out of necessity, discerning. And it was this emphasis on the ability to discriminate—to "treat fashion critically"—that made Soviet fashion ideologically acceptable.

Good, Clean Fun

This reentry of fashion into the language and symbols of everyday life was very clear in cinema. In A *Girl with Character*, Iudin had used a special costume designer, one M. Zhukova (one of the first instances in which costume design is marked as a special category in film credits). The same light touch and ironic awareness of the shifting poles of consumerism and style was evident in his next film, *Four Hearts* (*Serdtsa chetyrekh*, 1941), for which Zhukova was again responsible for costume. The film features two sisters, Galina and Shura. Galina, a mathematician, is serious and focused. Shura, her younger sister, is frivolous, a comic foil to her older sibling. At the beginning of the film, these differences are configured as much in the two women's clothes, as they are in their activities. Galina wears spectacles (a charged symbol of the intellectual—the politician Kirov had stopped wearing them in 1928, apparently in an attempt to shed his image of *intelligent*) and sensible suits and frocks.[33] We first see Shura dressed in a pajama suit, playing the piano while staring lovingly at a sketch of Pushkin. Galina is pictured as having no time for distractions such as love, poetry, and landscape; Shura is all distraction.

In the course of the film, however, the binary distinctions between the two sisters are overcome. Despairing of her sister's frivolity, Galina arranges for them to spend the summer away from the city, in a scientific research colony, where she will provide lessons in mathematics for servicemen from the Red Army. While there, almost against her will, she falls in love with a young soldier-scholar, Gleb. Through love, she enters a different symbolic sphere, and this is visually expressed in her clothing. Shura, meanwhile, while remaining firmly unserious in clothing and demeanor, herself falls into romance, and the two couples appear happily symmetrical at the end of the film. Thus, through the character of Galina, the distinction between so-called frivolity and so-called seriousness is overcome. Both, we understand, have a place in Soviet Russia.

In case this acceptance of glamour should go too far, however, Iudin makes sure to include a clear foil to his two positive heroines, in the form of their Moscow landlady, a manicurist. In this character, dress is a clear index of meaning: her style is a clear parody of bourgeois "high fashion." It is old-world, over the top—and this in direct contrast to the simple beauty of the implicitly Soviet dress of the other women. The manicurist, with her overly ornate outfits and caricatured chic (shading herself with a frilly parasol as she rides to the summer colony, for example, and usually with bows on both hat and dress), is part of that long line of women mocked for their excessive ornament and slavish following of Western style. In both profession and appearance, she represents a different ethical order, and it is against her that the other women's appearance is measured. Thus the apparent opposition between Shura and Galina is merely a generic trope, allowing for the neat symmetry of the film's final resolution; both, ultimately, remain firmly within the sphere of ideological acceptability.

The Material of Socialism

Four Hearts is an extremely visual film—it uses mise en scene, costume, and the visual impact of its heroines, to both thematic and visual effect. In scenes of the city, for example, Moscow appears *en fleurs*, as floral patterns on women's clothes, parasols, and flower sellers' stalls combine to create a softened vision of the city against which Galina's initial purposeful serious-ness is set. Changes in fashion shaped this overt use of floral motifs, tied to a broader shift in ideologically approved textile design. Debates on textile design form another important chapter of the history of Soviet fashion, and one that deserves further exploration. For the early avant-garde designers, this was the material sphere of ideological transformation, a means of bringing propaganda into everyday life, of quite literally clothing citizens in the Soviet message. During the 1920s, such designers had been united in a drive to eliminate "the plant motif" from textiles, and to create more politically appropriate designs. By the second half of the decade, this had assumed the most literal of forms: in 1928, at a major Exhibition of Textiles in Everyday Life, propaganda designs (such as factories, tractors) were very much in evidence. In 1933, however, thematic textiles of this kind were banned, and the floral reappeared as the dominant design. Floral summer dresses became a key signifier of the new leisure ideal in Soviet culture.

This debate made its appearance in cinema, too—and not only in the predominance of floral motifs in film comedies of the late 1930s and 1940s. Grigorii Alexandrov's 1939 version of the Cinderella story, *The Radiant Path* (*Svetlyi put'*), offers a direct and mocking glance back at the earlier craze for "thematic" textile design. His heroine Tania achieves her fairy-tale ending by becoming a prize-winning operator of weaving machines, employed by a textile factory. Thus we are plunged directly into the world of Soviet materials. The film itself is markedly floral in its visual impact and the floral acts as a signifier of the luxury and domesticity of the new Soviet civilization. In one striking scene, for example, Alexandrov consciously places three women in different floral designs side-by-side, as if "painting" by textile. In another, the question of textile design is the subject of a comic debate: we see the two directors of the factory discussing possible "thematic" textiles, and examining designs that feature factories ("Not enough smoke") and other clearly ideological "signs." In the end, as the dialogue makes clear, such textiles are "absolutely absurd," and they appear relegated to the design of our heroine's parasol as she travels by cart to Moscow, surrounded by house-plants, mirrors, hats, and other signs of domestic luxury.

Palatable Glamour

Produced in 1941, Iudin's *Four Hearts* was banned until the end of the war in 1944, judged to present the wrong kind of image of the Red Army for the period of war in which it was made. Its emphasis on leisure and its lightness of touch, although recognized by Andrei Zhdanov and the other censors as a valuable contribution to the quest for appropriate Soviet comedy, were simply too frivolous for the seriousness of the moment. In its drive to admit a softer element into the representation of the Soviet everyday, however, it was very much a film of its time.

Four Hearts was, like many other films of the period, explicitly concerned by the relationship between seriousness and pleasure, earnest endeavor and relaxed enjoyment, in the Soviet value system. Trauberg's *The Actress (Aktrisa)* of 1943 engaged more directly with similar questions. The heroine of the film, Zoia, is a successful actress and singer, first seen on stage in extraordinarily rich costume. The film is set during the war, and she has been evacuated from the city to the provinces, and temporarily housed in the home of the old-fashioned Agaf'ia. Her piano, glamorous clothes, and equally glamorous parrot sit uncomfortably within the domestic interior of ordinary provincial Russia. In parallel, her profession seems at odds with the serious business of war. As her landlady writes disparagingly of the actress to her son at the front: "She's a parrot herself."

In the first part of the film, Zoia is clothed in a series of remarkable outfits, and consciously pictured according to the aesthetic codes of Hollywood and glamour to which she belongs. We see her changing, for example, behind a dressing-room screen, tossing her clothes one by one over the screen as she argues with her director. On stage, in the film's opening sequences, her theatrical costumes frame her within a clear code of artifice. The narrative of the film tracks her rejection of that world. Beset by conscience, she abandons the theater and takes up work as a nurse, dissolving her former self into the anonymity of a white nurse's uniform. She falls in love with one of the patients (coincidentally the son of her former landlady) whose eyes have been damaged in battle; he is a lover of operetta—and more specifically of one particular singer, Zoia Vladimirovna herself, one of whose records he has carried with him into battle at all times. In one crucial scene, when the patients acquire a record player and they are about to play this cherished record, it breaks. In an attempt to hide this tragic fact from the blind patient, Zoia sings the song herself. Her patient recognizes her voice, and their romance is assured.

For our heroine, this enables a reappropriation of the world of the theater. Her blinded lover recognizes her voice, without seeing her, and in this way liberates her from the *kraski i kostiumy* (paints and costumes) of her former world—and allows her to return to them in a new way. In one scene, we see her dressing for a potential outing with her beloved patient, looking at herself in the mirror, testing outfits, and implicitly testing out different versions of herself. Gone is the confidently glamorous "parrot" of the earlier scenes; in its place we see a simple woman for whom beautiful clothes are a luxury rather than a necessity, a treat rather than a way of life. And this signals the key transformation: through her lover, and the other patients, Zoia recognizes the value and necessity of entertainment and glamour to the *collective* good. She reassumes her art (and her style) but—crucially—she does so "critically" and consciously. This, then, is a fashion version of the archetypal socialist realist path to consciousness that Julian Graffy discusses earlier in this volume. It creates a new, ideologically acceptable, version of style and entertainment, at the service of the collective.

Of course, the greatest fashion icon of the 1930s and 1940s was the film star Liubov' Orlova, wife of Grigorii Alexandrov and heroine of all his most successful films. In the 1936 film *The Circus*, when Orlova played the American trapeze artist Marion Dixon, Sovietness was configured as the rejection of the glamour, falsity, and individuality of the West, and the embracing of the plain white trouser suit of collectivity. In one scene, Marion Dixon throws away her impressive collection of evening dresses to assume the simplicity of her chosen world. She dissolves her stylish self into the anonymity—and implicitly the liberation—of the collective.[34]

Ten years after *The Circus*, however, Orlova starred in a film that treated the subject of clothing and belonging in quite different terms. This film was

Figure 3.3. Beauty Is a Terrible Thing.
From Grigorii Alexandrov's *Spring* (1947).

Alexandrov's *Spring* (*Vesna*) of 1947. It is, in a sense, a film about Orlova herself, and about the role and meaning of filmmaking, and of glamour. Like *The Actress*, it seeks to appropriate the tropes of entertainment, of frivolity, pleasure, and glamour, to the Soviet cause. And, like that film, and like *Four Hearts* it is explicitly concerned with blurring the distinctions between insiders and outsiders—with overcoming difference in an inclusive model of Sovietness.

In this film, Orlova plays two roles. She is Nikitina, a world-famous scientist, bespectacled, clothed in suits and sensible shoes. And also Shatrova, an actress, beautiful, innocent, and essentially lightweight, whose job it is to play the role of Nikitina in a film about Soviet science. At the beginning of the film, these two women could not be further apart. Nikitina is explicitly outside the world of fashion and glamour—indeed, she is sent a hat by a Moscow fashion store, and we see her reject it with a distaste echoed in her assistant's exclamation: "Ah yes, beauty is a terrible thing! (*Da, krasota—strashnoe delo*)."[35] (See fig. 3.3.) The film director, setting out to make a film about Soviet science, finds in her the perfect embodiment of his vision of the scientist—stern, serious, and entirely lacking in

Figure 3.4. Made Up and Clothed.
From Grigorii Alexandrov's *Spring* (1947).

femininity. She, in turn, is suitably disparaging about cinema itself, seeing in it a world directly opposed to her own: "You need not facts, but effects," she says to the director, "I am no fan of cinema."

The actress Shatrova, by contrast, is overtly styled as Nikitina's opposite. She is glamorous, certainly; but—and this is important—she is also clearly configured as a simple girl. Her glamour is not transgressive, her sexuality not threatening.[36] And this is the key to the film's representation of the world of female style. In the course of the film, polar opposites begin to blur, the binaries begin to collapse. When Shatrova is offered the lead role in a stage performance, on the same day as an initial meeting with the film director for whom she is to play Nikitina, she manages to persuade Nikitina to stand in for her—to pretend, that is, to be Shatrova playing Nikitina. In the confusing scenes of disguise and mistaken identity that ensue, Nikitina discovers the power and liberation of disguise. She is "made up, clothed, and filmed" as someone else playing herself, and these disguises enable her to enter a new, and implicitly softer, realm of emotions (see fig. 3.4).

First, she rejects the image of Soviet scientist as an emotionless automaton, insisting to the uncomprehending film director that: "Our Soviet scientist is a human being—with a human soul." Later, dressed in a full-length evening dress, Nikitina has a discussion about love with the film director whom she had earlier despised. As they talk, the film studio background shifts, creating layers of fantasy and make-believe. The pair move through fantastic sets, love scenes, dance sequences, and military parades, and finally into a dialogue between two Nikolai Gogols. "Only in a film studio," the director jokes, "could you see two Gogols—and neither of them real." Gradually, then, the unreality of film is transformed into a virtue; the world of effects acquires its own value. And its greatest effect is on Nikitina herself, for it allows her to enter the symbolic realm of romance. Costume and set combine to transport Nikitina into a world of femininity that she had previously rejected, and allow her to fall in love. When she returns to her apartment, her housekeeper does not recognize her: "Is it you?!" she exclaims. "It's me!" cries Nikitina joyously. She is lost in the euphoria of love—and, implicitly, in the consciousness of her own femininity that had been granted to her by dress and cinema combined.

At the end of the film, then, difference is overcome. Scientists can wear evening gowns, actresses can be serious. Cinema, too, has justified its own role: the film ends with a song, as Orlova appears in both her roles, and two happy couples sing together. This final song is both fact and symbol: its message is that the Soviet scientist has learned to sing, has learned to appreciate the value and necessity of the apparently frivolous. There is, it is implied, a place for artifice, for fantasy and "effects," and for glamour in Soviet culture. Ultimately, however, artifice and glamour are neutralized. They are not threatening. And in parallel, fashion loses its power to distinguish the individual, and is appropriated to a vision of collective homogeneity. In a sense, then, clothing means nothing in this film. It no longer carries ideological significance. It is reduced to an empty sign. And this neutralization ultimately excludes the very possibility of otherness—of using fashion as a means of being different. As in *Four Hearts*, the apparently binary opposites of seriousness and frivolity, so characteristic of the genre film, dissolve into one.

Conclusions—Clothing a Soviet Self

Four years after *Spring*, in 1951, an article in the magazine *Soviet Woman* (*Sovetskaia zhenshchina*), describing a scene in the newly opened Moscow House of Fashion, expressed this inclusive vision in clear terms: "Here we meet a worker from a city organization and the collective farm worker from a village outside Moscow, a teacher and a student, a professor and a housewife, a shift engineer from a Siberian metal works, who has come to Moscow for a few days, and a schoolgirl, choosing her first long dress to wear at her graduation dance."[37] This, then, is fashion for all; the luxury and beauty of the new clothing store is available to everyone, regardless of status. It is explicitly democratic.

Within this, however, a secondary message emerges, and one that lies at the center of the paradox of Soviet fashion: "The Soviet consumer doesn't want fancy clothes," the article continues, in familiar terms, but adds: "She wants clothes that are simple but not primitive, comfortable and dressy, practical for everyday life but far from standard. Even work suits must not be standard."[38] Thus, within the apparent rejection of the individual vagaries of what Roland Barthes has called the "Fashion System" of the West, a need for individuation remains. Soviet fashion must be at once collective and individual (not "standard"); it must, it seems, offer the opportunity to stand out, as well as to fit in. We return, then, to the very criteria that Simmel identified as essential to the hegemony of fashion — the coexistence of the desire to belong and the need for self-differentiation. The particularity of the Soviet case, however, is manifest. This was a centrally controlled clothing industry, which was seeking to create — *from above* — a model of fashion and consumerism that would answer these apparently contradictory needs.

In the combined story of fashion and film of the 1930s and 1940s, then, we begin to see how ideologically approved cultural texts negotiated the dangerous waters of individuality and "belonging." This fragile balance was essential to the formation of a peculiarly Soviet model of subjectivity, a fuller understanding of which demands much further research. The broader picture of fashion and clothing could, however, be one means of approaching this. In *The Fashion System*, Barthes described Western fashion as offering a form of personal liberation, allowing the subject to appear in different and shifting guises: "In the vision of Fashion," he writes, "the ludic motif [that is, disguise] does not involve what might be called a vertigo effect: it multiplies the person without any risk to her of losing herself, insofar as, for Fashion, clothing is not play but the *sign* of play." For Barthes, fashion neutralizes the act of disguise, making the self a fluid and changeable category: "The game of clothing is no longer the game of being, the agonizing question of the tragic universe, it is simply a keyboard of signs from among which an eternal persona chooses one day's amusement."[39] Picking and choosing between styles and "looks," the Western fashion consumer adopts and discards different modes of being, without threatening an apparently "eternal" self, which is implicitly separate from outward appearance. Whatever objections one might raise to this description within the Western context, it nevertheless provides a revealing counterpoint to the Soviet "fashion system." The restricted spectrum of Soviet fashion might be seen as a means of limiting this freedom of "play." For all its inclusivity and apparent democracy, Soviet style sought, in the end, to limit. In this case, the "game" that Barthes describes was one in which the stakes were high, and "dressing the part" really mattered. Ultimately, although the apparently all-inclusive model of Sovietness that I have revealed appeared to offer space for all, the effect of its studied neutrality was to make the price of real difference all the higher.

NOTES

1. *Komsomolskaia pravda*, June 30, 1928.
2. Anatolii Lunacharskii, "Svoevremenno li podimat' rabochemy ob iskusstve odevat'sia," *Iskusstvo odevat'sia* 1 (1928): 1.
3. N. B. Lebina, *Povsednevnaia zhizn' sovetskogo goroda 1920/1930 gody* (St. Petersburg: Zhurnal Neva', Izdatel'sko-torgovyi dom Letnii sad', 1999), 204–25 (220).
4. Ingrid Brenninkmeyer, *The Sociology of Fashion* (Keller: Winterthur, 1962), 84.
5. Ibid., 156.
6. Georg Simmel, "The Philosophy of Fashion," in David Frisby and Mike Featherstone, eds., *Simmel on Culture: Selected Writings* (London: Sage Publications, 1997), 187–206 (189).
7. Ibid., 191.
8. Ibid., 189.
9. Christine Ruane, "Clothes Shopping in Imperial Russia: The Development of a Consumer Culture," *Journal of Social History* 28, no. 4 (Summer 1995): 765–82. See also Christine Ruane, "Subjects into Citizens: The Politics of Clothing in Imperial Russia," in Wendy Parkins, ed., *Fashioning the Body Politic: Dress, Gender, Citizenship* (Oxford: Berg, 2002), 49–71.
10. T. Strizhenova, *Iz istorii sovetskogo kostiuma* (Moscow: Sov. Khudozhnik, 1972), 49.
11. *Komsomolskaia pravda*, June 30, 1928.
12. N. Mandel'shtam, *Vtoraia kniga*, cited in Lebina, *Povsednevnaia*, 210.13. From *Protokoly i Vserossiiskoi konferentsii po khudozhestvennoi promyshlennosti.* (Moscow: N.p., 1920), 37–38.
14. Varst (Varvara Stepanova), *LEF* 2 (1923): 65–68.
15. Ekaterina Degot, "Ot tovara k tovarishchu: k estetike nerynochnogo predmeta," in E. Degot and Iuliia Demidenko, eds., *Pamiat' tela: nizhnee bel'e sovetskoi epokhi: katalog vystavki* (Moscow: Gosudarstvennyi muzei istorii Sankt-Peterburg, 2000), 8–19.
16. Strizhenova, *Iz istorii sovetskogo kostiuma*, 29–30.
17. Central State Archive of Historical-Political Documents, fond 40000, opis 6, delo 352, 1.141.
18. Aleksandr Rodchenko, Letter to Stepanova from Paris. In A. M. Rodchenko, *Stat'i, vospominaniia, avtobiograficheskie zapiski, pis'ma*, ed, V. A. Rodchenko (Moscow: Sov. Khudozhnik, 1982), 93.

19. Lebina, *Povsednevnaia*, 217.

20. See Anne E. Gorsuch, "Moscow Chic: Silk Stockings and Soviet Youth," in William B. Husband, ed., *The Human Tradition in Modern Russia* (Wilmington, Del.: SR Books, 2000), 65–76.

21. Vlad Korolevich, *Zhenshchina v kino* (Moscow: Teakinopechat', 1928), offers a systematic account of female film stars, Western and Russian, according to different models of femininity. For information regarding the popularity of Western films in Soviet Russia of the 1920s, see Denise Youngblood, *Movies for the Masses: Popular Cinema and Soviet Society in the 1920s* (Cambridge, UK: Cambridge University Press, 1992).

22. Oksana Bulgakova, "The Hydra of Soviet Cinema: The Metamorphoses of the Soviet Film Heroine," in Lynne Atwood, ed., *Red Women on the Silver Screen: Soviet Women and Cinema from the Beginning to the End of the Communist Era* (London: Pandora, 1993),151.

23. Korolevich, *Zhenshchina v kino*, 90.

24. Sheila Fitzpatrick, *Everyday Stalinism: Ordinary Life in Extraordinary Times: Soviet Russia in the 1930s* (Oxford: Oxford University Press, 1999), 92.

25. Ibid., 103.

26. Jukka Gronow, *Caviar with Champagne: Common Luxury and the Ideals of the Good Life in Stalin's Russia* (London: Berg, 2003), 94.

27. V. Lebedev, "Krasivaia veshch," *Nashi dostizheniia* 6 (1934): 101–103.

28. Ibid., 102.

29. Elena Eikhengol'ts, "Problema massovoi odezhdy," in P. I. Novitskii, ed., *Izo-front: klassovaia bor'ba na fronte prostranstvennykh iskusstv. Sbornik statei ob"edineniia Oktiabr'* (Moscow: Ogiz Izogiz, 1931), 55–69.

30. Pavel Nilin, "O roskoshnoi zhizni," *Nashi dostizhenii* 6 (1934): 56–61. Also cited in Fitzpatrick, *Everyday Stalinism*, 92–93.

31. Nilin, "O roskoshnoi zhizni," 61.

32. N. Kal'ma, "Novyi pokupatel," *Nashi dostizhenii* 6 (1934): 106. For detailed discussion on Soviet consumption, and in particular on the campaign for "cultured trade" of which this emphasis on discernment was a part, see Julie Hessler, *A Social History of Soviet Trade: Trade Policy, Retail Practices, and Consumption, 1917–1953* (Princeton, N.J.: Princeton University Press, 2004).

33. Lebina, *Povsednevnaia*, 218.

34. For more on Alexandrov's film *The Circus* as a staging of "otherness," see Josephine Woll's essay in this volume.

35. This is an echo of the famous scene in Ernst Lubitsch's Hollywood film, *Ninotchka* (1939), where Greta Garbo, Soviet Commissar in Paris, is initially shocked by the "confection" of a French milliner, but ends the film converted to the glamour that it represents.

36. Ol'ga Vainshtein emphasizes the importance of "modesty" in Soviet discourses on female style in her analysis of women's fashion in the last decades of Soviet power. Ol'ga Vainshtein, "Female Fashion, Soviet Style: Bodies of Ideology," in Helena Goscilo and Beth Holmgren, eds., *Russia-Women-Culture* (Bloomington: Indiana University Press, 1996), 64–94 (70).

37. "Dom modelei," in *Sovetskaia zhenshchina* 1 (1951): 63–64 (63).

38. Ibid., 64.

39. Roland Barthes, *The Fashion System* (Berkeley: University of California Press, 1990), 257.

Under the Big Top

America Goes to the Circus

Josephine Woll

Foreigners, as Peter Kenez argues in this volume, frequently appear in the more than two hundred feature films produced by Soviet studios between 1933 and 1940, usually as negative characters.[1] In the historical spectacles glorifying Russia's past (for example, Vladimir Petrov's 1937–1938 *Peter the First* and Sergei Eisenstein's 1938 *Alexander Nevskii*), foreigners challenge the wisdom of Russia's far-sighted rulers or invade Russia's territory. In the substantial number of adventure films made about the October revolution and Civil War, most famously Sergei and Georgii Vasil'ev's *Chapaev* (1934), Efim Dzigan's *We Are from Kronstadt* (1936), and Leonid Trauberg's and Grigorii Kozintsev's trilogy of films starring the revolutionary hero Maxim (1935's *The Youth of Maxim*, 1937's *The Return of Maxim*, and 1939's *The Vyborg Side*), Bolsheviks typically triumph over local opponents (White Army officers, remnants of the pre-Revolutionary bourgeoisie, recalcitrant kulaks), but foreigners are either understood or are actually shown to offer political and financial support to enemies of Bolshevism, even when they remain on the margins of the story.

Similarly, the "construction dramas" dealing with heavy industry, the *kolkhoz* movies portraying collective farm life, or the popular aviation and border-guard adventure movies, all of which concentrate on contemporary domestic Soviet life, pit the protagonists against inimical forces at every turn, most dangerously the homegrown saboteurs and wreckers who pretend to pious loyalty as they work to undermine their society. As the decade wore on, however, Japanese and German enemies multiplied: more than thirty films from the 1930s involve devious foreign agents penetrating Soviet borders.[2] At the same time, foreigners (or returning émigrés) who reject their own profoundly flawed societies to come to the Soviet Union for a better, more meaningful life—a trope developed ten years earlier—figure in a number of films from the decade. Grigorii Alexandrov's *The Circus* (1936) offers both—enemy and convert—in an engaging package that entranced audiences at the time, and continues to do so seven decades later.

Of the four musical comedies Grigorii Alexandrov made together with composer Isaac Dunaevskii, all starring Alexandrov's wife Liubov' Orlova, only *The Circus* involves foreigners. The first, *Jolly Fellows* (1934), "a loose chain of *èstrada* [revue or cabaret] numbers . . . Soviet Hollywood with white pianos and pearl-studded cellos," wears its politics lightly, preferring tuneful jazz and slapstick humor: "The only Marxism in the movie was that of Groucho and his brothers at the moment when the jazzmen created havoc in the Bolshoi Theater."[3] In *Volga-Volga* (1938), Stalin's favorite, Orlova's provincial postal carrier and songwriter defeats a recalcitrant bureaucrat, Byvalov ("man of the past," a favorite screen villain, here played by the brilliant Igor Il'inskii). *Radiant Path* (1940), Alexandrov's Soviet version of the Cinderella story, stars Orlova as an uneducated servant girl who becomes a textile worker and overcomes her own ignorance and the malice of first a jealous boss and then yet another hidebound bureaucrat to reach Stakhanovite bliss and recognition in the Kremlin. There are no outsiders in these three films, only insiders who obstruct the heroines' steady progress toward success and happiness.

The Circus makes use of several patterns from the other films, but adds the "insider/outsider" element to the mix. Two outsiders penetrate its utopian world. One, Marion Dixon, is American. Stone-throwing racists literally drive her out of the American heartland: she barely escapes the lynch mob by pulling herself onto the train that will carry her away. Distraught, clutching her blanketed bundle, Marion tumbles into the arms of the other foreigner. Even before we learn his name—Franz von Kneischutz—we know he is German, for although he is reading an English-language newspaper, his first words to Marion are "Was wollen Sie?" Mistakenly believing she has found safe haven with Von Kneischutz, Marion closes her eyes with relief. As the caboose recedes, the globe spins; English letters "USA" convert to Cyrillic letters "СССР," and the audience finds itself in the Moscow circus, where Von Kneischutz and Marion are preparing to perform their remarkable feat, "The Flight to the Moon." The remainder of the film details their experiences in the USSR.

Both Marion and Von Kneischutz, then, begin as outsiders to the Soviet Union. But by the end of *The Circus*, their stances vis-à-vis Soviet society diverge radically. Marion sheds her outsider status to become a part of the Soviet collective, proudly marching in the May Day parade, while Von Kneischutz has been neutralized, excluded from and rendered entirely irrelevant to the society whose values he never understood, even as he spurned them contemptuously (see fig. 4.1).

"Other," *chuzhoi*, implies its opposite, *svoi*, the entity or group or society whose values constitute the norm against which the "other" is defined. The

Figure 4.1. The Neutralized Enemy.
From Grigorii Alexandrov's *The Circus* (1936).

specific nature of "otherness" personified in Marion Dixon and Franz von Kneischutz can only be understood against and in terms of the *svoi* that Alexandrov depicts in *The Circus*. The film intends both the behind-the-scenes circus world, consisting of manager, performers, and crew (even animals), and the onstage world, which includes the audience as well as the circus performers, to represent the values and composition of Soviet society. Exploiting the entertainment potential of his genre exceptionally well, Alexandrov melds comedy, music, and melodrama to package familiar ideological messages, part of the bundle of quasi-political, quasi-mythic patterns that consistently characterize official Soviet culture of the 1930s, both "high" and popular culture.[4]

Svoi

So who and what constitute the *svoi* in *The Circus*? First of all, those who work under the big top form a symbolic *malaia sem'ia*, or "little family."[5] The round ring of the circus functions as visually appropriate for an apparent absence of hierarchy. Theoretically the circus director is boss—as he

Figure 4.2. From Grigorii Alexandrov's *The Circus* (1936).

suggests when he embraces the hero Martynov or, much later, Marion, "in the name of the central administration (*glavnoe upravlenie*)"—or when he vehemently refuses to allow a "talking dog" act in the ring. But his sputtering irascibility highlights rather than disguises his good nature, and his relationship to other characters is far more egalitarian than his position might imply. Indeed, though he has but one biological daughter, Raika, he regards with paternal affection nearly everyone else, especially Ivan Petrovich Martynov and, eventually, Marion Dixon. He consults Martynov as a peer—indeed, as a supplicant—when he beseeches Martynov to devise a Soviet equivalent to Marion's "Flight to the Moon." The performers, his nominal subordinates, keep him waiting two hours when he calls a rehearsal for 10 AM. Raika pretends to bow to his fatherly rule but she, he, and we all know the truth: she manipulates him no less adroitly than any daughter in a Molière comedy. Toward the end of the film, to kill time until the bruited "Flight to the Stratosphere" can begin, the director performs a unicycle number along with his backstage crew. All of them—superannuated circus performers who perfected their creaky act decades before—work together cheerfully, if with increasing exhaustion, for the good of the circus. Even the "talking dog" act triumphs, sneaking onto the ring while the director's back is turned. He enforces his "authority" only with the aid of a lasso that literally drags the performers into the wings. During the thematic culmination of the film, the lullaby scene, the director stands level with the manager/announcer, the two men happily united in their approval of what they see.

The close-knit geniality of the circus performers' *malaia sem'ia* includes animals too: the seals who propel the globe on their snouts, the monkey itself taken aback at the shot it fires, the goose that obligingly gives up a feather so the director can sign a document, the elephant who tenderly nudges Marion in the hay, even the cowardly—if fearsome—lions with whom Skameikin, Raika's fiancé, is trapped. Skameikin himself, though his roving eye follows any and every pretty girl, is the most innocent sort of lecher, and he willingly puts his skills as a builder at the service of the circus. Like Skameikin, Martynov, Raika, and the others happily dedicate themselves to the greater glory of the circus/state, demonstrated by their commitment to create the "Flight to the Stratosphere," superior in every way to the "Flight to the Moon."

Martynov himself exemplifies all the qualities of a socialist realist positive hero, slightly humanized by love: what film critic Maia Turovskaia calls "the chaste monk in a quasi-military uniform (*tselomudrennyi monakh v poluvoennoi forme*)."[6] (See fig. 4.2.) Martynov, who wears this uniform despite his profession as a circus star, enters the film with a display of skilled marksmanship: both outfit and ability link him to the military forces that defend the USSR, thus illustrating Emma Widdis's argument that clothing identified Sovietness. He displays the determination of the Stakhanovite worker and the derring-do of other heroes of the 1930s: the polar explorers; the crews of ice breakers; the pilot Valerii Chkalov, who flew across the North Pole in 1937. The film consistently associates Martynov with the technological innovation so valorized during the First Five Year Plan; yet—in line with the shifting emphases of the mid-1930s—he remains in control of them, and implicitly of nature.[7] When Martynov and Marion finally perform the "Flight to the Stratosphere," Martynov circles the big top in a flight suit and aviator's helmet, ultimately defeating gravity itself. Outstripping the capitalist "Flight to the Moon" in its audacity, its technical skill, its sheer ostentation, the Soviet "Flight to the Stratosphere" promises comparable triumphs in other international rivalries.

Martynov demonstrates no less facility as Marion's instructor, a role perhaps even more important ideologically than his circus feat. Standing next to her at the piano in her opulent suite at the newly built Metropol Hotel—a source of pride for Soviet viewers—Martynov teaches Marion the words to the film's anthem, "The Song of the Motherland." The camera frames them in full frontal shot, Martynov a few inches taller than Marion—enough to reinforce his superiority—his square face and high forehead a physical manifestation of his integrity, clarity, and dedication. Patiently he enunciates the crucial words of the song, a tuneful paean of praise to the values of *svoi* and to the collateral values enshrined in the Stalinist Constitution of 1936,[8] and Marion instantly learns them, her voice "increasingly loud and confident, . . . blending with the strong, pure voice of her beloved."[9] Her eager mastery is, however, still contingent: she does not trust the song's sentiments enough to reveal her secret to Martynov, instead drowning out her baby's crying with a crashing chordal elaboration of the song on the piano.

Like the Constitution, the song emphasizes Soviet egalitarianism ("For us there are no black or colored races [*Net dlia nas ni chernykh, ni tsvet-nykh*]"), its freedom ("I know no other land / Where a man can breathe so freely [*Ia drugoi takoi strany ne znaiu / Gde tak vol'no dyshit chelovek*]"), its superiority to other systems ("And no one on earth knows better than us/ How to laugh and love [*I nikto na svete ne umeet / Luchshe nas smeiat'sia i liubit'*]"), its ability to protect itself from hostile outsiders ("But if an enemy wants to break us / We will sternly frown / We love our motherland like a bride, / We'll protect her like a dear mother! [*No surovo brovi my nasupim / Esli vrag zakhochet nas slomat' / Kak nevestu, rodinu my liubim, / Berezhem, kak laskovuiu mat'!*]"). Nor should the conflation of document and lyrics surprise: Orlova, hearing radio reports of the ongoing revisions of the Constitution, would notify lyricist Vasilii Lebedev-Kumach, who in turn "would then compose his own 'musical declaration' of the Constitution to include in the movie's score."[10] The final version celebrates the extrapolation of those values already exemplified by the *malaia sem'ia* of the circus collective to the large Soviet family, society as a whole.

Alexandrov reserves his portrait of the *bol'shaia sem'ia*, the "great family" or Soviet society writ large, for the climactic lullaby scene. Von Kneischutz has revealed Marion's secret, thrusting her interracial child, product of an affair with a Negro, at the Soviet circus audience. He assumes the audience will respond with appropriate revulsion. Instead, people laugh and welcome the child with literally open arms. When Von Kneischutz attempts to climb the steps alongside the seats to retrieve the little boy, both official and unofficial Soviets prevent him: two uniformed men—the movie's equivalent of the border guards so exalted in the mid-1930s—stand up to block him, joined by a solid wall of civilians ranged against him. (At the February 1936 Plenum of the Writers' Union, a border guard was marched into the auditorium, to the applause of the audience and praise of the plenary speakers, and marched out again.[11]) As Von Kneischutz backs away in confusion and then slinks out in defeat, two armed men, also in uniform, make sure he really leaves.

Ordinary Soviet citizens enjoying the delights of Soviet achievement, circus-style, demonstrate strength and solidarity no less powerfully protective than the armed might of the security forces. They pass the child from one set of cradling arms to another, singing to him all the while. Alexandrov carefully constructs the baby-brigade to showcase individuals of different ethnicities, as demonstrated by their distinctive physical features, their distinctive clothing, and their various languages. Men—father-figures comparable to the director—dominate the scene visually, as the camera pans from Slavic faces to a beak-nosed type from the Caucasus, a Central Asian, a tender Jew, a black sailor—the latter framed together with a white wife or girlfriend, forming a triangle with the child at its apex. The audience, itself a microcosm of Soviet "friendship of nations" (*druzhba narodov*), exemplifies vaunted Soviet values of cohesiveness, inclusiveness and tolerance as it generously welcomes the baby and, by implication, his mother.

Chuzhoi

Although initially an outsider, and certainly a foreigner, Marion conforms to the paradigm of socialist realist heroes or more often heroines, who begin in ignorance and/or innocence and progress to knowledge and understanding, under the tutelage of a seasoned and experienced mentor. In Marion's case she arrives in Moscow scarred by her American experience and pinioned by what she believes to be the inevitable cost of her "mistake," social ostracism if not actual physical threat. She learns otherwise: from Raika, from Martynov, from the audience at the circus.

In fact Marion joins the roster of cinematic "outsiders" of the 1920s, foreigners who, in Julian Graffy's words, "come to watch, stay to learn."[12] Films of the 1920s did not define outsiders a priori as enemies. Whether initially suspicious of the Soviet Union, like Mr. West from Kuleshov's *The Extraordinary Adventures of Mr. West in the Land of the Bolsheviks* (1924), or simply curious about it, like the Queen of Mars (*Aelita*, 1924), these outsiders eventually become enamored of the Soviet state's patent advantages. By the 1930s, as Peter Kenez argues, the scene had changed.[13] While the spectrum and quantity of domestic enemies had grown exponentially, the international political situation did offer potential menace, with the rise of fascism to the west and Japanese militarism to the east. *The Circus* borrows from both realities to create a clear dichotomy between the sympathetic stranger, Marion Dixon, and the sly, unscrupulous enemy, Von Kneischutz.

In Marion's case, romantic attraction triggers her education (not sex: her romance with Martynov lacks all eroticism). Marion's skill and talent immediately impress Martynov, who tosses Skameikin's bouquet to her as she circles the circus tent, and Martynov's pictures, spilling out of the suitcase delivered by mistake to Marion's dressing room, intrigue and impress Marion. But romance immediately takes a back seat to ideology, and once enlightenment begins, Marion rapidly shifts from outsider to insider; love merely stimulates learning. Marion assimilates native custom so quickly that when she caresses Martynov after he crashes to the circus floor, a casualty of his first, failed "Flight to the Stratosphere," she calls him by his patronymic, Petrovich, a sign of both acculturation and intimacy.

Shame about her past, and fear of exposure, compel Marion to follow the jealous Von Kneischutz out of the circus arena before he can make his threat to expose her secret. But once in her hotel suite, she rejects his impassioned pleas. He offers California and sunshine; she retorts that she wants to stay in Moscow. He jerks off their hangers clothing worth "thousands of dollars," all of which he bought "for you, Mary, for you." "The Mary you bought them for is no more," she solemnly intones, signifying that she too has learned a lesson about fashion and its uses in Soviet Russia. Earlier, Marion pulled off her black wig to reveal her blond hair, a stark visualization of the lie she has been forced to live, and the opportunity Moscow presents to reveal her true self. By the time she spurns Von Kneischutz in the hotel, she has shed much of that alien skin. Indeed, when the baby toddles out and Von Kneischutz roughly points to his kinky hair and black skin, Marion retorts that "they" will forgive her—"they" meaning the citizens of what she wants to be her new home.

Her hope that Martynov will, indeed, forgive her, emboldens her to risk openly declaring her love, in a letter that propels the plot for the rest of the film. But when Von Kneischutz proclaims the truth to the circus audience, residual fear and shame send her running to the wings, to weep into a bale of straw. She emerges, under Martynov's sheltering arm, only when the audience has demonstrated its absolute, unified acceptance of the baby (see fig. 4.3). Even then, she asks the circus manager what it all means, giving him the chance to declaim that "in *our* land" all children are precious and loved, whether they are black, white, pink, purple, or polka-dotted.

The director's explanation nearly completes Marion's enlightenment. She smiles in wonderment, holding her son without the shame that disfigured her love for him earlier. Full transformation requires the transition

Figure 4.3. Welcoming with Open Arms.
From Grigorii Alexandrov's *The Circus* (1936).

from consciousness to action, however, here presented via a dissolve from the circus into Red Square, from the dark robe that Marion shrugs off to raiment of bridal white, from cowering under Martynov's sheltering arm to standing straight, her head up and her shoulders back. Marion may not have fully mastered Russian verb forms, but when Raika asks her if she now "understands," she can wholeheartedly assent. She strides along with thousands of members of the joyously marching "great family" (*bol'shaia sem'ia*), an image that in turn dissolves into a lengthy and extravagant celebration of Soviet military and ideological power via superimposed images—banners adorned with Marx, Lenin, and Stalin, rows of synchronized marchers and military machinery—all enhanced by the repetition of the "Song of the Motherland," which by now the theater audience has learned as well as the characters have and can hardly help but join in singing.

The other outsider in *The Circus*, Von Kneischutz, both diametrically opposes Martynov's virtues and totally lacks Marion's potential for conversion to insider status. He combines the physical features of the moustache-twirling villain of silent melodramas, the ruthlessness of a fairy-tale ogre, and the ideological beliefs of several categories of enemies of the Soviet state. Typically, films of the 1930s set in Siberia or the Far East involve Japanese spies who easily manage to find local saboteurs with whom to conspire, while films set in central Russia link Soviet saboteurs with Germans. Von Kneischutz's interspersing of German phrases reminds us of his nationality, while his views on racial purity and the sin of miscegenation partake more or less equally of Nazi ideology and American racism, Klan variety. Germany's menacing militarism finds symbolic expression in the row of torpedo-shaped objects behind which Von Kneischutz crouches in the hotel room; appropriately, when his pleas fail, he turns to threats. His absorption of American materialism also contributes to his belief that everything has a price tag, as in his crude equation of buying clothes for Marion and buying Marion.

Like nearly all the domestic enemies who received public attention in the 1930s, Von Kneischutz can adeptly disguise himself and his real feelings and intentions. Yet his apparent physical strength is illusory, as the inflation of his otherwise puny chest with a pneumatic pump attests, and his psychological domination of Marion, at first so effective, proves equally ephemeral. Some of his deceptions are inconsequential—he smilingly accepts Skameikin's flowers before contemptuously tossing them into the gutter. But the deceits, trivial or decisive, characterize a malignant mendacity directed against the circus itself, and by extension against the Soviet system.

Thus Von Kneischutz pretends to commiserate when the "Flight to the Stratosphere" initially fails, yet he himself deliberately caused its failure by plying Raika with cake so she would gain weight and throw off the critical balance in the cannon shot. Von Kneischutz's heavy-handed flirtation can seduce only a girl as innocent, if willful, as Raika. The notion that naive but loyal Soviet citizens could fall victim to foreign entrapment, thereby becoming tools in the hands of the enemy, featured all too often in the Soviet press of the 1930s and 1940s, engendering narratives that helped explain the otherwise inexplicable involvement in espionage and antistate activity of so many people. Lydia Chukovskaia's novella *Sofia Petrovna*, written within two years of the Terror (and three years after *The Circus's* release), effectively illustrates the importance of such narratives in manipulating popular opinion and in transforming disbelief to acceptance. Chukovskaia's protagonist, the excruciatingly naive eponymous heroine, learns of the shocking arrest of the director of the publishing house where she works. She simply cannot believe the news. Her friend, Natasha, more politically savvy, helps her understand:

> Natasha took a carefully folded newspaper out of her old briefcase. . . .
> "Understand, my dear, he could have been seduced," said Natasha in a whisper, "a woman . . ."
> Sofia Petrovna began to read.

The article recounted the case of a certain Soviet citizen, A., a loyal party member, who was sent by the Soviet government on a mission to Germany to study the use of a new chemical. In Germany, he fulfilled his duties conscientiously, but soon became involved with a certain S., an elegant young woman who professed to be sympathetic to the Soviet Union. [After S. steals important documents] A. had sufficient courage to break off with S. immediately but not sufficient courage to tell his comrades about the disappearance of the documents. He went back to the USSR, hoping by his honest work as a Soviet engineer to atone for the crime against his homeland. For a whole year he worked peacefully and was already beginning to forget about his crime. But hidden agents of the Gestapo, infiltrating into our country, began to blackmail him. Terrorized, A. handed over to them secret plans from the factory at which he worked. . . . "Do you understand?" Natasha asked in a whisper. "Our director is, of course, a fine person, a loyal party member. But citizen A., they write here, was also a loyal party member at first. . . . They say our director has been abroad."[14]

Typically, such narratives involve an ordinary Soviet citizen who follows his suspicions to discover the truth, foils the enemy's plans, and strips away his mask. At that point the NKVD, coming as if from nowhere, takes over, and the saboteur/enemy simply disappears. *The Circus* wholly conforms to this pattern. When Von Kneischutz makes one last attempt to present his worldview to the circus audience—namely, that miscegenation is a crime against civilization—the united collective laughs with good-natured derision. He asks in genuine bewilderment, "Why are you laughing, ladies and gentlemen?" to which the director replies, with a sideways spit for emphasis, "What should we do, cry?" Von Kneischutz sinks into his coat and exits, his departure ensured by the two armed and uniformed men who follow behind.

Where he goes and what happens to him become quite irrelevant to the circus audience, the theater audience, and the film, whose focus returns to Marion, now emboldened to return to the ring, and on to the final montage. Lilia Mamatova, discussing this near-magical evaporation of menace in films of the 1930s, comments, "By the end the saboteur [*vreditel'*] is completely forgotten, all memory of him supplanted by the spectacle of the violent exultation of simple people at their major victory in the workplace. The massive repressions of the 30s were difficult to square with any understanding of legality, so the film viewer was not encouraged to consider what awaited the saboteur—trial or extra-judicial punishment. The sentence, naturally, remained secret as well."[15]

Alexandrov's portrayal of the *svoi/chuzhoi* dichotomy in *The Circus* has particular piquancy because the film's mélange of comedy and melodrama renders quasi-official, quasi-mythic patterns so palatable and indeed appealing, not only to Soviet audiences of the 1930s but to those of subsequent generations. Of the divergence between what he calls "political" and "expressive" worlds in the Soviet Union of the 1930s, Richard Stites writes:

> If one views the popular culture of the 1930s only as an immense mask or an engine of fraud, then no further analysis is needed. Those who interpret the function of mass culture in purely ideological terms are inclined to read it as simply an imposed system of mystification. Common sense and evidence belie such a reading. . . . In many realms of culture . . . there is no necessary contradiction between fraud, deceit, and manipulation on the one hand and authentic popular enjoyment on the other. The violation of reality, the call for suspension of disbelief, the assault on plausibility are central to popular genres, even "realistic" ones. When people read or watch something that is palpably untrue . . . they do not "believe" it; they do or do not enjoy it. But they do not "disbelieve" it either: they look for a core of truth inside the art they consume, whether or not it is objectively true. And a core of truth indubitably existed for millions of people in the popular culture of the Stalinist 1930s.[16]

Audiences in the 1930s derived pleasure from *The Circus* in large part because it celebrates values they identified as their own, values obviously superior to those espoused by the film's representative of an alien, hostile world. To be sure, the reality of Soviet life often contradicted those values. Its vaunted unity concealed glaring fissures, while its acceptance of the "other" was highly conditional and unstable. *The Circus* itself exemplified these vicissitudes: after Stalin ordered the murder of the great Jewish actor Solomon Mikhoels in 1948—a murder passed off as an accident—the footage of Mikhoels singing the lullaby in Yiddish was cut from prints of the film until after 1956.[17] Nevertheless, the values honored in *The Circus*—tolerance, egalitarianism, acceptance, harmony—should defeat those of Von Kneischutz and his ilk, and in the film, at least, they easily do.

NOTES

1. Peter Kenez identifies three broad categories of feature films for this period: historical spectacle, revolutionary, and contemporary drama. See also his *Cinema and Soviet Society, 1917–1953*, 2d ed. (London and New York: I. B. Tauris, 2001), 147.

2. Ibid., 149.

3. Richard Stites, *Russian Popular Culture: Entertainment and Society since 1900* (Cambridge, U.K.: Cambridge University Press, 1992), 88–89.

4. The most useful sources on this subject are Rufus Mathewson, *The Positive Hero in Russian Literature*, 2d ed. (Stanford: Stanford University Press, 1975); Katerina Clark, *The Soviet Novel: History as Ritual* (Chicago and London: University of Chicago

Press, 1985); and essays by Lilia Mamatova, "Model' kinomifov 30-ykh godov"; Maia Turovskaia, "Kino totalitarnoi epokhi'"; and Liliana Mal'kova, "Litso vraga," in Maia Turovskaia, Lilia Mamatova, and Liliana Mal'kova, eds., *Kino: Politika i liudi (30-e gody)* (Moscow: Materik, 1995).

5. On the "Great" and "small" family, see Clark, *Soviet Novel*, 114–17.

6. Mamatova, "Model' kinomifov 30-ykh godov," 62.

7. Clark, *Soviet Novel*, 104–11.

8. According to the venerable conservative film critic Rostislav Iurenev, Martynov inspires in Marion "a keen awareness of that great, strong, and kind country where people live joyfully and freely." Cited by Moira Ratchford, "*Circus* of 1936: Ideology and Entertainment under the Big Top," in Andrew Horton, ed., *Inside Soviet Film Satire: Laughter with a Lash* (Cambridge, U.K.: Cambridge University Press), 88.

9. Ibid., 90.

10. Ibid., 85–86.

11. Clark, *Soviet Novel*, 114.

12. See Julian Graffy's essay in this volume.

13. See Peter Kenez's essay in this volume.

14. Lydia Chukovskaya, *Sofia Petrovna*, trans. Eliza Klose (Evanston, Ill.: Northwestern University Press, 1992), 40–41.

15. Mamatova, "Model' kinomifov 30-ykh godov," 66.

16. Stites, *Russian Popular Culture*, 95–96.

17. See Stites, *Russian Popular Culture*, 128, which mentions that the Jewish protagonist in Iulian Semenov's thriller *In the Performance of Duty* (1962) "is even permitted to sing the Shlomo Mikhoels's Yiddish lullaby that had just been restored to the footage of *Circus*."

Eisenstein's Cosmopolitan Kremlin

Drag Queens, Circus Clowns, Slugs, and Foreigners in Ivan the Terrible

Joan Neuberger

Sergei Eisenstein's *Ivan the Terrible* has almost as many foreigners as Russian characters and, while everyone in this film acts in ways meant to seem *strange*, the foreigners are especially marked. Caricatured, parodied, ridiculed and dehumanized, sexually ambiguous, demonic, and animal-like, the foreigners in *Ivan the Terrible* would seem to be the quintessential "other." But this menagerie of exotic creatures exemplifies Eisenstein's most characteristic strategy for making meaning in film. In *Ivan the Terrible* Eisenstein creates a visual universe that both presents and complicates binary conceptions of self and other. Rather than a polarized world of Russians and others, Eisenstein's Muscovy is occupied by people intricately linked to one another. Exoticized images of "others" project meanings back onto Russian characters. They challenge stereotypes about Russians and foreigners both. The often juvenile, sometimes sadistic ridicule and vaudevillian humor, with which these characters are portrayed, has the effect of parodying and subverting expectations. As with every other element of this film, things are not what they seem.

Russians, Foreigners, and the "Unity of Opposites"

Before looking in detail at specific examples, we should take a quick tour around the visual universe of the film to survey the bizarre international circus Ivan and his subjects inhabit.[1]

The Prologue (Ivan's childhood) features greedy European traders, among whom the sinister figure of the Livonian ambassador stands out (see fig. 5.1).[2] A "slimy" character, he turns out to resemble a slug, and appears to have a tail (see fig. 5.2). As Part I begins, we meet several delegations of foreigners at Ivan's sumptuous coronation: ruffled and bejeweled envoys from the Vatican (see fig. 5.3), haughty representations of the Western

Figure 5.1. The Livonian Ambassador: Close-Up.
From Sergei Eisenstein's *Ivan the Terrible*.

Figure 5.2. The Livonian Ambassador as a Slug.
From Sergei Eisenstein's *Ivan the Terrible*.

Figure 5.3. The Vatican's Ambassadors.
From Sergei Eisenstein's *Ivan the Terrible*.

powers, and again the Livonian ambassador, with savvy political advice and sans tail. Ivan's wedding and the rebellion that interrupts it are largely domestic affairs, though our Livonian friend stirs up trouble in the hallways. Foreigners are implicated in the rebellion that follows and then, before the crowd is fully subdued, a new menace appears in the form of a threatening messenger from Kazan', but Ivan makes quick work of him, with his famous rallying cry "To Kazan'!" During the war, Tatar prisoners are treated with callous brutality by Andrei Kurbskii, giving Eisenstein an opportunity to linger over the Tatar boys' beautiful bodies, alive and then dead.[3]

Back in Moscow, the rest of Part I proceeds without much foreign intervention, though there are foreigners hanging around at key moments, as during Ivan's illness. There were to be several scenes featuring Queen Elizabeth, which were cut for political reasons connected with World War II when the United Kingdom and the USSR were allies, but Eisenstein had cast his friend, the director Mikhail Romm, in the part and had completed the screen tests. Ivan was to be shown outsmarting Elizabeth politically, while she dallied with her own sexy young courtiers, a sexual in-joke for those who might recognize Romm in the role.[4]

Part II opens in the court of the Polish King Sigismund (see fig. 5.4), which is a hotbed of all kinds of sexual vamping. We see Sigismund himself,

Figure 5.4. King Sigismund's Court.
From Sergei Eisenstein's *Ivan the Terrible*.

Figure 5.5. Sigismund's Courtiers.
From Sergei Eisenstein's *Ivan the Terrible*.

Figure 5.6. The Spy's Eye.
From Sergei Eisenstein's *Ivan the Terrible*.

his own courtiers, his women, and we have Andrei Kurbskii on his knees, suggestively handling his sword (see fig. 5.5). Foreigners appear prominently in one more scene in Part II. When Metropolitan Filipp stages "The Fiery Furnace," a liturgical play about the martyrdom of three Jewish boys who refuse to pay homage to the tyrant Nebuchadnezzar (with obvious allusions to the Stalinist terror), the Chaldean guards are represented as grotesque and sinister circus clowns.

In Part III (which, though unfilmed, exists in the form of the screenplay, some stills, and a few minutes of extant footage), Ivan's foreign enemies are depicted as ridiculously incompetent, cowardly, and disloyal, and they are defeated with laughable ease in the final battle for the sea. We meet one formidable foreigner, however, in the historical figure Heinrich von Shtaden, a German mercenary who joined the *oprichniki* (Ivan's infamous personal army) and served under Ivan during some of the brutal campaigns of oprichnik terror. Shtaden wrote a book about his experiences, which Eisenstein used in preparation for the film.[5]

Eisenstein begins to complicate the binaries these characters imply by using the foreigners as mirrors of the Russian characters. For all their oddities, inversions, and alien, antinormative dress and demeanor, the foreigners in the film are *paired* with Russians of equivalent strangeness. The Livonian ambassador skulks around the Kremlin with an eye open for intrigue that mirrors the stealthy Maliuta Skuratov's eye (see fig. 5.6). This is, of course, a fun-house mirror: the eyes of Livonian and Maliuta do not match exactly, but they suggest each other and remind us of each other, though at first their connection is unclear. The Chaldeans' clown outfits include straw beards, tall pointed caps, and caftans of fabric resembling the boyars' caftans. They evoke another pair of clowns, the two bickering boyars from the prologue, Belskii and Shuiskii. In the prologue, their contrasting physical types, clownish banter, and cruel jokes at Ivan's expense push the young Ivan to assert his authority as tsar. And Sigismund's image is meant to remind us of Ivan and mirror Ivan in an intriguing, but initially indeterminate way.

These off-kilter pairings are typical of Eisenstein's method. Central to his aesthetic and philosophy in this period was a belief that both life and art were structured by a dialectical "unity of opposites." But while Eisenstein searched high and low for examples of the universal structures of dialectics, he was anything but rigid in his application. In other words, the *unity* or *synthesis* of dialectical processes is always in creative tension with the dualistic, contradictory, centrifugal, varied nature of the conflict between *thesis* and *antithesis*. In applying this to the visual contrast between Russianness and foreignness in *Ivan the Terrible*, difference and synthesis are in constant tension with one another, but the paired opposites are also always in progress toward an explosive, transformative, transcendent moment of synthesis, which Eisenstein called *ekstasis*. Foreigners and Russians are different from one another, opposites even, but they are clearly related to one another, they repeatedly mirror each other. They *complete* each other. Let us see how this creative tension is realized in specific instances.

At first glance, everything in Sigismund's court seems designed to suggest an alternative to Moscow, and a parody at that. The hall is spacious and uncrowded in contrast to the Kremlin's low arched ceilings and mousehole doorways. Even where the Russian interiors are spacious as in the Dormition Cathedral, they are crowded with people and paintings, and they are rounded and sensuous compared to the geometric shape and decoration of the Polish court. The Polish courtiers and attendants are arrayed in static, isolated, formal groups, and their interaction unfolds with a stiffness and ceremony that contrasts with the more fluid and emotional relationships between Ivan and his court. The enormous knights behind the throne are Renaissance Gobelin tapestries, secular warriors to the Kremlin's sacred icons and frescos. The dialogue makes the contrast explicit. King Sigismund declares: "God in his wisdom decreed that Lithuania, Poland, and the Baltic States should serve as the outposts of Europe in order that the civilized nations of the west might be protected from the Muscovite barbarians." One of the ladies punctuates this speech with melodramatic indignation, adding, "The Muscovites eat children alive." The same ladies, however, swoon and flirt when Kurbskii appears and the camera zooms in on their heart-shaped headdresses (Kurbskii also wears his heart on his chest). Kremlin sexuality by contrast is all honorable and chaste, Anastasia is more mother than lover to Ivan, and while she too loves Kurbskii, she denies herself in order to support her husband and his great cause.

These contrasts could hardly be more obvious. Russia is barbaric, backward, religious, straitlaced, and apparently weak, but really strong; whereas Poland, a protector of Europe, is civilized, advanced, secular, decadent, and apparently strong, but really weak. Difference reigns: or does it? Underlying the binary distinction is one of Eisenstein's prime examples of the unity of opposites—what he always designated as "b.s." in his notes, short for bisexuality. Eisenstein's use of bisexuality here is not only, or even primarily, intended to signal sexual orientation but is rather one of his favorite examples of human inner contradiction and anxiety about contradiction.[6] Sigismund and his men visually personify the fusion of masculine and feminine in unstable, strange, and evocative ways.

Decades before the appearance of gender theory, Eisenstein understood the uses of gendered images in asserting claims to power and civilization: Sigismund's grandiose, manly claim to be the protector of Western civilization is mirrored by the effeminacy of his costume and manner. Sigismund's mixed gender markers provide a counterpoint to the masculine ideal of the medieval knight looming large above him. The king makes his speech standing in girlish declamatory pose, proclaiming Poland a beacon of civilization. His dress is a hyper-effeminate version of common dress of the period. Although Sigismund appears in more sober guise in historical portraits, a ruffled collar, earrings, pantaloons and tights, feathers, jewels, and lace were standard aristocratic male dress in early modern Europe.[7] On Sigismund, however, the collar, lace, and jewels are flamboyantly ornate. Whereas early in his film career, Eisenstein used actors with recognizable, conventional characteristics as physical "types" to *fix* meaning, in *Ivan the Terrible*, he endowed characters with exaggerated conventional attributes to raise doubts about fixed meanings and convey ambiguity and contradiction. The king's two male courtiers are dressed in an exaggeratedly effeminate and stylized manner. They mirror and parody the oprichniks' somber black costume, which Eisenstein derived from the dynastic double-headed eagle. Sigismund's courtiers almost resemble angels—Eisenstein sometimes called his oprichniki "fallen angels." The oprichniki are also pretty boys in velvet and feathers but they suggest sinister vitality and power. Kurbskii himself performs a frankly homoerotic ritual of exchange and fealty to Sigismund (which is, of course, at the same time an act of treason to Ivan) (see fig. 5.7). Kurbskii hands his sword to the king, who inspects it with supercilious desire, affecting his full expectation of being desired, and hands it back.

Figure 5.7. Kurbskii Vowing Loyalty to Sigismund.
From Sergei Eisenstein's *Ivan the Terrible*.

Kurbskii caresses and kisses it—a Judas kiss, replicating his disingenuous kiss of the cross on pledging loyalty to Ivan after his illness.

I propose, first, that this whole ensemble of sexual, gender, cultural, and political exchanges stands not only for the Polish court but for the "West" as a whole and is meant to evoke not only the specific foreigners in question but Western Europeans in general. The sexual innuendo of the scene is based not on Polish or Livonian sources but on Eisenstein's reading about Elizabeth's flirtations with younger men and a generally racy environment at her court.[8] A later production note links "Bess and Sigismund," and the chessboard floor of the hall recalls the chessboard Ivan sent to Elizabeth in Part I as a threat and a gift.[9] This larger context is further supported by published images linking Sigismund's court with Elizabeth's court, engravings of the Polish Sejm and the English Queen appearing before Parliament.[10]

Second, Eisenstein is doing much more here than representing the West as effeminate and weak or making insider jokes about homoeroticism. Some viewers have seen homophobic strains in the film and interpreted them as a Freudian "return of the repressed." Marie Seton, an unreliable but influential biographer, saw Eisenstein as a self-hating homosexual, unable to suppress his fear of his own homosexuality, mocking homoeroticism on screen.[11] In contrast, others read this scene as a positive celebration of male homoeroticism or homosexuality.[12] But both miss the point (or at least Eisenstein's point). In addition to whatever these scenes might tell us about Eisenstein's sexuality, bisexuality was a key category in his investigation of the unity of opposites as an aesthetic and philosophical problem. The blurring or reversal of gender binaries is connected in Eisenstein's work with other binaries, including the moral (good and evil), the political (tsar and slave, master and dog), and the national or cultural (us and them).

Eisenstein believed that human nature was bifurcated in numerous ways (sexuality among them) and that we seek continually to erase inner divisions by imagining and acting out rituals of merger and reversal. This fact and our anxiety about it are expressed in culture in ways meant to erase difference and resolve anxiety. Eisenstein was fascinated by the ritual exchange of clothing in the wedding ceremonies of some ancient cultures (of which the exchange of rings today is a survival). Such rituals represent a symbolic form of sex reversal, which captures difference, anxiety about difference, and the synthesizing of difference in the unity of opposites that marriage and sexual unions of all kinds signify.[13] Bisexuality is a great example for Eisenstein in part because it is so easy to represent visually. In Sigismund's court Eisenstein presents multiple examples of sexual ambiguity, blending, crossed lines of homosexual and heterosexual desire, and play that function as a visual repository of images that suggest other binaries and their complications. It is not difficult to see how the gendered dialectics can be applied to deepen both Ivan's own individual inner divisions as well as the conflict between Russia and the West or Russia's ambivalence about its position straddling East and West.

Eisenstein conceptualized Ivan as a man torn by inner conflicts, political conflicts, and by conflicts between his public and private lives. The trick was, as Eisenstein put it, to dramatize this dialectical "inner monologue" in film images.[14] Ivan's inner divisions are depicted onscreen through his encounters and relationships with other characters, each of whom represents some conflicted aspect of Ivan himself: *dédoublement.*[15] Ivan's inner conflict and his struggle to assert Russia's power vis-à-vis the West is projected twice in the conflict/mirroring/farce inscribed in pairing Ivan and Sigismund and in the bisexual dialectic embodied by Sigismund and his courtiers. Eisenstein connected this kind of doubling and reversal with circus and carnival, and masquerade and disguise. Rituals of sex reversal have "social" implications in addition to individual ones, Eisenstein wrote, because "the play of [hierarchical] social categories (tsar-slave) in carnival disguises [occurs] in the same forms as in biological (b.s.) cases; primarily to achieve a unity of the divided sexes (*edinstva razobshcheniia sex'ov*)."[16] Social, cultural, and political differences all function the way sex role differences function—they differentiate but in a way that is problematized and subverted in order to resolve contradictory desires within ourselves. When faced with difference, people (as individuals and as cultures) find ways both to accentuate difference and transform themselves into their counterparts, rivals, mirror opposites, if only temporarily (at carnival) or symbolically (through ritual) or metaphorically (in myth, story, and now cinema). The individual, sexual, social, political, and cultural all contain these patterns: conflict between binary oppositions leads to merger or reversal, synthesis, and ultimately transformation into a higher synthesis that shortly breaks down into renewed conflict.

As overly complicated as it might seem, this fusion of Freudian psychoanalysis and Marxian dialectics is a typical device in *Ivan the Terrible* and is fundamental in Eisenstein's aesthetics, philosophy, and filmmaking method during this period. Eisenstein strove to construct this entire unwieldy film on the basis of a single, structural "principle" reiterated in infinite variations: the dialectical bisection and synthesis, conflict and transformation. By representing Sigismund and company as men in drag, Eisenstein sets them up as emblems of cultural difference (Western versus Russian), who contain within themselves the universal bisexual dialectic. The Polish men in drag parody Ivan's own guard, the oprichniki: but they complete each other as mirror images, and create something new in the process. The very ludicrousness of their frilly costume draws attention to the deadly seriousness of their mirror counterparts, the oprichniki, and in so doing reveals what Eisenstein represents as the inherent link between humor and sadism.

Ivan the Terrible gave Eisenstein an opportunity to explore the myriad ways in which opposition and resolution play themselves out in history and in art. He had long been interested in ancient Chinese principles of yin and yang, especially their application in formal qualities of Chinese painting. His work on *Ivan* inspired him to revise a long, unpublished essay on the subject in 1945–1946 as he was finishing the film; one of his prime examples of the intended and unintended ways in which the yin/yang principles of conflict and harmony are inscribed in art was his own set construction and shot composition of Sigismund's checkerboard court.[17] The prevalence of such dialectical structures connected with sex, power, individual personality, morality, history, and so many other aspects of the film suggests that it can be applied to understanding the function of foreigners in Eisenstein's film. Foreigners in *Ivan the Terrible* may be different but their difference is not foreign. The values implied by the cultural conflict are contained within the Russians in the film and more important, it completes them, by providing synthesis. In Eisenstein's thought and practice, difference, resolution, and conflict are natural and necessary. The foreigners here are both a ridiculous form of "them" and they are the feared contradictions within "us." In this way, Eisenstein uses the Western view of Russia as backward and barbaric to set up an inner division between the Russians' ridicule of that view and fear of its essential truth.

Sadism and Humor, a Political Dialectic

All this, believe it or not, is meant to be funny. Eisenstein often displayed a fairly puerile sense of humor and that comes into play here. But there were serious reasons for imbuing this portrait of sexual and cultural difference, conflict, and mirroring with satire and campy humor. The satire hints at something unspeakable about the foreigners, and not only in the antinormative sex-play on the surface. The model for understanding Eisenstein's use of humor here is that same dialectical unity of opposites that structures the sexual, class, and cultural issues in the film. Courtiers in frills and assassins in velvet point to another factor in Eisenstein's method—his dialectical sadistic humor. We laugh at his foreigners because they are ridiculed, patronized, humiliated, contorted, and diminished. The combination of sadism and humor that is evident in all his films works in *Ivan the Terrible* to illustrate particularly insidious features of Stalinism by pairing it in dialectic tension with Nazism.

Here Eisenstein introduces Heinrich von Shtaden, the German mercenary and author, as the very embodiment of pitiless oprichnik cruelty. He appears only briefly in the completed film, but was slated to play a key role in two scenes of the unfinished Part III. Eisenstein wrote a great deal about Shtaden in his production notes, and while one of his scenes only exists in the screenplay and Eisenstein's notes, the other was shot and survives.[18] The extant footage shows Ivan's interrogation of Shtaden when he appears at Alexandrova Sloboda as a spy for Kurbskii and his Livonian masters. Ivan, it seems, suspects Shtaden is a spy and treats him to a kind of cat-and-mouse humiliation that mimics the treatment Ivan gave the rebellious crowd in Part I, and is familiar to all who know (and knew) Stalin's treatment of his enemies (and his friends). Alternating jokes and threats, Ivan easily manipulates the crowd of oprichniki (the former rebels, by the way), egging them on to laugh at Shtaden as he becomes increasingly sullen, scared that Ivan is on to him. After intimidating and testing Shtaden, Ivan suddenly drops the hostility, pretending the whole thing was a harm-

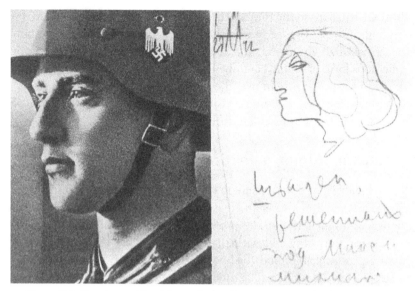

Figure 5.8. Shtaden as Nazi Maximilian in Eisenstein's Notebook.
From Sergei Eisenstein's *Ivan the Terrible.*

less prank, and Shtaden is accepted into the oprichnina. Andrei Moskvin's
brilliant cinematography in this scene—the lighting, shot composition, and
especially the use of shadows—highlight the play of dialectics by making
all the laughter seem sinister, and the threats funny.[19]

Originally, Eisenstein wrote, he had introduced Shtaden purely for
the "wolfish" atmosphere of the oprichnina, based in part on Shtaden's
blood-curdling memoir and in part on his role as an outsider and a spy
inside the oprichnina.[20] But the director realized that if he made Shtaden
the source of evil that leads to the corruption and downfall of Aleksei and
Fedor Basmanov he could deepen and complicate his depiction of Ivan's
most vicious moment. When Ivan discovers that his oprichnik leader, Aleksei
Basmanov, has been stealing from him, Ivan has Fedor kill his father as a
display of loyalty to the tsar, and then has Fedor killed for his disloyalty to
his father. Shtaden sets off this horrifying chain of events by informing on
Aleksei and then killing Fedor.

Eisenstein based Shtaden's visual appearance on Nazi soldiers (see
fig. 5.8). Morally, Eisenstein noted, "Shtaden [was] the 'evil genius' of
Basmanov family." Politically he brought about the Basmanov's downfall
and Ivan's also:

And it turns out very well that this is done by a German-Livonian—in typical German-fascist style . . . that is, it is *typical* of the Germans to exploit every contradiction in the countries they invade . . . this would be great for contrasting . . . the theme of Ivan and the theme of the German *dictatorship*. . . . Give the Germany *a bit* of prophesy about the unleashing of instincts and appetites—the dark element, the *worst*—while Ivan heeds the *best* in the people. . . . *Great* of course that Ivan's "trick" at Alexandrova Sloboda [when Ivan "tricks" the people into recalling him to Moscow to rule over them] here grows into tragic pathos.[21]

Shtaden turns out to be another mirror of Ivan. The Nazis and Russians (here I read: Soviets) are both predators. The Russian case is tragic, though, because it began in utopian revolution based on an excessively optimistic ideology.

Conclusions

Eisenstein's portraits of foreigners—the ridiculous, sinister, and evil—were not created in order to demonstrate the Russians' moral or cultural superiority. On the contrary, Eisenstein's use of the dialectical unity of opposites turns the film's foreigners into mirrors who reflect (and cruelly at times) the variety of ambivalent divisions and conflicts that Russians experienced as Russians.

As necessary components of Russian identity, the foreigners in *Ivan the Terrible* insist on difference—though ironically and surreptitiously. This stance is deeply subversive but in a classic Eisensteinian through-the-looking-glass way. By ridiculing the foreigners and making them essential for the construction of a sense of national identity, Eisenstein defies the pervading Stalinist xenophobia present in other films from the time and pays tribute to cosmopolitan multiplicity.[22] All the examples discussed here position Russia in a broader Eurasian context to explore fundamental ambiguities about Russian autocracy and Russia's place between East and West. With images of sadistic mockery and parody, *Ivan's* foreigners complicate the unitary cultural norms of Stalinist society, reject "static" Bolshevik nationalism, and represent Russian court society as a thoroughly cosmopolitan circus. And finally, Eisenstein uses the conflict about cultural difference to examine tensions between meaning and representation; to show us the power of images to reach into our deepest sources of anxiety about forming our own identity and finding our place in the world.

NOTES

1. For a plot summary see Joan Neuberger, *Ivan the Terrible: The Film Companion* (London: I. B Tauris, 2003).

2. Until one month before the release of *Ivan the Terrible* Part I, the Prologue appeared at the beginning of Part I immediately after the credits. It was deleted in the censorship process, but Eisenstein later inserted it as a flashback in Part II. For a concise production history of *Ivan the Terrible*, see Neuberger, *Ivan the Terrible*, 13–24.

3. Young, beautiful, bare-chested young men, pierced by arrows or other implements, are a feature in Eisenstein's earlier films as well. For a relevant discussion of Saint Sebastian as a model for martyred young men including these Tatar captives, see Richard A. Kaye, "Losing His Religion: Saint Sebastian as Contemporary Gay Martyr," in *Outlooks: Lesbian and Gay Sexualities and Visual Cultures*, ed. Peter Horne and Reina Lewis (London: Routledge, 1996).

4. The Elizabeth/Romm screen-test footage can be seen on "Deleted Scenes," compiled by Naum Kleiman, on *Ivan the Terrible, Part II*, in the compilation boxed set, *Eisenstein: The Sound Years* (The Criterion Collection, 2001).

5. Eisenstein's notes on this and the other subjects discussed in this article are located in his personal archive at Rossiiskii gosudarstvennyi arkhiv literatury i iskusstva (RGALI), fond 1923. Eisenstein's reading notes on Shtaden are in 1923/1/561, 569, 570 and 1923/2/125.

6. On Eisenstein's uses of bisexuality and cross-dressing, see S. M. Eizenshtein, *Metod*, vol. 2 (Moscow: Muzei-kino, Eizenshtein-tsentr, 2002), 494–97; Yuri Tsivian, *Ivan the Terrible* (London: British Film Institute, 2002), 60–73; Anne Nesbet, "Inanimations: Snow White and Ivan the Terrible," *Film Quarterly* 50, no. 4 (1997): 25–26; and Neuberger, *Ivan the Terrible*, 83–84, 94–96.

7. Sigismund III, however, who ruled later in the sixteenth century, was often portrayed in fancy ruffs and fussy goatee, but these portraits lack the girlish poses and complicated coiffure; see Mariusy Trąba and Lech Bielski, *Poczet królów i książąt polskich* (Bielsko Bialla; PARK, 2005), 411, 431. I am indebted to Valerie Kivelson for bringing these portraits and the Polish sources in note 10 to my attention.

8. RGALI, 1923/1/561/5 (October 1, 1941).

9. RGALI, 1923/2/1169/20 (April 20, 1942).

10. *Nobilitas Politica vel Civilis* (London: N,p., 1608). Reprinted in Robin Winks and Lee Palmer Wandel, *Europe in a Wider World, 1350–1650* (New York: Oxford University Press, 2003), 196; see also the checkerboard Sejm in Antoni Mączak, *W czasach "potopu"* (Wrocław: Wydawnictwo Dolnośląskie, 1999), 96.

11. Marie Seton, *Sergei M. Eisenstein, A Biography* (New York: Grove Press, 1960), 437.

12. See, for example, Thomas Waugh, "A Fag-Spotter's Guide to Eisenstein," *Body Politic* 35 (1977): 14–17. For a more balanced view, see Parker Tyler, *Screening the Sexes: Homosexuality in the Movies* (Garden City, N.Y.: Anchor Books, 1972); also Al LaValley, "Maintaining, Blurring and Transcending Gender Lines in Eisenstein," in *Eisenstein at 100: A Reconsideration*, Al LaValley and Barry P. Scherr, eds. (New Brunswick, N.J.: Rutgers University Press, 2001), 57–63.

13. RGALI, 1923/2/1166/42–43 (November 14, 1943); S. M. Eisenstein, *Selected Works*, vol. 4, in *Beyond the Stars: The Memoirs of Sergei Eisenstein*, ed. Richard Taylor,

trans. William Powell (London: British Film Institute, 1995), 604–15; V. V. Ivanov, "Perevertysh i karnaval," in *Izbrannye trudy po semiotike i istorii kul'tury* (Moscow: N.p., 1998), 343–47. Eisenstein double-marked an incident he noted from Shtaden's memoir, in which some opponents of the oprichniki changed into the oprichnik clothes "and carried out a lot of harm and mischief" (RGALI, 1923/1/561/57).

14. RGALI, 1923/2/128/3.

15. Tsivian, *Ivan the Terrible*, 51.

16. RGALI, 1923/2/128/3. "Sex" appears in English with the Russian genitive case ending in the original.

17. S. M. Eizenshtein, *Metod*, vol. 2 (Moscow: Muzei-Kino, Eizenshtein-tsentr, 2002), 150–91, 457–59, 599–600, 645.

18. See "Deleted Scenes," compiled by Naum Kleiman, on *Ivan the Terrible, Part II*, in the compilation boxed set, *Eisenstein: The Sound Years* (The Criterion Collection, 2001).

19. For a discussion of the lighting and shooting of this scene, see Ia. L. Butovsky, *Andrei Moskvin, Kinooperator* (St. Petersburg: Dimitri Blanin, 2000), 212–16.

20. Sergei Eizenshtein, *Izbrannye proizvedeniia v shosti tomalch* (Moscow: Iskusstvo, 1964–1971), vol. 6, *Production Notes, March–April 1942*, 504.

21. Eizenshtein, *Izbrannye proizvedeniia*, vol. 6, 505–506; see also RGALI 1923/2/125/5–6.

22. See Josephine Woll's and Peter Kenez's essays in this volume.

The Picture of the Enemy in Stalinist Films
Peter Kenez

The Setting: Socialist Realism and Identifying Enemies in Stalinist Cinema

At the end of the 1920s Soviet film enjoyed a well-deserved worldwide reputation, but within a short time the fame and influence of the great directors were lost; the golden age was brief and the eclipse sudden and long-lasting.[1] The coming of the sound film made the famous "Russian montage" outdated, and therefore it was a factor in the decline, but far more important in destroying the reputation of Soviet cinema were the political changes that took place in the early 1930s. From 1928 to 1932 the Soviet Union experienced an extraordinary transformation, touching on all aspects of life. The changes introduced in the cultural sphere were part and parcel of the changes that included forced collectivization of the countryside, liquidating the kulaks, and attempting to build an industrial civilization in the shortest possible time.

The destruction of the moderate pluralism in intellectual life that had existed in the 1920s came to be called, by the Stalinists, perversely, as "cultural revolution." In the period artists were cajoled and coerced to come up with principles and methods that would be suitable in the new order. Only rarely were they passive victims; most of the time they collaborated. Although in its golden age Soviet film was widely admired, the Stalinist leadership was dissatisfied. The Bolsheviks considered film to be an excellent instrument for bringing their message to the people, and they intended to use it, more than any other medium of art, for creating the "new socialist man." These excessively high expectations were bound to lead to disappointment: films that were artistically successful and made in a communist spirit did not attract a large enough audience. The Bolsheviks wanted artistically worthwhile, commercially successful, and politically correct films. It turned out that these requirements pointed in different directions and no director could possibly satisfy them all.

The Cultural Revolution in cinema aimed to remedy what seemed a fault to the Bolshevik leaders: artistically most interesting and experimental works remained inaccessible to simple people. In order to make an impact on workers and peasants audiences had to be attracted. Bolshevik policies brought about some of the desired results, and in the course of the 1930s moviegoing for the first time became a part of the life of the average citizen. In the 1920s cinema was basically an urban entertainment, however, the bulk of the people lived in villages. Now the peasantry was coerced to join collective farms and the collectives were pressured to buy projectors. From 1928 to 1940 the number of films made per year fell to thirty-five and for the rest of the 1940s it remained stationary.

The numerical decline went hand in hand with a reduction of stylistic variety, because Stalinist leaders imposed socialist realism on all Soviet artists. The doctrine of socialist realism was first defined—and imposed on all artists—at the 1934 first all-union Congress of Soviet Writers. The Congress included in its statutes this classic definition: "Socialist realism is the basic method of Soviet literature and literary criticism. It demands of the artist the truthful, historically concrete representation of reality in its revolutionary development. Moreover, the truthfulness and historical concreteness of the artistic representation of reality must be linked with the task of ideological transformation and education of workers in the spirit of socialism."[2]

Socialist realism, as defined by the 1934 Congress, seemed to be a very simple concept, yet it is striking that many intelligent commentators have found it necessary to struggle with a definition, and have by no means agreed with one another. Katerina Clark offers a most helpful approach to the question in her book, *The Soviet Novel*. Clark suggests that since the socialist realist novels are formulaic, the best way to appreciate these works is to present the master plot on which the novels were based. Those novels that follow the master plot are socialist realist, and those that do not are not, regardless of the intentions of the author. As she points out, a socialist realist novel is always a *Bildungsroman*, that is, it is about the acquisition of consciousness. In the process of fulfilling a task, the hero, under the tutelage of a seasoned Party worker, acquires an increased understanding of himself, the world around him, the tasks of building communism, class struggle, and the need for vigilance.[3] Indeed, the same master plot can be found in films, as Julian Graffy demonstrates in this volume. Clark argues that socialist realist art is best compared not with the classics of literature but with cheap novels and Hollywood films. Low- and middle-brow art tend to be formulaic not only in the Soviet Union, but everywhere.

For socialist realist art to carry out its assigned social function, it had to enjoy complete monopoly. Socialist realism could not coexist with other literary trends; the phenomenon had to dominate the artistic world completely. This domination was the source of its power: the consumer of art had to get the impression that there was no other way to look at the world than the one presented. As long as the reader or the viewer had a choice, he or she did not yet live in the world of socialist realist culture. Genuine socialist realism presupposes concentration camps in the not very distant background. Under the circumstances, no honest contemplation of the human predicament was possible; no genuine issues that society faced could be examined. The Stalinist 1930s was the age of socialist realism not because a new doctrine was suddenly discovered; the crucial variable was the willingness of the political system to suppress every portrayal of the world that did not conform to the current doctrinal "reality." Classics of socialist realism, novels such as Dmitrii Furmanov's *Chapaev* and Maxim Gorky's *Mother*, and S. Iutkevich and Fridrikh Ermler's film *Counterplan* (1932), appeared years before the concept of socialist realism was defined. One might plausibly argue that these precursors became truly socialist realist only in the mid-1930s. Soviet cultural life was unique; it could be compared with nothing that had ever existed before.

Socialist realist films include three stock figures with depressing regularity: the Party leader, the simple person, and the enemy. The Party leader is almost always male, ascetic, dressed in a semimilitary style, unencumbered by a family or love affairs. The simple person can be male or female, and is allowed to have an interest in the opposite sex. Sexual relations are always chaste, the viewer can never see more than a kiss, and these relations often need to be straightened out by the Party leader. The enemy, whose function is to wreck and destroy what the Communists are building, is always male. On occasion, but rarely, he attempts to win over the simple person to his side by lying and subterfuge, but mostly he limits his activities to blowing things up.

By far the most frequent theme in films dealing with contemporary life was the struggle against saboteurs. This is hardly surprising. It was an age of denunciations, phony trials, and the "uncovering" of unbelievable plots. Although it is likely that sabotage did not exist at all in the 1930s, in the world of Stalinist discourse the unmasking of the hidden enemy was a dominant theme. Film directors lent their talents to the creation of an atmosphere of hysteria and paranoia. Their scenarios closely resembled the tales of the most vicious storyteller of them all, Andrei Vyshinskii, the infamous prosecutor at the purge trials. In the films, as in the confessions at the trials, the "enemy" carried out the most dastardly acts out of unreasoned hatred for decent socialist society.[4] The film *The Great Citizen*, made in 1937, was a fictionalized version of the Kirov murder and the trials that followed it. The story of the film is no more or no less believable than the trial transcripts. We know that Stalin took the matter of the depiction of the enemy very seriously indeed. When he received the script of the film he made copious comments. He instructed the director, Ermler, how the "enemies of the people" should look in the film: "They should not be depicted as old and venerable, there should be nothing admirable about them, etc."[5]

In the seven-year period 1933–1939, Soviet directors made eighty-five films that dealt with contemporary life. (This number does not include some films for children and about military adventures, or about the exploits of border guards.) In thirty-three of these, the socialist hero has to overcome difficulties, including bureaucracy, arrogance, or stupidity, or natural obstacles, such as storms or cold. But in more than half the films, fifty-two, the hero unmasks hidden enemies who have committed criminal acts. The hero can never be too vigilant: in Aleksandr Dovzhenko's *Aerograd* (1935), the enemy turns out to be his best friend; in Sergei Eisenstein's unfinished *Bezhin Meadow* (1935–1937) it is the protagonist's father; and in Ivan Pyr'ev's *The Party Card* (1936) it is the heroine's husband. We may make some generalizations about the antihero. He always comes from a "class alien" family: most often kulak, but sometimes bourgeois. He never changes, that is, there never was a time when he turned against the people. There could never be evolution. The bad were always bad and by analogy, the good always good.

Few movies had fully developed negative characters, and in many they were completely absent. For reasons of dramaturgy it was easier to combat nature than a human enemy, and therefore a large number of films dealt with the heroic deeds of Soviet people against natural obstacles. By contrast, films with negative heroes, such as Ermler's *Great Citizen* (1937–1939) and especially Pyr'ev's *The Party Card*, are the most repellent and morally reprehensible products of the decade because they explicitly and consciously justified mass murder. *The Party Card*, completed in 1936, was about the need for vigilance. The enemy, the son of a kulak, hides his real essence and feelings, pretending to be an honest Soviet citizen. He steals the Party card of his wife and then uses it for a nefarious purpose. The film was made at the time of a national campaign to renew Party cards, thereby purging undesirable elements. Among the goals of the film was to contribute to the cult of the Party card, the losing of which was considered a major infraction of Party discipline. The enemy of *The Party Card* is unmasked at the end by his wife. The leadership of Mosfilm for some reason found this film "unsuccessful, false, and distorting Soviet reality." Stalin had a different opinion. He changed the title of the film from the proposed *Anka* to *The Party Card* and approved its distribution.[6]

The Internal Enemy: 1932's *Counterplan*

Let us now examine the depiction of the enemy in one typical production film, *Counterplan*. It was a very important product in the history of Soviet cinema, one that was widely discussed at the time. The leaders of the film industry considered it a pattern to be followed, and therefore its release can be regarded as the beginning of an era. Ermler and Iutkevich were instructed to make a film on industrialization in January 1932, but they were given neither a script nor precise instructions. Although *Counterplan* (*Vstrechnyi*) is one of the milestones of Soviet cinema, it remains almost entirely unknown in the West, and is distinguished neither by artistic quality nor aesthetic innovation. When the film was completed in October 1932, it was heavily criticized by the collective at Sovkino, and had to be hurriedly recut. Even contemporary critics agreed that it contained nothing new artistically. The film was to be completed for the fifteenth anniversary of the Revolution. It was important, however, because it offered a model and set the tone for many future films.[7] Significantly, *Counterplan* was made two years before the official doctrine of socialist realism was articulated. But that should not be surprising. Socialist realism did not come down from on high as a fully developed theory imposed on entirely unwilling artists. The doctrine grew out of a mixture of influences: Russian literary tradition, Marxist-Leninist ideology, and the political atmosphere prevailing in the country.

Like all socialist realist films, it had a veneer of realism. No strange juxtapositions or cuttings disturb a plausible urban locale. We see familiar landmarks of Leningrad, a factory interior, and apartments, which are, to be sure, nicer than most people in the audience had ever seen, but believable nonetheless. Yet the world depicted here is completely imagined: people in the film do not behave as human beings have ever behaved. Instead they represent types and talk and act, as they should according to Stalinist myths.

The action of *Counterplan* takes place in a factory. The choice of locale was slightly unusual: none of the major films of the previous decade had dealt with production problems in a contemporary factory. However, during the period of industrialization it was inevitable that production dramas would play a role in the film world, albeit not as large as one might have expected. The obvious purpose of these works was to mobilize the people to work with greater enthusiasm for the grand task of industrialization. Unfortunately the English title *Counterplan* gives no hint of the meaning of the Russian *Vstrechnyi*, a well-known term in the ideological jargon of the period of the First Five Year Plan. The workers of a factory express their enthusiasm for industrialization by presenting their own *vstrechnyi* plan to the authorities, a "counterplan" by definition more ambitious than the original. The action of the film revolves around the difficulties of fulfilling this counterplan, the completion of an electricity-generating turbine ahead of schedule. The film has a *Perils of Pauline* quality: when one difficulty is successfully surmounted another appears.[8] Will our heroes, in spite of all, succeed in carrying out the ambitious counterplan?

A socialist realist film is always about the acquisition of consciousness. In the film not only are the difficulties overcome, but also in the process some of the heroes acquire a superior understanding of the world. This higher degree of consciousness never arrives by itself, simply as learning from experience. There is always an instructor, representing the Party. In *Counterplan* there are two processes of education going on at the same time.

One story line concerns an old skilled worker, Babchenko. He is a respected and devoted worker, but he represents the old world: he drinks, and instead of measuring the finished product he simply estimates. He is entrusted with making a crucial part of the turbine, but the part is spoiled because Babchenko makes a mistake. In the course of the film he learns to give up his daily vodka, acquires respect for the Party leadership, and learns to work properly according to modern methods. At the end of the film he is ready to join the Party.

The other student is Pasha, the head of a section in the factory, a young cadre and a good friend of the Party Secretary. He is a devoted Party member and there is nothing more important in his life than carrying out his responsibilities. Yet he is not on the same level of consciousness as the Party Secretary, Vasia. Vasia intuits that a saboteur is at work. He knows how to talk to the workers and motivate the downcast Babchenko (see fig. 6.1). Above all, unlike Pasha, he would never admit defeat. He articulates the message of the day: "Numbers! If numbers are against the fulfillment of the plan then they are hostile numbers! And the people who bring them forward are not our people, but they are enemies. . . . How is it that you did not know numbers can also be Party numbers?" So when we discuss the topic of the "enemy" in Soviet films, we must not forget "numbers." Under Vasia's tutelage, Pasha becomes a better communist.

Figure 6.1. Vasia and Babchenko.
From Fridrikh Ermler's *Counterplan* (1932).

During the Cultural Revolution directors were attacked for dehumanizing history by presenting the masses as heroes and not providing Soviet audiences with worthwhile models to follow. Critics correctly maintained that heroless movies were boring for mass audiences. Socialist realist films always provided an individual hero. In *Counterplan* Vasia, the progenitor of dozens of future heroes, plays this essential role. His job, Secretary of the factory Party organization, was the appropriate job for a positive hero, while he also is an attractive man (there were no physically unattractive positive heroes in Soviet films). Moreover, his clothes identify him as a positive hero—in his military uniform he looks a bit like the young Stalin. He has a nice sense of humor, and he loves to sing and play the guitar.

If it was difficult to make the positive hero lifelike, it was entirely impossible to create a believable negative character. The problem was that the Party line, to say nothing of Soviet power, could not possibly be opposed on morally acceptable grounds. A negative hero in a socialist realist film, therefore, is always an Iago-like character, who wants to do evil for the sake of evil. But Shakespeare's Iago had grandeur; he is intelligent, perceptive, and a skillful manipulator of his antagonists. In his desire to harm Othello,

Figure 6.2. The Internal Enemy.
From Fridrikh Ermler's *Counterplan* (1932).

he is a figure of superhuman proportions. A Soviet director, however, could not give to his negative character majesty and courage, thereby making him a worthy opponent.

Counterplan has a typical negative hero. He is a member of the old intelligentsia, the engineer Aleksei Skvortsov (see fig. 6.2). In explaining his wicked motives to his mother, all he can say is: "They are eliminating us as a class. If there will be no electricity, there will be no communists!" He is a relatively unimportant figure and appears only for a few minutes on the screen. He does not even carry out active sabotage. He simply knows that the drawings are incorrect and he fails to correct them. He is a small, cringing figure, dominated by his mother, who calls him Aleshen'ka. In the 1920s, Ermler, the only Party member among the major directors, had made several appealing films about the plight of the old intelligentsia. But in this film, made at the time of specialist baiting and phony trials, he lent his talent and reputation to the unattractive task of justifying the murderous policies of the regime. Ultimately, the dramaturgical weakness of *Counterplan* is that the adversaries are unevenly matched. There is little tension, for it is easy to defeat an enemy such as Skvortsov. In this respect also the film is typical of Soviet cinematography of the 1930s.

The Soviet system, as it developed in the 1930s, destroyed millions of its own citizens and, contrary to the views of some Western historians, the terror affected all layers of society. Cinema both reflected the terror and also contributed to an atmosphere of hysteria. One needs no particularly sophisticated methods of analysis to recognize that Soviet films made in the 1930s convey the message that the enemy was everywhere: the parents, children, friends, and lovers of the naive heroes turn out to be traitors. The enemy can appear in the guise of a good worker and even show false enthusiasm for the building of socialism. No one can be trusted. Films, of course, did not exist in a vacuum: Soviet reality confirmed their vicious message.

The External Enemy: Foreigners in Stalinist Cinema

By 1940, however, we witness a curious phenomenon: the internal enemy suddenly and completely disappears. Of the thirty films dealing with contemporary topics made in 1940, not a single one focuses on traitors. The enemy, to be sure, remained, but now the wicked people were agents smuggled over the border. The country was preparing to face a foreign foe. Instead of encouraging the Soviet people to ferret out nonexistent internal saboteurs, the films now preached how Russian and Georgian, Armenian and Azerbaijani, must work together for the common good.

Perhaps not surprisingly, the opinion-formers were obsessed with the danger posed by the foreign foe. In the 1930s, more films were made about border guards than about workers. Twenty-one films dealt with catching foreign agents. Most of these agents were Japanese, and were caught by border guards. Eleven other films tell more or less the same story: the enemy, most often German, but sometimes Polish, attacks without a declaration of war. The Soviet people respond quickly and decisively. The war is taken to enemy territory, where it is rapidly and victoriously concluded. In retrospect, one gets the impression that Soviet publicists were whistling in the dark.

Soviet films depicted the outside world as undifferentiated and threatening, but also uniformly miserable. The outside world as it appeared on the screen was unrecognizable. In this world people were starving to death; brutal police were suppressing a mighty Communist movement; and the foreign workers' ultimate concern was the security of the Soviet Union. Again and again they would rather strike and starve than allow an attack on the fatherland of all workers. Given these premises, it is not surprising that a recurring motif was foreigners, whether of Russian extraction of not, coming to the USSR and finding there a happy and worthwhile life. On the basis of these works one might conclude that a basic problem of the USSR was how to keep out all the foreigners who wanted to come and live there. The action of twenty films took place entirely or partially outside of the borders of the USSR. The foreign locales clearly reflected the twists and turns of Soviet foreign policy. Before 1935, an unnamed Western country was usually portrayed; this was a synthetic place, having signs in English, French, and German.

Ivan Pyr'ev's 1933 *The Conveyor Belt of Death*, for example, received rather favorable reviews. The film has a confused and complicated story, the consequence, perhaps, of its having been written and rewritten by several people over a period of three years. It attempts to show the crisis of bourgeois society, to unmask "the beauties of bourgeois life," and to show the role of the Communist Parties in contemporary Western Europe. Pyr'ev's film, unlike Vsevolod Pudovkin's *Deserter* (1933) (more on this film below), does deal explicitly with fascism.

However, the location of the story is not only not specified, but also deliberately obfuscated. Pyr'ev created a synthetic West. He conveys the impression that fascism is a general problem in all capitalist societies. In this director's presentation, the working classes of the West are unbendingly loyal to the Soviet Union. In the climactic turning-point of the film, the workers go on strike rather than produce weapons that could be used against the Soviet Union. The film is an interesting example of the Soviet perception of the West, a perception that has changed remarkably little over the decades (see the essays by Anthony Anemone and Oleg Sulkin in this volume). For a Soviet observer the most horrifying aspect of life in a capitalist society is lack of security, the ever-present fear of unemployment, and of the various social ills prostitution has an unusual fascination. Sometimes, however, Germany or the United States was specified. Films set in Germany in the early 1930s, such as Pudovkin's *The Deserter* (made in 1933) not only did not comment on the Nazi danger but also portrayed the socialists as the main enemies of the working class. In 1935, Soviet foreign policy shifted. The Comintern called for a popular front of all progressive forces against Nazism. Soviet studios made six anti-Nazi films between the congress of the Comintern in 1935 and the signing of the Nazi-Soviet Pact in 1939. Of these, the best and most prominent were A. Minkin and Gerbert Rappaport's *Professor Mamlock* (1938) and Grigorii Roshal's *The Oppenheim Family* (1939). By 1940, audiences could see several new films showing the joy of Ukrainians and Belorussians being liberated from Polish oppression (for example, *Wind from the East* and *The Voice of Taras*).

Enemies Within:
Germans, Collaborators, and Wartime Films

The period of World War II is a curious interlude in the history of Soviet cinema.[9] Paradoxically the directors became freer in the sense that they could express their genuine sentiments. When they depicted Germans as the enemy and depicted them as merciless, cruel, and inhumane, they had a boundless source of raw material to select from. They had no reason to lie. A realistic depiction of German behavior was in itself good propaganda.

Once again, the Soviet regime, like no political system before, was able to mobilize its well-developed propaganda machine and focus its message. During the war seventy films were made and with a very few exceptions all served a political purpose. In order to mobilize people for a just war the enemy was depicted as one that had to be fought. Vigilance, a major theme in prewar films, once again came to the fore. The picture of the enemy went through some transformation. In the very earliest shorts, made in 1941, Germans were depicted as inhumane and cruel, but also at times as silly and foolish. Such light-heartedness, however, quickly disappeared. As it became clear all too soon, this enemy should not be underestimated. This was not to be an easy struggle. There was nothing to laugh at in the Germans. In one of the earliest war films, Ermler's *She Defends the Motherland* (1943), the Germans destroy everything in their wake, and commit the greatest crime a Russian can imagine by knowingly crushing a child under a tank. In Russian war films, as this scene indicates, the director could never go over the top in depicting German beastliness.

German inhumanity was also projected back into the past and it was explicitly racial. Eisenstein's *Aleksandr Nevskii*, made in 1937, already reflected this pattern. The Teutonic Knights were depicted as proto-Nazis. The Germans were always inhuman, even those Germans who had lived for centuries in Russia. Moreover, the deportation of the Volga Germans during the war was rationalized by making a film showing the beastliness of the Volga Germans at the time of the Russian Civil War. There could be no good Germans. Pudovkin even attempted to make a film in 1942, *The Murderers Go Out to the Street*, on the basis of a Bertolt Brecht story, which was about the persecution of German communists by the Nazis. But in the prevailing atmosphere there could be no good Germans. Communist internationalism went out the window. The proper allies of the Russian people in this struggle according to the propagandists were the other Slavic people.

There were, however, enemies in Soviet films who were depicted with even greater venom than the Germans, and these were the collaborators. In the film *Rainbow* (Mark Donskoi, 1944) the village elder who collaborated is killed at the end, and the Soviet officer husband who returns with the partisans kills his wife who had cohabited with a German. The audience accepts these murders as necessary and just. *The Rainbow* has a powerful effect even on today's audiences, largely because of its unusually graphic and detailed depiction of Nazi barbarities. For example, the Germans murder a young boy who tries to smuggle food to a prisoner, and they kill a newborn babe. The enemy as pictured in wartime films like *The Rainbow* had tremendous staying power—long after the war ended, as Stephen Norris reminds us in his essay, Soviet film directors continued to depict Germans and collaborators as uniformly vicious and stupid while the Soviet people always remained clever and heroic.

Cold War Enemies: The External Enemy Recast

The postwar period (1946–1953) was once again distinct in its depiction of enemies. The war exposed a large number of Soviet citizens to the outside world. And that from the point of view of the political leadership represented a great danger of subversion that had to be counteracted. The cutting of the contacts with the Western world, and the introduction of an anticosmopolitan campaign that was almost lunatic in its extremism, could be explained by the concern of Stalin and his followers for the stability of the regime. A corollary of the anticosmopolitan campaign was intense xenophobia with pronounced anti-Semitic elements. The films naturally reflected this spirit. Jewish directors felt the consequences of discrimination; however, anti-Semitic themes did not appear in Soviet films of the period.

The postwar Soviet regime did not hold purge trials. As those murderous spectacles disappeared from public life, so did the fixation on spies, saboteurs, and internal enemies of various sorts. Judging purely on the basis of contemporary films, the regime that murdered millions of its citizens ruled over a conflict-free society. The "enemy," so very important both for good drama and also for the cohesion of the Soviet order, was now almost always foreign. In those postwar films that were made as contributions to various Soviet propaganda campaigns, the Soviet hero always defeated a foreign enemy.

Films such as *The Russian Question* (Mikhail Romm, 1948), *The Court of Honor* (Abram Room, 1948), *The Secret Mission* (Abram Room, 1950), and *The Conspiracy of the Doomed* (Mikhail Kalatozov, 1950) were among the best-known works of the period. These films each dealt with a contemporary issue: *The Court of Honor* was a contribution to the struggle against cosmopolitans; *The Russian Question* showed how anti-Sovietism was created and encouraged by the American imperialists; *Conspiracy of the Doomed* was a peculiar, Soviet version of the political struggles that had recently occurred in occupied Eastern Europe; *The Secret Mission* deals with Anglo-American treachery during the past war. In spite of their widely different topics, the message is always the same: Russian ways are superior; the Soviet people are courageous, patriotic, and handsome; foreigners are treacherous and infinitely mean and cruel. These foreigners, unlike their earlier cinematic counterparts discussed by Julian Graffy, could never become "ours," and always remained outsiders.

The most ambitious of these films was Grigorii Alexandrov's 1949 *Meeting on the Elbe*, which gave the Soviet version of the events leading to the outbreak of the Cold War. Let us look at this work in some detail. The film contrasts the two worlds at the moment of victory over Hitler and in the immediate postwar period. One would not expect subtlety in such juxtaposition, and indeed there is none. In Alexandrov's version the Red Army brings peaceful reconstruction to the inhabitants of an imaginary German town, Altenstadt. In the Soviet zone the munitions factories are converted to produce consumer goods. Soviet soldiers are ready to help in all sorts of good causes. As the Soviet general puts it: "we must find a way to the hearts of the German people." This general gives machine-gun oil to the nuns for making candles. The soldiers and officers are heroic, physically attractive, and immensely proud of their nation. They suffer homesickness. There is no need to worry that the Red Army would impose communism on the unwilling Germans. This is the way an officer explains Soviet policy to his American interlocutor: "You must deserve the Soviet system!"

Far more interesting than the Soviet figures, all knights in shining armor, are the Americans. During World War II, Soviet directors had always depicted Germans as evil. By contrast, the Americans were now presented as a varied lot. The simple Americans love and admire the Russians and want peace above all. They well understand that it was the Russians, rather than the Western Allies, who won the war. The enemy is the capitalists and their hirelings. Obviously, Soviet scenarists and directors knew little about America, and they made no effort to expose the genuine failings of capitalist society. They created an image of an enemy that bore as little similarity to reality as their version of the Soviet man.

The directors put together their picture of the Americans from various sources. Some features of that picture go back to the earliest days of the

Figure 6.3. The Cold War Enemy.
From Grigorii Alexandrov's *Meeting on the Elbe* (1949).

Soviet regime, as Julian Graffy's article makes clear. For example, the notion of debauchery has always fascinated Soviet observers. Many of them
imagined modern-day America as Rome just before its fall. In *Meeting on
the Elbe*, as in many other films, the capitalist chomps on his cigar, listens
to jazz, and is entertained by scantily dressed young women (in this era
jazz is always a symptom of corruption). The idea that sexual seduction
is a weapon in the hands of the class enemy is one that goes back to the
first Soviet films. In *Meeting on the Elbe*, needless to say, our Soviet hero
indignantly rejects the approach of the beautiful spy-journalist, played by
the director's wife, Liubov" Orlova (who also starred in Alexandrov's musical comedy, *The Circus*) (see fig. 6.3).

   This film is interesting because it is so unconsciously self-revelatory; the
director projects on the enemy what he knew the Red Army was doing or
was accused of doing. In the 1930s the Soviet regime successfully cut off its
own people from the outside world. The war broke down the barriers, and
millions of Soviet citizens came to learn something about the way of life of
foreigners and their high standard of living. From the point of view of the

Soviet authorities, contacts between their own people and Europeans and Americans were dangerously subversive and had to be minimized. *Meeting on the Elbe* starts out with a depiction of a joyful meeting of Soviet and American soldiers. The American general, watching the scene, remarks: "This is the most unfortunate consequence of war." He is afraid that Americans, getting to know Russians, will become immune to capitalist, anti-Soviet propaganda. The Russians, encountering Westerners, especially Americans, have always been painfully conscious of their technological backwardness. In this film it is the Americans who envy Soviet achievements in optics and steal a German invention in order to turn it to military use. The choice of optics is a particularly interesting example, because the most famous Russian booty was the famous Zeiss factory, which was moved from Jena to the Ukraine, lock, stock, and barrel. Hundreds of thousands of Soviet citizens were sent to camps because of their dangerous exposure to Western ways. In this film the decent American officer, Major Hill, who befriended his Russian counterpart, is excluded from the U.S. Army and sent home to face the committee investigating un-American activities. The Soviet Union was in the embarrassing situation of having to explain why millions of its citizens after the war did not want to return home. Here we see an American soldier of Ukrainian background who forever pines for his abandoned motherland.

The most frequently heard—and justified—charge against Soviet occupation forces was that they looted and raped.[10] In this film, of course, it is the Americans who loot. The wife of General McDermot says to her husband: "Be a man, and not a chicken in uniform. You are not in a general's uniform in order to nurse the Germans. There is a beautiful forest around us and the leaves murmur like dollars. Cut down the forest and sell the wood to the British before it is too late!" It is, of course, especially demeaning that it is a woman, a Lady Macbeth, who gives commands to her husband (we also see how American soldiers abuse and exploit German women).

The Germans in this film have a dramatic role. They have to choose between the two ways of life: the Soviet way, which represents the future, or the American, which is the past. The ex-Nazis, the criminals, feel more at home with the Americans. The Communists, the most progressive people, identify with the Soviet Union to such an extent that we see them coming out of prison, singing in Russian. The battle is for the allegiance of the non-Communist, decent Germans. Otto Dietrich, the mayor of the town and a scientist, stands for the soul of Germany. This honest and elderly professor has opposed the fascists, but, unlike his son, has not sympathized with the

Communists. Now he sees the constructive work that is going on in the Soviet zone; he understands that Soviet policy aims at the unification of Germany under democratic rule; and he becomes fully conscious of the corruption and viciousness of the Americans. He wholeheartedly chooses the Soviet side.

This relatively positive portrayal of the recent enemy almost got the film into trouble. When the completed work was shown to the Ministry of the Film Industry (the censorship committee), it was heavily criticized. The next day the film was shown to the entire Central Committee of the Communist Party of the Soviet Union. Stalin once again came to the aid of Alexandrov. He uttered a single sentence: "This film was made with great knowledge of the material!"[11] The success of the film was assured.

The Soviet propaganda machinery, of which cinema was a significant part, was an absolutely essential feature of the Stalinist regime. It is not too much to say that it could not have existed without it. From internal enemies to external ones and back again, Stalinist cinema pictured the enemy as an integral part of defining who belonged to the USSR and who did not. How films depicted the "enemy" thus reveals much about the conscious and unconscious fears of the political elite.

NOTES

1. This article is largely based on my book, *Cinema and Soviet Society, 1917–1953* (Cambridge, UK: Cambridge University Press, 1992); revised edition published as *Cinema and Soviet Society: From the Revolution to the Death of Stalin* (London: I. B. Tauris, 2001).

2. Abram Terz, *The Trial Begins and On Socialist Realism* (New York: Vintage, 1960), 148.

3. Katerina Clark, *The Soviet Novel: History as Ritual*, 3d ed. (Bloomington: Indiana University Press, 2000).

4. Julie Cassiday connects Soviet show trials to cinematic and theatrical techniques in her *The Enemy on Trial: Early Soviet Courts on Stage and on Screen* (De Kalb, Ill.: Northern Illinois University Press, 2000).

5. Quoted in Vance Kepley, *In the Service of the State: The Cinema of A. Dovzhenko* (Madison: University of Wisconsin Press, 1986), 494.

6. I. D. Pyr'ev, *Izbrannye proizvedenia* (Moscow: Iskusstvo, 1978), vol. 1, 74–84.

7. See Denise Youngblood, "Cinema as Social Criticism: The Early Films of Fridrich Ermler," in Anna Lawton, ed., *The Red Screen: Politics, Society, Art in Soviet Cinema* (New York: HarperCollins, 1991), 66–89.

8. *The Perils of Pauline* is perhaps the best-known serial film of the silent era. Released in 1914, the eighteen-episode series follows Pauline, a recent heir to a fortune,

and her attempts not to fall victim to those who want her fortune. *Perils* was filmed again in 1934, in 1947, and in 1967 for television.

9. See also Denise Youngblood, "A War Remembered: Soviet Films of the Great Patriotic War," *American Historical Review* 106, no. 3 (June 2001): 839–56.

10. For the extent of Red Army rapes in Germany, see Norman Naimark, *The Russians in Germany: A History of the Soviet Zone of Occupation, 1945–1949* (Cambridge, Mass.: Harvard University Press, 1995), 69–140.

11. G. V. Alexandrov, *Epokha i kino* (Moscow: Politizdat, 1983), 297–98.

Identifying the Enemy
in Contemporary Russian Film

Oleg Sulkin

Let me start with a parable, as befits the Russian tradition, one that is more shocking than edifying.

It takes place during World War II. A wounded soldier is taken to a Soviet hospital. He's in a coma, with terrible burns, his arms and legs are gone, and he has become no more than a mute hunk of flesh. He's given the best possible care, a nurse's aide is assigned to him, and surgeons perform a series of delicate operations. Months go by. He regains consciousness. Then he begins to speak—*in German*, which plunges his whole medical team into a funk.

This bit of Soviet military folklore from the 1940s clearly resonates with the sometimes daunting challenge of identifying the enemy in contemporary Russian film. As Peter Kenez has written in the preceding chapter, picturing the enemy in Stalinist cinema involved constant changes that kept up with the shifting political landscape of the 1930s. Who are the good guys? Who are the bad guys? What are the identifying features of the first group? What features are used to encode the second group? This essay seeks to provide some answers to these vexing questions by surveying the multiple ways in which enemies appear on post-Soviet screens.

One fact is indisputable: The dissolution of the Soviet Union and the toppling of its communist doctrine have left a yawning hole where once there was an official ideology. Ever since, starting in 1991, a struggle to claim the role of dominant ideology has been underway between two leading contenders. The first is a rather incoherent blend of imperialist thinking, Russian Orthodoxy, and elements of "state capitalism." The second is a more intelligible liberal-democratic ideology based on market and bourgeois values and individual liberties. Each of these competing doctrines has its direct and indirect adherents in the world of Russian film.

For all the striking changes Russia has undergone, the tendency for singling out an enemy, for "scapegoating," is still alive and fully engaged today. It is nurtured by the sentiments of the millions of Russians embittered by the economic "perestroika," or restructuring, that left them impoverished, by the suspicious rise of a handful of "oligarchs," by the protracted war in Chechnya and increasingly frequent terrorist attacks, by rampant crime in the cities and by environmental degradation. Deeply rooted in Russia's protracted experience of serfdom and intensified by the Bolshevik doctrine of class antagonism, the dichotomous Russian mentality still pulsates to the anxious binary rhythm of Us and Them, Our Guys and Their Guys, Russian and Foreign. In filmmaking, the most intensive efforts to seek and destroy the "enemy" are now being made by two distinct ideological camps: the pro-Putin "new statists" and the nostalgic conservatives, including the neocommunists. In life and politics, these two camps can be sworn enemies, but in the world of film they are united first and foremost by nationalism and pan-Slavism.

Wartime Enemies: Chechens and Germans on Film

One surefire catalyst for identifying the enemy is the war in Chechnya. The war functions as a litmus test for the political and ethical positions of Russian filmmakers. Why? Because the old pattern that we all knew as the crucial question of revolutionary films—"Who are you for, the Whites or the Reds?"—has been reprojected onto a new reality and become the question "Who are you for, the federals or the Chechens?"[1] Typically, films representing a pro-Chechen position are automatically out of the question in the Russian film industry: no one would even consider funding and producing such a film. What we see instead is the humanistic theme of equal responsibility for the war on both sides and a simply neutral depiction of the rebels—and even *this* is immediately interpreted as unqualified support for them.

This "even-handed" position was visualized by director Sergei Bodrov Sr. in his 1996 film *Prisoner of the Caucasus* (*Kavkazskii plennik*), a kind of loose interpretation of Leo Tolstoy's story by that title. Bodrov depicts abstract, generalized Caucasus highlanders, rather than Chechens specifically, and does so with sympathy and compassion. "Both sides are in the right, and both sides are to blame," the director said of his film. "But when a large country wages war against a small ethnic group, it assumes a far greater share of the responsibility."[2]

We see the same generalized humanistic position in director Aleksandr Rogozhkin's war drama *Checkpoint* (*Blokpost*, 1998), which tells of the daily lives of a Russian patrol in a Caucasus "hot spot." The setting is identifiable, of course, as Chechnya, but the director makes a point of never referring

Figure 7.1. Sympathetic Soldiers.
From Aleksandr Rogozhkin's *Checkpoint* (1998).

to the republic by name, evidently in the interests of making his story as universal as possible. Rogozhkin's highlanders do not speak Chechen but rather Circassian, a language common to a number of North Caucasus republics. Both the Russians and the highlanders are portrayed sympathetically (see fig. 7.1). For Rogozhkin, the origins of the war are "a mystery," and he does not divide his characters into "good" and "bad."[3]

In Fedor Popov's chamber melodrama *Caucasian Roulette* (*Kavkazskaia ruletka*, 2002), a young Russian woman named Anna, a rebel Chechen sniper, and Maria, the mother of a soldier taken captive by the rebels, meet in a train headed for Russia. Anna is trying to get her infant son out of the war zone; Maria tries to get Anna to return her baby to Chechnya—if she does, then the rebels will release her son. Neither mother will give in. Each has powerful arguments on her side; each is partly right, and each partly to blame. Popov sides with neither one, giving their conflict a sense of tragic indeterminacy. The title well conveys the film's fatalist mood.

The soldier's mother in Natalia Piankova's *Slavic Woman's March* (*Marsh slavianki*, 2003) is traveling in the opposite direction: into Chechnya. She's going there to free her captive son. When she arrives she learns that another woman, aged forty, has nursed her wounded son back to health but been unable to save her own boy from drug addiction. We see only victims, no enemies, but it is clear from the film's ecstatic poetics that un-named and undefined enemies certainly exist offscreen, and that they are the malignant forces that have unleashed this gruesome war that is claiming the lives of innocent boys.

The most famous example of the humanist, "balanced" approach to Chechnya is Andrei Konchalovskii's *House of Fools* (*Dom durakov*, 2002). Somewhere in the Chechen war zone is a mental institution that is visited by Chechen and federal forces by turns. The director does not side with either army but rather identifies with a third, passive party to their conflict, namely the inmates of the madhouse. This film is a kind of extended and updated quotation from Andrei Tarkovskii's *Andrei Rublev*: the story of Durochka, the holy fool of the church, who is threatened by raiding Tatars. Only the "Tatars" are now doubled: their function is performed by both the Russian federal troops and the Chechen militants.[4]

The national-chauvinist position, on the other hand, is clearly manifest in Aleksei Balabanov's 2002 action film *War* (*Voina*). That same position was marked out still earlier, in the mid-1990s, by Aleksandr Nevzorov, a Peters-burg-based TV journalist, muckraker, and shrill demagogue. Nevzorov em-ployed a quasi-documentary style to the film *Purgatory* (*Chistilishche*, 1997), about the January 1995 fighting for a hospital in the Chechen capital city of Grozny. The director clearly supported the central Russian government's position. To illustrate the depravity and cruelty of the Chechen militants, he has his female snipers on the Chechen side—evidently lesbians from the Baltics—deliberately aim for the genitals of the male federal troops. Nevzorov's Chechens are wild beasts, killing and mauling their prey. And there is only one thing to do about them: they must be destroyed.

Few people recall now that it was Nevzorov who first precipitated back in 1991 the "ideological revolution" in film with his documentary *Our Guys* (*Nashi*), which gave the concept of national chauvinism its first aesthetic expression. As Soviet troops seized the TV center in the Lithu-anian capital, Vilnius, in January 1991 and Soviet tanks were deployed on the scene, Nevzorov shot a film that clearly delineated Us and Them. In one shot, Nevzorov puts aside his motion picture camera and picks up an assault rifle, symbolizing the ultimate degree of solidarity with the "people's cause." The ethnic and political polarization of the former Soviet Union has led yesterday's liberals and Bohemian artists more and more often to take up arms for a cause. I will never forget a conversation I had with the wonderful Georgian director Temur Babluani, who told me he'd grown to hate the Abkhaz so much that he'd gone off to fight them himself and had fired on them with an assault rifle. Earlier, this director created one of

Georgian cinema's most humanistic films, *Sun of the Wakeful* (*Udzinarta mze*, 1992), a film suffused with the idea of all-forgiveness. It is very sad and even frightening to see former intelligentsia vanishing and joining the ranks of the so-called patriots.

In Balabanov's *War*, we see the same black-and-white framework as in Nevzorov—Us and Them—only complicated by psychological depth, convincing motivations, and the significant presence of a third party: foreign hostages. The Chechens are depicted without the slightest empathy, as cruel and cunning enemies. To drive home the idea that the Chechens are treacherous sadists and nothing more, Balabanov graphically recreates the beheading by knife of a captive Russian soldier. At one point, documentary footage of a similar scene had been posted on a rebel Chechen website. The main Chechen figure, the captor of the main character, Ivan, is also given a monologue certain to enrage Russian audiences. The Chechen boasts that he knows his lineage to the seventh generation, that this is *his* land, and that he will fight on until "there's not a single Russian left from here to Astrakhan."[5]

As for the West, unlike *Brother 2* (*Brat 2*, 2000), in which a debased, complacent, oblivious, stagnant, violent, and hypocritical America is condemned by Danila Bagrov (the main character) to be wiped out by an ascendant and lawless Russia, *War* portrays the West as neither friend nor foe, but something indeterminate. Both foreign hostages, a British actor and his fiancée taken captive together with Ivan, are passively cartoonish and pathetic figures jerked this way and that throughout the plotline by the powerful will of the young Russian avenger.

I do not mean to simplify and flatten Balabanov's position by reducing it to an easily discernible primitivism. In fact, as a narrative artist he is far from straightforward. His film *Brother* (*Brat*, 1997), the story of a fair-minded young Russian who devastates the crime organization that wronged his older brother, can be interpreted in two ways. On the one hand, it is a parable of "might for right"; on the other hand, it is nearly a manifesto for Russian fascism. *Brother 2* is a vicious satire on an America that crumbles beneath the blows of a Russian Rambo. At the same time it is a "double-barreled" parody of both the Hollywood action genre and the Russian folkloric hero—Ivan the Fool—who travels the world astride an oven. But the subject of Chechnya is too serious to ignore the obvious impulses of ethnic hatred that emanate from the film *War*.

Given the dramatic divergence in portrayals of the enemy in Russia's current conflict with Chechnya, it is hardly surprising that the ideological vectors of recent cinematic treatments of World War II—which Russian citizens still regard as the Great Patriotic War—have also diverged widely. After the dissolution of the Soviet Union there was a long hiatus during which this entire topic was regarded as closed and irrelevant. But during the early years of the new century several noteworthy films on World War II have been released, each of them with its own distinctive image of the enemy.

Nikolai Lebedev's film *The Star* (*Zvezda*, 2002), the second film version of Emmanuil Kazakevich's story by that title, tells the story of a Soviet scout team suffering heavy casualties on a reconnaissance mission. The film combines the hallmarks of both Hollywood action movies and the Soviet heroic army story; it portrays the Nazis in the finest Soviet tradition—as an impersonal, uniform, and alien mass. In contrast with, say, the late Elem Klimov's *Come and See* (*Idi i smotri*, 1985), an apotheosis of hatred for the German fascists, where they are portrayed as insatiable, gleeful ghouls with Boschian, almost paranoid interest in the details of their cannibal practices, for this young director, the Nazis are once again a malignant monolith, a teeming swarm of locusts unworthy of close inspection.

In Aleksandr Rogozhkin's *The Cuckoo* (*Kukushka*, 2002), by contrast, the direct clash of traditional enemies is given a quirky modernist treatment and ultimately turned inside out. In September 1944 two soldiers, a Russian and a Finn, lock horns on the farm of a Lapp (Saami) reindeer herder, a woman whose husband has been "disappeared" by the authorities. The Russian and the Finn are both renegades and outsiders. The Russian has been falsely charged with anti-Sovietism and barely escaped execution by his Red Army comrades. The Finn is a committed pacifist and intellectual whom the Nazis have dressed in a German uniform, given a sniper's rifle, and chained to a rock, leaving him to die shooting it out with approaching Russian troops. Since the three characters have no language in common, their interactions are strictly carnal. The men sleep with the herder by turns, remaining enemies to one another. To be more precise, their enmity is maintained by the inflexibility of the Russian, who cannot see in this mild former student, a devotee of Tolstoy and Dostoevsky, anything but a "Fritz" and a "fascist." Rogozhkin absolutizes the Russian soldier's xenophobia, his blind, instinctive hatred for the enemy; he forces him to commit acts that are impossible to motivate convincingly based on elementary laws of small-group behavior. The Russian makes two attempts to kill the Finn, wounding him grievously, despite the fact that the Finn gives him every possible signal of peaceful intentions, signals that can be understood even without a common language. Rogozhkin's point is to sound the full depth of the zombification of "mass consciousness" under Stalinism, a phenomenon that he treats with wistful irony.[6]

Figure 7.2. Mercy for the Fallen.
From Aleksei German Jr.'s *Last Train* (2003).

While Rogozhkin insists on Russians' singular fury toward their enemies, Aleksei German Jr., the son of the famous director, shot a 2003
debut film, *The Last Train* (*Poslednii poezd*), in which a Nazi is for the
first time depicted as an "enemy with a human face." Elements of tentative
humanistic reflections on the occupying army were found in a few scattered
Soviet and post-Soviet films, while this tradition as a whole stems from Boris
Barnet's brilliant *Outskirts* (*Okraina*, 1933; U.S. title *The Patriots*), in which
a German POW of World War I is portrayed as a decent young guy who
wins the love of a Russian working-class girl.

As in Rogozhkin's film, German's heroes are outsiders in the war. An
aging and corpulent German army doctor arrives on the Eastern Front
toward the end of the war and finds himself in absolute hell. The Russian
winter is raging, the field hospital is in a shambles, officers and soldiers alike
are sick, coughing, suffering; Russian bombs fall without letup. If this is
the enemy, then it is a helpless and pathetic one. The army doctor enters
the war zone together with a staff clerk. We will see the Russian camp as
well, represented by a civilian troop entertainment unit—a group of equally
wretched, disoriented, ailing, and coughing people. The cruelty of both
sides' treatment of one another is depicted in German's film as if dictated
from on high, by the immutable laws of war, but his characters have no faith
in the justice of those laws. Both the Germans and the Russians talk of more
or less the same things—of peacetime, of the idyllic past lives stolen from

them by the war. Since German is concerned primarily with the senseless-ness of war, seen as a "dark Satanic mill" that grinds individuals to dust, he makes a point of demolishing one of the hoariest Russian stereotypes of Germany's fascist enemy that Peter Kenez has identified in his essay. To paraphrase Pushkin, German urges mercy for all the fallen—whatever their nationality, whosoever uniform they wear (see fig. 7.2).[7]

By contrast, it should be full steam ahead for jingoistic agitprop military and espionage action features like *Man's Work* (*Muzhskaia rabota*, 2001–2002), the popular two-part TV miniseries *Special Forces* (*Spetsnaz*, 2002), or the series *In The Service of My Country* (*Rodina zhdet*, 2003). Another recent example of this strengthening trend is a pretentious epic *72 Meters* (2004) by Vladimir Khotinenko. It is a tour de force story of a sinking Russian submarine, of the heroism of its crew, made with a clear intention to overpower the effect of *K-19: The Widowmaker* (2002), a Hol-lywood flick starring Harrison Ford. The guys are spotless and idealized; they are typical Soviet-like martyrs dying for "the people's cause." The only black sheep in this angelic milieu is a character of a "rotten" intellectual being sent to the submarine as a guest expert. He is weak, ambivalent, and pathetic, which creates a sharp contrast to the monolithically united and morally healthy Navy guys.

What set this genre apart are its rough-hewn heroes in the Rambo mold and the relocation of its theater of hostilities to the Near and Middle East. Islamic extremism and Islamic international terrorism are now the main suppliers of enemies for Russian film. It is typical for films and series of this kind to portray such attributes of Islam as head- and face-covering gar-ments, prostrated prayer, and long beards as inherently alien to the Russian mentality. We see a gradual exoticization of the Other, of an inimical way of life, as described by Mikhail Bakhtin.[8]

Us and Them:
Russianness and Otherness on the Big Screen

It is likewise typical that the increasingly negative interpretation of Islam has been paralleled by the rapid sacralization of Russian Orthodoxy as the "great-powerist" religion of the new Russia. In the absence of any new and intelligible "national idea," many directors proffer Orthodoxy as a surro-gate. The series *Special Forces 2* has a subplot about a special forces soldier who joins a monastery after his wife and daughter are tragically killed; he then journeys to Yugoslavia to rebuild an Orthodox church destroyed by Albanian Muslims. Critics, naturally, could make ironical observations about an Orthodox monk/ninja warrior as the paradigmatic superhero of today's mass Russian culture. But one cannot help being struck by the ferocious, total hostility of this culture's portrayal of its opponent, hostility suggesting an "ethnic instinct" not intimated since the films made during World War II.

As one would expect, in recent Russian films of a "neocommunist" bent, Russia's progress toward capitalism is condemned. But whereas in earlier decades, as Peter Kenez argues, capitalism was viewed as an external enemy, now it is an internal enemy, exulting in its triumph over the honest men and women it has reduced to an underground existence.

For example, in Stanislav Govorukhin's programmatic film of 1999, *The Voroshilov Sharpshooter* (*Voroshilovskii strelok*), three young men lure a neighbor girl into an apartment and rape her. Her grandfather, Ivan Fedorovich, after giving up on the legal system, buys a rifle with a telescopic sight and metes out vigilante justice. With one shot he castrates one of his granddaughter's molesters; with his next shot he blows up another one's car, leaving him terribly burned; the third molester then loses his mind. The main culprit, a wealthy businessman, runs a string of retail kiosks and speaks in the slang of the prosperous "new Russians." His buddy, a student majoring in "structural linguistics," is obviously an enemy just for pursuing such interests. Finally, the third culprit is the most decent of them all, but very weak-willed and cowardly. Soviet films, as Emma Widdis has argued earlier in this volume, frequently used the clothing and mannerisms of negative characters to alert viewers that they were encountering an alien, an enemy. The enemies in Govorukhin's *Sharpshooter* are young men in dark glasses, wearing shorts, with a fitness machine in the room, Western blockbusters and pornography on the television, and loud, aggressive rock music playing on the stereo (by contrast, the sympathetic heroine sings Soviet songs of the thirties and forties) (see fig. 7.3). They drink tequila instead of vodka. They smoke pot instead of the Belomor brand of cigarettes. The main culprit buys a brand new BMW, which the broad Russian public views as the ultimate emblem of Western consumerism. In post-Soviet Russian films made between 1992 and 2002, the act of locking or unlocking a foreign car with its remote control became a sure signal that the car owner is a member of the new criminalized business elite, a major player. The odds are that a character who locks his car by remote control is either a negative or ambiguous figure. Even if a positive character happens to drive a foreign car, the audience will virtually never see him use the remote. There is something aggressive about that gesture, something that doesn't sit well with Russian viewers.

Figure 7.3. The New Russian Enemy.
From Stanislav Govorukhin's *Voroshilov Sharpshooter* (1999).

The familiar, collectivist class antagonism of Us versus Them that served as a refrain for generations of Soviet directors does yeoman service for Govorukhin as well. "Us" is represented by the poor but honest retired railroad worker Ivan Fedorovich, his beat-policeman friend—from the same working-class stock—who helps him evade punishment by concealing his rifle, a rough-mannered police captain who hates wealthy and educated scum, and Ivan's granddaughter Katia with her long pigtail symbolizing Russian/Slavic beauty. "Them" is represented by the pro-Western rapists, corrupt government officials, and the "new Russians."

Shooting at the genitals of his granddaughter's molester (as in Nevzorov's *Purgatory*) and the frequent references to the male role in procreation suggests an unconscious desire on the part of the filmmaker to nip Russia's nascent capitalism in the bud. Physiologism is typical, in fact, of all extreme manifestations of hatred.

Physiological revulsion is sure to be evinced by another "new Russian" in Lidia Bobrova's affecting melodrama *Granny* (*Babusia*, 2003). This story of a neglected old woman who is disowned by her ingrate children and grandchildren is peopled by characters who are far from angelic. But the only figure that the director portrays with unqualified disapproval is a heavyset oaf in a sheepskin jacket, the "new Russian" husband of one of Granny's daughters, who lives in an upscale detached house and drives an SUV. Naturally, we see him locking his car with its remote keypad.

The new enemy—soulless bourgeois pragmatism—can also be invisible, as in Vadim Abdrashitov's *Magnetic Storms* (*Magnitnye buri*, 2003). We are meant to be deceived, in certain respects, by the feud we see unfolding between two opposing clans of workers, each supporting its "own" patron oligarch. But the scenes of hand-to-hand combat between the clans are as mechanized as a conveyor belt—clearly implying that this entire mass of working stiffs is being manipulated by unseen puppet masters. Russia has been duped by the new capitalism and must reconsider what it has to gain from that capitalism and find a solution for mutual enmity.

One such solution can be found in Gennadii Sidorov's film *Old Women* (*Starukhi*, 2003), a powerful and rare antithesis to all types of social and ethnic intolerance. In 1995, Vladimir Khotinenko's *The Muslim* (*Musul'manin*) had portrayed a Russian POW returning from the war in Afghanistan to his native village after having converted to Islam while in captivity; typologically, this figure is no longer fully Russian, if only for the fact that he does not drink or smoke (and what kind of red-blooded Russian male would give up vodka and cigarettes?). In *Old Women*, in a run-down Russian village where a community of half-destitute old women are living out their days in dilapidated huts, Russian typological fears meet head on with the materialized object of those fears. A family of Islamic refugees from an ethnic conflict in a Soviet Central Asian republic settles in the village. At first, the old women employ the village idiot to torch their house, but then they take pity on the family and become great friends with them. The refugees are enemies, or aliens, only by virtue of such external differences as their language and way of life. In essence, however, they are the saviors of Russian civilization: the male refugee builds a power station and arranges a celebration in the finale in which all the characters get up and dance together to Eastern rhythms. *Old Women* is essentially an instructive and therapeutic film about Russians managing to overcome their ethnic xenophobia. The real enemy is within these old women, within the Russian mentality, and the sooner it is exorcised and defeated, the closer the Russian nation comes to renewal.

The reflective consciousness of Russia's intelligentsia has grown equally disenchanted with the romanticization of "honest communism," with Western-style democratization, with the rapacious capitalism of the "new Russians," and with the resurgence of a chauvinist Russian Orthodoxy; it is

Figure 7.4. Indicator of an Outsider? The BMW.
From Petr Buslov's *Bimmer* (2003).

therefore keeping the greatest possible distance from all forms of engagement. In the world of these films no one is just, and no one is to blame, exactly as in the world of Aleksei German Sr.'s *Khrustalev, My Car!* (*Khrustalev, mashinu!* 1998), which depicts the Stalin era as a hyperrealistic fairy tale with elements of black humor and satirical mythology. As Oleg Aronson aptly observed, "This is not so much a film as an anthropological study, or better still, a medical assessment of a disease which afflicts each and every one of us, but which we are unable to fully recognize in ourselves."[9]

Conclusion: Identifying Enemies as Plot Device

In certain types of genre film the problem of identifying the enemy is the very thing that drives the plot. One example of this is Petr Buslov's *Bimmer* (*Bumer*, 2003), a youth crime drama heavily influenced by Quentin Tarantino in which four young gangster wannabes tour a lumpenized and volatile post-Soviet frontier in a stolen BMW (see fig. 7.4). Since everyone who inhabits this landscape is resentful and treacherous, every new encounter is fraught with potential violence. The four must quickly decide on the basis of clothing and conversational styles whether they're among friends or foes, whether they'll soon be fighting for their lives or tossing back shots of vodka. Essentially, the heroes of this road movie are constantly testing different social milieus for receptivity. The point of each new contact is to flush out the new person's or group's attitude toward the four main characters. The initial encounter consists of a nearly physiological ritual of sniffing one another out. Make a mistake, and you end up robbed or dead. A second, similar example is Aleksandr Proshkin's *Trio* (*Trio*, 2003), in which undercover policemen drive a truck through Russia's southern provinces, acting as bait for a gang of murderers preying on long-distance truckers. Distinguishing killers from cops proves very difficult in the turbulent Russian heartland. This is not, of course, a problem for Russian society alone, but the fact that Russian directors are now concentrating on it is quite telling. The Russian film industry has grown tired of blurred distinctions between "good guys" and "bad guys" and has decided to exploit this very confusion and fence-straddling as a plot-driving device.

Let us try to sum up, then, at least as far as possible given that we have been examining trends in a state of rapid and contradictory evolution. There have emerged three main discourses of identification of the enemy. The first affirms that the enemy never sleeps: he is here among us, and must be physically destroyed without pity or reflection. The second—that the enemy *is*, in fact, "asleep," that is, he is undercover, unexposed, and must be flushed out and analyzed, to which end society must be constantly on its guard. The third—that in principle there is no such thing as the enemy: the enemy is actually a phantom, a vestige of the past, or if there *is* an "enemy," then he is within each of us, and the sooner we can purge ourselves of him, the better for all concerned. Each of these three discourses has its adherents and promoters in Russian cinema and this fact in and of itself is probably all to the good, as an index of pluralism of opinion. If democratization has borne real fruits in today's Russia, look for them in the world of film. However, it seems that with Putin's antiperestroika in full swing, the base for pluralism has been gradually diminishing. Nobody can predict the consequences of such a transition in the sphere of film industry, or in how the enemy will be identified in future Russian films.

TRANSLATED BY TIMOTHY D. SERGAY

NOTES

1. For an example of the revolutionary film question and its meanings, see Julian Graffy's essay in this volume.

2. Quoted in *Iskusstvo kino* (*Cinema Art*), no. 7 (2000): 6.

3. Ibid.

4. See the essay by Stephen Norris in this volume for more on the film and the reactions to it.

5. Astrakhan is a city on the Volga delta, which is ancient Russian territory, seized from nomads by the Russian Tsar in the mid-sixteenth century.

6. Stephen Norris's essay also explores Rogozhkin's film in more detail.

7. Pushkin's famous poem "Exegi Monumentum (1836)" includes the stanza:

> In centuries to come I shall be loved by the people
> For having awakened noble thoughts with my lyre,
> For having glorified freedom in my harsh age
> And called for mercy towards the fallen.

8. Mikhail Bakhtin, *Voprosy literatury i estetiki* (*Questions of Literature and Aesthetics*) (Moscow: Khudozhestvennaia literatura, 1975), 251.

9. Oleg Aronson, *Metakino* (Moscow: Ad Marginem, 2003), 223.

About Killers, Freaks, and Real Men
The Vigilante Hero of Aleksei Balabanov's Films
Anthony Anemone

Since his directorial debut in 1992, Aleksei Balabanov has established a reputation as one of post-Soviet Russia's most versatile and successful film-makers.[1] From low-budget contemporary urban gangster thriller to literary adaptation and art house stylization, big-budget action films to quirky contemporary urban romance, ethnographic documentary to over-the-top parody, Balabanov's films combine an astonishing stylistic versatility with an equally striking thematic consistency. All of his films feature prominently characters who live on the margins of Russian society: from creators and consumers of pornography in turn of the century St. Petersburg to contemporary urban gangsters, hit men, hobos, punks, pimps and prostitutes, demobilized soldiers, Chechen terrorists and their hostages.[2]

In Balabanov's world, heroes are tested and measured in two ways: by their willingness to use violence in defense of the weak and innocent and their ability to endure violence and suffering. By virtue of his selfless, and sometimes self-sacrificial, struggle against the unscrupulous and powerful elements that dominate a lawless society, the vigilante emerges as Balabanov's ideal post-Soviet hero in what I will call the Vigilante Trilogy, *Brother* (1997), *Brother 2* (2000), and *War* (2002). By tracing the development of this motif in Balabanov's films, we may be able to illuminate some of the problems and paradoxes of creating new heroes and values in post-Soviet cinema.[3]

Russians and Brothers

Born as a low-budget take-off on the gangster movie, Balabanov's *Brother* became the surprise hit of 1997: the movie's gross from theatrical release was higher than any other Russian movie, and it led all movies, domestic and foreign, in video rental receipts for the year.[4] The film's plot is simple and reminiscent of a post-Soviet fairy tale: into a lawless and violent post-Soviet St. Petersburg wanders, quite by accident, the film's young hero, the recently

Figure 8.1. The Vigilante Hero.
From Aleksei Balabanov's *Brother* (1997).

demobilized Danila Bagrov (see fig. 8.1). A kind of post-Soviet *Ivan durachok* recently roused from his stove,[5] in a few astonishingly violent days he manages to eliminate a good proportion of the local mobsters who threaten his brother and friends. Although he doesn't kill anyone who doesn't deserve it, the film ends on an ambivalent note as his two best friends, Hoffman and Sveta, both reject Danila and the violence that he has used so freely to protect them. Influenced by both American vigilante films of the 1970s and the rampant criminality and breakdown in public order in the Yeltsin 1990s, Balabanov put a version of Dostoevsky's "eternal" question at the center of the film: that is, in a world where the authorities are unable to maintain order and justice, is an individual morally and ethically justified in using violence in defense of the weak and vulnerable? Or will vigilante violence eventually corrupt even the best intentioned?

In *Brother 2*, Balabanov's hero resumes his vigilante adventures in Moscow and then the United States. Rather than modifying Danila's personal code from the original movie, *Brother 2* combines the familiar theme of loyalty to a "brother," in this case a fellow soldier from Chechnya, with the need for a new national spirit of Russian patriotism. Perhaps the most important difference between the original and the sequel is that no matter how many people Danila maims or kills in *Brother 2*, no one, on the screen or behind the camera, challenges or questions his right to do so and his innocence and absolute moral rectitude remain untouched.[6] *Brother 2* is more explicit than the original about Danila's army service and suggests that the values that Danila brought back from the war in Chechnya—self-reliance, physical bravery, loyalty, patriotism, and the willingness to use violence in a worthy cause—are precisely what Russia needs to extricate itself from its assorted post-Soviet crises. Danila is the hero precisely because he is the only character who understands that, despite appearances, Russia is at war and must fight to defend itself.

More striking than the necessity of applying the lessons and the values of war to the problems of peace is the role played by Soviet ideological images and motifs in the film. Several critics have described *Brother 2* as the first post-Soviet movie to "recycle" or "reanimate" Soviet ideology.[7] Indeed, the film is suffused in kitschy visual images and sentimental clichés reminiscent of the Soviet period: the characters surrounded by paintings, posters, and sculptures of Lenin and Stalin and a Civil War vintage Maxim gun that transforms a stolen Volvo into a post-Soviet *tachanka*.[8] Another example is Balabanov's filming Russian crime boss Belkin in Lenin's office at Gorki. On the ideological level, Balabanov uses the hoary Soviet myth of working-class solidarity in his characterization of the friendship between Danila and Ben Johnson, the truck driver who drives Danila to Chicago and helps him and Dasha escape from America back to Moscow at the film's end.[9] More important still is the cult of the motherland and the myth of total national fraternity expressed in the poem recited by the young son of Sergei Makovetskii's crime boss, and quoted by Danila at several points in the film.[10]

The final element of this retro Soviet Patriotism is xenophobia and, especially, anti-Americanism. Although Danila had no love lost for Americans, Jews, or Caucasians/Chechens in the original, anti-Americanism, as Oleg Sulkin also argues, plays a more central and serious role in *Brother 2*, both in the depiction of individual characters and as a structural support of Danila's new Russian patriotism. In a sense, the worst crimes of the significantly named American crime boss Mennis (that is, larceny, prostitution, murder, snuff movies) are less a sign of anti-Americanism than the corruption of Russians by America's "terrible essence (*strashnaia sila*)"—in typical Soviet propaganda fashion, women (Dasha) are threatened with prostitution, while men (such as Mitia Gromov and Vitia) are more likely to be lost to greed and alcohol. Balabanov combines anti-Semitism, anti-Ukrainianism, and anti-Americanism to create an image of an American

Figure 8.2. Goodbye, America: Danila and Dasha Leave Chicago.
From Aleksei Balabanov's *Brother 2* (2000).

"Evil Empire" whose corruption, criminality, greed, and limitless financial
resources represent a serious threat to an economically weakened but morally and culturally superior Russia.[11]

To this old and familiar critique of soulless American materialism, Danila
opposes the equally traditional Russian, and Soviet, notion that strength is
in truth or righteousness (*Pravda*). Rooted in folk utopian tales, the symbolism of a struggle between *Pravda* (the light of truth and justice) and *Krivda*
(falsehood, injustice) was also used by Bolshevik propagandists in introducing the new revolutionary icon of the Red Star.[12] This theme is resolved in
Mennis's office, when Danila reduces the American criminal boss to tears and
"convinces" him that strength is indeed in righteousness, not in money. The
paradoxes of Danila killing Mennis's bodyguards in order to convince him
that "strength is in righteousness" are, apparently, lost on both the director
and his domestic audience. Although viewers may question whether returning money to the selfish, ungrateful, and thoroughly Americanized hockey
player, Mitia Gromov, was worth Danila's efforts, the ambivalence of the
original *Brother* is completely missing from *Brother 2*. Danila and Dasha's
triumphant return to Russia is scored to Nautilus Pompilius's song "Goodbye,
America," which, apparently, is used by Balabanov to punctuate the end of
the "utopian dream" of America for Balabanov's audience (see fig. 8.2).[13]

Wartime Brothers: *War* as Sequel

Despite Balabanov's remark that there would be no sequel to *Brother 2* because he had exhausted the theme,[14] his next film, *War*, demands to be read as the third installation of the *Brother* franchise. Although the characters are different, *War* picks up where *Brother 2* ended, depicting, in essence, a surprisingly tragic version of the Russian homecoming of the vigilante hero. Indeed, almost all of the themes of *War* are familiar from the *Brother* films: like Danila Bagrov, the central hero Ivan (Aleksei Chadov) is a vigilante, whose violent actions are motivated out of loyalty to a metaphorical brother and comrade, in this case the heroic hostage Captain Medvedyev (Sergei Bodrov Jr.), and frustration with the inability of the State to uphold justice.[15] Again like Danila, the recently demobilized Ivan uses the skills and lessons learned during military service to defeat a brutal band of Chechen criminals in a vigilante action that violates all the laws of civilian society. Finally, even more so than in the *Brother* films, nationalist values, xenophobic discourse, and nostalgia for the lost power of the Soviet State dominate *War*'s ideology: the Chechen fighters are depicted as brutal and subhuman monsters who deserve no more mercy than the American criminals and pimps whom Danila guns down without any hesitation.[16]

Nevertheless, the characters, situations and the violence of *War* are less cartoonish and the fate of the "hero" more tragic than we would expect from the director of the *Brother* films. The crux of the matter is that in order to free hostages from a band of brutal Chechen fighters, the everyman hero Ivan must adopt the methods of his enemy: by killing anyone who gets in his way and enslaving and brutalizing a Chechen shepherd, this Russian Rambo accomplishes his mission, but at what cost? (See fig. 8.3.) In order to defeat a primitive and brutal enemy in the name of a "higher" and more humane civilization, Ivan must abandon the values of that "higher" civilization and descend to the level of his enemy. His "successful" adaptation is recognized by Aslan Gugaev (Georgii Gurgulia), the commander of the Chechen fighters, who says admiringly: "Ivan, you're a real mountain fighter (*Ivan, ty nastoiashchii gorets*)." In the end, however, instead of being rewarded, Ivan's vigilante heroism is rejected and he is arrested and charged with kidnapping and murdering civilians.

Ivan's fate, unresolved at the end of the film, can be read as Balabanov's critique of a society that can neither ensure justice nor recognize its true heroes. Alternately, it may reflect Balabanov's abiding ambivalence about the ultimate morality of vigilante violence even when committed in an

Figure 8.3. A Russian Rambo?
From Aleksei Balabanov's *War* (2002).

unquestionably worthwhile cause. The director attempts to get around
this lingering ambivalence about the vigilante hero through the character
of Captain Medvedyev, the embodiment of a more politically correct and
more traditionally Russian version of heroism. Because of paralyzing injuries
suffered when he was captured, Captain Medvedyev's heroism can only be
expressed passively: in his indomitable spirit, his insistence on remaining a
soldier in spirit, and his refusal to be broken. Because his heroism resides in
his ability to survive brutalization by his captors, Medvedyev avoids Ivan's
fate, and his heroism is intact at the movie's end. With its deep roots in
Russian cultural and religious traditions, especially "Martyr Saints" of the
Orthodox Church like Saints Boris and Gleb,[17] Medvedyev's passive heroism
suggests not only the director and screenwriter's desire for an authentically
Russian, and ethically unassailable, form of heroism, but also the practical
difficulties involved in bringing such a hero to life on the screen or in real
life. The vigilante theme, then, moves in a spiral, from the ambivalence
of the first *Brother* to the triumphalism of *Brother 2* and back to the tragic
ambivalence of *War*. By the end of *War*, there are two possible resolutions of
the theme: either the vigilante hero will be rehabilitated or a new "passive"
hero will take his place. What direction Balabanov takes his new Russian
hero will, perhaps, become clear in his next movie, *Cargo-200*.[18] One question that can be answered at this point concerns the role Balabanov's 1998

Of Freaks and Men plays in the development of the motif of a new Russian hero for the post-Soviet world.

Identifying Us: Russians as Freaks?

Often dismissed by short-sighted critics as an exercise in pure style lacking in content,[19] or as an opportunistic and scandalous provocation,[20] *Of Freaks and Men* is not only Balabanov's most complex and provocative film but also supplies a critical missing link in Balabanov's vigilante trilogy.[21] Despite its setting in a sepia-toned, fin de siècle St. Petersburg associated with the prerevolutionary silent film era, the characters, situations, and themes of *Freaks and Men* are surprisingly contemporary and familiar to viewers of Balabanov's films set in the present. Like Balabanov's post-Soviet characters, his freaks and men are all, literally or metaphorically, outsiders, living in the shadows of a bourgeois capitalist St. Petersburg that is undergoing massive social and economic change. In the lawless conditions of both periods of Russian fin de siècle urban capitalism, the weak and innocent find themselves at the mercy of the strong and unscrupulous, while kidnappers, pornographers, and murderers ply their trades without any concern for the police or any other form of government authority.

Through a series of complex plot twists and turns, *Of Freaks and Men* depicts, without the slightest moralizing or preaching, the corruption and violation of innocence and "normality" as two sexually repressed middle-class families, the Radlovs and Stasovs, fall apart as a result of their coming into contact with a band of criminal pornographers. The end of the insular middle-class idyll of the Radlov and Stasov families is brought about by a combination of political, economic, sociological, technological, and psychological forces that are as relevant to the post-Soviet present as to the prerevolutionary past. Among the causes of this revolution are the absence of police authority; class tensions between rich and poor, masters and servants; corrupting foreign influences; new media technologies that allow new people, influences, and images into the hitherto closed and protected world of the family; and the sexual perversities and illicit desires of the Russian Victorians themselves. Among the hidden weaknesses and secret vices that Balabanov finds in Russia's prerevolutionary middle class are sexual frigidity and repression, voyeurism and masochism, and blindness to their own desires and the desires of others. In its depiction of the collapse of the bourgeois family, *Freaks and Men* suggests not only the "terrible force" of the modern city, but also an aestheticized and psychologized "End of St. Petersburg": a domestic revolution influenced not only by Marx and Lenin but also by the Marquis de Sade, Freud, Leopold von Sacher-Masoch, and Friedrich Nietzsche, whose well-known provocation—"Are you visiting women? Do not forget your whip!"[22]—could serve as the epigraph to the film.[23]

In addition to the unscrupulous machinations of the pornographers and the sexual dysfunctions of the St. Petersburg bourgeoisie, Balabanov locates another significant cause of the fall of the bourgeoisie in the weakness and passivity of male characters like Engineer Radlov (Igor' Shibanov), Dr. Stasov (Aleksandr Mezentsev), and Putilov (Vadim Prokhorov), the young and feckless filmmaker who works for the pornographers. For example, although his intentions in love and in art, are honorable, Putilov's failure to oppose the forces of evil or to act as a morally conscious and responsible adult, reinforced by the repeated phrases "*Putilov, Vam pora* (Putilov, it's time for you)," "*Liza, ia spasu vas* (Liza, I am rescuing you)," and "Putilov, *uzhe popozdno* (Putilov, it's already too late)," seals the fate of Liza, his would-be lover (Dinara Drukarova). Worse still, while Putilov eventually succeeds in freeing himself from the clutches of Johan (Sergei Makovetskii) and Victor Ivanovich (Viktor Sukhorukov), he abandons Liza to her fate. The weakness of the "respectable" bourgeois professionals is emphasized by the energy and decisiveness that Johan and Viktor Ivanovich use to dominate others and to attain what they want.

Perhaps the most interesting and original aspect of Balabanov's vision of the fall of the houses of Radlov and Stasov is the role played by the new technologies of sound and image recording: photography, cinema, and phonography, the technologies that have, more than anything else, created the modern media-saturated world in which we live today. Balabanov sees revolutionary changes in the technologies of recording and representing reality as a critical similarity between the ends of the nineteenth and twentieth centuries: then, the dawn of photography and the cinema and now, the birth of the Internet, video, and digital technology. Rather than serving simply as props to suggest a particular historical period, phonographs, still and movie cameras, CD walkmen, VCRs, computer games, digital camcorders, and satellite phones actually influence the style and themes of Balabanov's films. From the music video and video game stylistics of the *Brother* films, to the handheld digital cinematography of *War*, and the sepia tones of early photography of *Freaks and Men*, each movie borrows its distinctive style from technological innovations contemporary with the film's action.[24]

The thematic use of media technologies in Balabanov's films is even more pervasive. In *Brother*, for example, Danila's obsession with the CD *Kryl'ia* (Wings) by Nautilus Pompilius, overheard during the introductory credit sequence of the filming of the music video, provides one of the main organizing motifs of the film. Danila's failure to find the Nautilus CD *Kryl'ia* serves as a metaphor not only for his failed search for "wings," for some form of transport—both literally and metaphorically—out of the violent material world in which he lives,[25] but for a father figure, love, and a community of like-minded friends as well. The narcissistic videos and empty pop music of pop star Irina Saltykova featured in *Brother 2* symbolizes the hedonistic and empty lifestyles of the post-Soviet Muscovite urban elite. In *War* Balabanov focuses on different aspects of our media-saturated modern life: rather than CDs and walkmen, in the center of the film's action are Internet Web sites, satellite phones, and handheld digital camcorders.[26]

Much like music videos and digital technology in the vigilante trilogy, early photography and the silent cinema are critical to the style and the themes of *Freaks and Men*. Through the use of sepia tones, intertitles, and slightly speeded-up action, Balabanov conjures up the atmosphere of a decadent prerevolutionary St. Petersburg. By ignoring the usual prerevolutionary roots of Russian cinema—silent romantic melodrama (Bauer), historical and literary adaptations (Chardynin), and monumental propaganda (Eisenstein)—and choosing instead to focus on the early pornography industry, Balabanov questions traditional intelligentsia accounts of Russian cinema's historical origins and its continuing role in Russian society and culture. Despite Engineer Radlov's naïve belief in the cinema's unique ability to convey truth to the masses, the movie shows the early cinema enriching the unscrupulous, humiliating the weak, and pandering to the worst instincts of a new anonymous urban audience, but never raising the spiritual level of the masses.

Balabanov emphasizes the moral and psychological freakishness of the cinema's creators and the perversity of its consumers in ways that are reminiscent of David Lynch's 1986 masterpiece *Blue Velvet*.[27] In addition to the obvious perversity of the criminal pornographers, the affectless Johan and the leering Viktor Ivanovich, who corrupt, kidnap, and murder without any qualms in pursuit of their economic interests and their pathological psychological needs, Balabanov stresses the complicit perversity of their accomplices, victims, and audience. For example, while the photographer Putilov began working for Johan out of economic need, Balabanov suggests that his fascination with cameras is a manifestation of a voyeurism that lies at the heart not only of pornography and the cinema, but of love and sexuality as well. Indeed, Putilov's love for Liza is expressed exclusively through repeated acts of photographing her. Not surprisingly, pornography's consumers are no less perverted than its purveyors: the sublimation of sexual energy

Figure 8.4. Freaks or Insiders?
From Aleksei Balabanov's *Of Freaks and Men* (1999).

into the perverse pleasures of the voyeuristic gaze in the main consumers of pornography, nondescript and expressionless men in black suits and bowler hats, hardly needs to be demonstrated. More interestingly the very distinction between producers and consumers of pornography disappears before our eyes: while both Liza and the Stasov maid Dar'ia (Tat'iana Polonskaia) begin as consumers of pornographic still images, they eventually become participants in the production of pornographic movies, the former as a masochist, the later as a sadist.

Ironically, but also appropriately, the most normal and human of all the characters in the film are the adopted Siamese twins, Tolia (Chingiz Dydendambaev) and Kolia Stasov (Aleksei De) (see fig. 8.4). Kolia is an innocent and a romantic, the closest thing to a hero in the entire movie: not only does he try to teach Liza that to love a woman you don't have to beat her, but he frees the "hostages" by shooting Viktor Ivanovich with Johan's revolver. Tolia is weaker, allowing himself to be corrupted, first by sex, then alcohol, which ultimately kills him.

Fascinated with the twins' anatomical freakishness, the Stasovs and Viktor Ivanovich try to aestheticize them through music and photography. While the audience initially perceives the Stasovs' musical pedagogy as positive, but Viktor Ivanovich's use of the boys in pornographic photography as exploitative, these distinctions ultimately break down as the secret connections between the Stasovs and Viktor Ivanovich are revealed: Dr. Stasov and Viktor Ivanovich are united by their shared fascination with the boys' freakish anatomy while the frigid Ekaterina Stasova (Lika Nevolina) discovers her true sexual identity through her masochistic relationship with the sinister Viktor Ivanovich. After they kidnap the twins from the Stasovs, Johan and Viktor Ivanovich arrange for them to sing in public. The impossibility of separating the pleasures of their singing from the unhealthy obsession with their physical freakishness suggests the dual nature of visual culture, the positive attraction to beauty, and the negative tendency toward fetishism and voyeurism.

In other words, the singing Siamese twins occupy the thematic center of the film because they embody, literally, the contradictory appeal of the cinema and, perhaps, of art itself: the "singing freaks (*poiushchie urody*)" are fascinating because of the combination of the beauty of their voices with the voyeuristic attraction of their freakish bodies. The combination of a fascination with the freakish with an aesthetic sensibility explains not only the various forms of sexual perversion but, Balabanov suggests, the power of the cinema as well. The combination of aesthetics and voyeurism becomes a metaphor for the power of the cinema. That the twins suffer a horrible and lonely death, while Putilov becomes a celebrity director of pornographic films provides a striking indictment of the moral vacuity of the cinema as well as the dilemmas of the artist in a capitalist economy, forced to pander to the degraded taste of a mass audience. Indeed, it is almost impossible not to read into this motif Balabanov's own ambivalence about contemporary Russian cinema and the price of popular success, perhaps including his own, in the new free market economy of post-Soviet Russia.

By setting *Freaks and Men* in fin de siècle St. Petersburg, Balabanov associates the film with the dual revolutions that have defined Russian ideological, social, economic, and cultural life for the last century: the Revolution of 1917 and the invention of the cinema. By putting pornography and the spectacle of "singing freaks" at the center of his film, Balabanov raises difficult questions about any art that ignores its moral and ethical responsibilities. And by portraying the crises of the bourgeois family as the clash between well-intentioned but weak and morally corrupt liberals with unscrupulous criminals and psychopaths, Balabanov suggests at least two interpretations of *Freaks and Men*: a warning of the criminal threat to the new Russian bourgeois and professional elites and an allegory of the Revolution of 1917. In either sense, the disastrous results of Radlov's, Stasov's, and Putilov's failure to oppose evil can be seen to justify Danila Bagrov's vigilante violence in the post-Soviet world.

At the heart, then, of *Freaks and Men* are at least three interrelated critiques. Balabanov suggests that the root cause of the disasters of Russian twentieth-century history can be found in the failure of the liberal middle class to defend itself and its values against the violence and fanaticism of revolutionaries and criminals. He also criticizes the moral bankruptcy of an art that ignores its ethical responsibilities and he scorns artists who compromise out of economic self-interest and a desire to make a career. At the center of this theme is an examination of the ethical and moral justification of vigilante violence, defined as the willingness to use violence when the State has proven itself incapable of establishing minimal security and social justice. Balabanov's films all reflect the raging anarchy of post-Communist Russian life, the desperate desire of many ordinary Russians for simple solutions to complex problems, and the power of nationalist discourse in contemporary Russian culture. In the course of Balabanov's films, the vigilante evolves from a naive and innocent hero of contemporary urban folklore into a tragic figure, who sacrifices himself, metaphorically and literally, to save the rest of us. Balabanov interrogates the consequences of the vigilante's active opposition to evil, comparing them to the costs of the liberal middle class's weakness and passivity. Despite all of his flaws, the vigilante remains an extremely attractive figure to Balabanov and his audience. While many viewers recognize, and are repelled by, Balabanov's use of the traditional tricks of the demagogue (for example, the reliance on simple solutions to complex and intractable problems, the willingness to trade in xenophobic stereotypes, the privileging of action and emotion over reason), given the power of the cinema to model reality, it would be unwise to underestimate the power of Balabanov's vigilante critique of Russian history and contemporary society.

NOTES

1. In addition to the films discussed in this essay, Balabanov has written and directed the 1989 documentary *Egor and Nastia* (*Egor' i Nastia*); the 1992 *Happy Days* (*Schastlivye dni*), based on motifs from Samuel Beckett's works; a 1994 adaptation of Kafka's *The Castle* (*Zamok*); a 1995 short *Trofim* (*Trofim*); a parody of the gangster film *Dead Man's Bluff* (*Zhmurki*, 2005); and, most recently, the off-beat contemporary love story *It Doesn't Hurt* (*Mne ne bol'no*, 2006). Fragments of *The River* (*Reka*), the filming of which was cut short by the death of the leading actress, were released in 2002. Balabanov's new film, entitled *Cargo 200* (*Gruz 200*), was released in 2007.

2. Even the aspiring young urban professional architects and designers of Balabanov's 2006 film, *It Doesn't Hurt*, are represented as socially marginal. Balabanov's

most recent film, *Cargo 200* (*Gruz 200*), was released in summer 2007, after this book went to press.

3. For a very different type of vigilante hero, see the 1999 feature by Stanislav Govorukhin, *The Voroshilov Sharpshooter* (*Voroshilovskii strelok*).

4. Despite its popular success, *Brother's* reception by critics and reviewers was, on the whole, far less positive. Andrew Horton, for example, writing in the *Central European Review* dismissed the movie as a "cheap" and "adolescent" version of Martin Scorsese's 1976 classic *Taxi Driver:* "Balabanov's view of Danila has none of the irony or ambiguity that Scorsese employs. His grassroots philosophy, simple-minded approach to vigilante violence and pathetic forgiveness of his brother for betraying him are designed to increase audience sympathy for Danila. This makes *Brother* [*Brat*] a surprisingly adolescent film with an artificial view of modern Russian life which opportunistically glosses over the real issues behind Mafia violence and a dispossessed youth to make the film more 'watchable.' If this is not a description of cinematic cheapness, then I don't know what is." Online at http://www.ce-review.org/00/18/kinoeye18_horton.html (April 10, 2005).

5. *Ivan durachok*, or Ivan the Fool, is a folkloric character in Russian tales who always manages to triumph because of (and not in spite of) his simplicity.

6. Many critics have commented on the disparity between Danila's rhetoric of "Strength is in righteousness" (*Sila v pravde*) and his actions, which are based on using violence to gain his ends. See, for example, Mark Lipovetskii, "Vsekh liubliu na svete ia!" *Iskusstvo kino* 11 (2000): 56.

7. Lipovetskii, "Vsekh liubliu na svete ia!" See also Evgenii Gusiatinskii, "Brat zhil, brat zhiv, brat budet zhit," *Iskusstvo kino* 3 (2001): 30–33.

8. The Maxim gun is an obvious reference (even brother Vitia recognizes it!) to perhaps the most popular Soviet movie of all time, the 1934 *Chapaev*, directed by the Vasil'ev "brothers." The tachanka was a horse-driven cart that carried a Maxim gun on it—it was used extensively during the Russian Civil War.

9. I am indebted to my colleague Alexander Prokhorov for the suggestion that Balabanov may be referring here to another famous cinematic "escape from America," Marion Dixon's (Liubov' Orlova) escape from a lynch mob at the beginning of Grigorii Alexandrov's 1936 Stalinist classic *The Circus* (*Tsirk*).

10. "*Ia uznal, chto u menia / Est' orgromnaia sem'ia— / I tropinka i lesok, / V pole kazhdyi kolosok. / Rechka, nebo goluboe— / Eto vse moe, rodnoe! / Eto Rodina moia! / Vsekh liubliu na svtee ia!*" For a discussion of the ideological importance of this poem, see Lipovetskii, "Vsekh liubliu na svete ia."

11. For a different perspective on the film's anti-Americanism, see the unsigned review from the 2001 University of Pittsburgh Russian Film Symposium: available online at http://www.rusfilm.pitt.edu/2001/brat.html (April 10, 2005).

12. Richard Stites, *Revolutionary Dreams: Utopian Vision and Experimental Life in the Russian Revolution* (New York: Oxford University Press, 1989), 15, 85. Nina Tumarkin, *Lenin Lives: The Lenin Cult in Soviet Russia* (Cambridge, Mass.: Harvard University Press, 1983), 70–72.

13. The Russian lyrics are: "*Kogda umolknut vse pesni / Kotorykh ia ne znaiu / V terpkom vozdukhe kriknet / Poslednii moi bumazhnyi parokhod. / Gud-bai Amerika—o / Gde ia ne byl nikogda. / Proshchai navsegda / Voz'mi bandzho sygrai mne na proshchan'e. / Mne stali slishkom maly/ Tvoi tertye dzhinsy. / Nas tak dolgo uchili / Liubit' tvoi zapretnye*

plody. / Gud-bai Amerika—o / Gde ia ne budu nikogda / Uslyshu li ia pesniu, / Kotoruiu zapomniu navsegda." Interestingly, when the song was released in 1985, it sounded like an ironic lament for the loss of the idealized image of America and American culture, which was based on its pre-Perestroika inaccessibility and status as "forbidden fruit."

14. http://brat2.film.ru/q&a2.asp. *Brother 2* official website (accessed April 10, 2005).

15. Actually, Ivan is forced to act by the inability and the refusal of both the British and Russian governments to defend their own citizens.

16. Like the *Brother* movies, *War* has been repeatedly criticized for its racist portrayal of the Chechens. See, for example, Andrew Horton's review in *Kinoeye*, available online at http://www.kinoeye.org/02/18/horton18_no3.php (accessed April 10, 2005).

17. For a discussion of the origins of this Orthodox tradition, see G. P. Fedotov, *The Russian Religious Mind* (New York: Harper and Row, 1960), 94–110.

18. *Cargo 200* (*Gruz 200*), a love triangle about a girl who loves a soldier killed in Afghanistan and the militiaman in love with the girl, seems perfectly positioned to continue Balabanov's search for a new Russian hero. The title is a code term for coffins of soldiers killed in action. For an interview with the filmmaker about his new film in production, see http://www.trud.ru/trud.php?id=200609021610501 (accessed April 10, 2005).

19. Jonathan Romney's review in *The New Statesman* is typical: "Maintaining a tone of coldly bemused detachment throughout, *Of Freaks and Men* succeeds in being elegantly sordid from start to finish: an altogether liberating gesture, surely, for a national cinema that from its very early days has been obliged to present itself as high-minded and ideologically weighty. There's no danger of that with Balabanov: his films can't easily be made to yield straightforward lessons either about morality or about the state of Russian society." Online at: http://www.findarticles.com/cf_dls/m0FQP/4481_129/61945858/p1/article.jhtml (accessed April 10, 2005).

20. "It seems more logical to the author of this review to take *Of Freaks and Men* as a calculated, cynical provocation which has, and this is critical, achieved its goal." Iurii Gladil'shchikov, *Itogi*, July 6, 1998. Available online at http://www.ctb.ru/base/films/9/3 (accessed April 10, 2005).

21. For a more serious analysis of the film, see Igor' Mantsov, "Posetitel' muzeia," *Iskusstvo kino* 2 (1999), available online at http://www.kinoart.ru/1999/2/2.html (accessed April 10, 2005).

22. Friedrich Nietzsche, *Thus Spoke Zarathustra* (Baltimore: Penguin, 1978), 93.

23. For a fascinating analysis of the theme of masochism in this film, see Mantsov, "Posetitel' muzeia."

24. Danila's wanderings through the city are usually shot without dialogue but with music, in the style of an MTV music video. The best example of this is the massacre at the music club in *Brother 2*, where Balabanov recreates the typical point of view of video shooting games (i.e., a point-of-view shot of a raised arm holding a gun, as the shooter navigates through corridors and adjacent rooms) thereby inviting viewers to identify with the killer while suppressing their ability to question the justification of his actions.

25. Susan Larsen, "National Identity, Cultural Authority, and the Post-Soviet Blockbusters: Nikita Mikhalkov and Aleksei Balabanov," *Slavic Review* 62, no. 3 (Fall 2003): 506.

26. The use of the Internet by the Chechen fighters to broadcast their partisan version of the war and John's use of the digital footage from their incursion into Chechnya suggest that greater access to digital media technology may result in nothing more than an increased number of partisan and partial digital realities.

27. "A story of sexual bondage, of how Isabella Rossellini's husband and son have been kidnapped by Dennis Hopper, who makes her his sexual slave. The twist is that the kidnapping taps into the woman's deepest feelings: She finds that she is a masochist who responds with great sexual passion to this situation." Review of *Blue Velvet* by Roger Ebert, available online at http://www.geocities.com/~mikehartmann/bluevelvet/bvreviews.html (accessed April 10, 2005).

9.

Fools and Cuckoos

The Outsider as Insider in Post-Soviet War Films

Stephen M. Norris

Post-Soviet cinema has frequently turned to the outsider, a reflection of the chaos that has defined life after 1991. Cinematic outsiders regularly serve as a means to explore crime, racism, poverty, and even tsarist history. Aleksei Balabanov's immensely popular *Brother* films (*Brat*, 1997 and *Brat 2*, 2000), as Anthony Anemone has argued in the previous chapter, follow the adventures of Danila Bagrov, a former soldier who becomes caught up in the crime scene of St. Petersburg and then Moscow (and even later, Chicago). He is, in Julian Graffy's words, "a representative of a post-Soviet generation unexpectedly released from the cage of moral and social certainties."[1] Danila is an embodiment of the crime, racism, excitement, and ambiguities of Russia since 1992. He is an outsider in that most contradictory of Russian cities, St. Petersburg. Yet Danila is not the only outsider that stands as a symbol for post-Soviet culture, just the most convenient one—the use of outsiders in contemporary Russian cinema is such a prevalent theme that it qualifies as a cult.[2]

The army certainly helped to shape Danila's personality and his search for meaning in Russia in the 1990s. Although his past is only hinted at, the audience knows that Danila has returned from a war region and has learned how to handle weapons. Chechnya is not specifically mentioned, but Balabanov's film implies that Danila has seen action there. His status as an outsider rests on his view of the war, the new Russian state that sent him to fight, and his ideas about Russia's future—Danila comes across as a Russian nationalist who resists the invasion of American culture. *Brother* is not a traditional war film, but its action necessitates an understanding of the Chechen War in particular and Russian history in general.

Danila illustrates some interesting connections between the cult of outsiders in post-Soviet Russia and the role of war in defining Russian-ness. In 2002, a controversy arose about two war films that made these connections the subject for intense debate. This chapter will examine the debates that erupted over 2002's "Oscar Affair" as a means of exploring post-Soviet culture, the role of war in Russian historical memory, and the use of cinema as a means of identifying national belonging (or "us"). Like Danila, Aleksandr Rogozhkin's *The Cuckoo* (*Kukushka*, 2002) and Andrei Konchalovskii's *House of Fools* (*Dom durakov*, 2002), the two films at the center of the controversy, tell us a great deal about the role of outsiders in the post-Soviet cultural atmosphere.

Outsiders as Insiders in Post-Soviet Russia

Post-Soviet cultural life, as several scholars have argued, has attempted to search for a usable past that will serve as a means for Russians to create a better future.[3] Not surprisingly, one of the most important arenas in which this search has taken place is cinema. Russian filmmakers have trained their cameras on all aspects of the Soviet era and started to reclaim certain aspects of the tsarist past as a source for a renewed nationhood. From blockbusters such as Nikita Mikhalkov's *Barber of Siberia* (*Sibirskii tsiriul'nik*, 1998) to Alexander Sokurov's art house success, *Russian Ark* (*Russkii kovcheg*, 2002), the past has provided fertile soil for Russian directors.[4]

One of the most important genres used in any attempt to deal with the past is the war film. As both Denise Youngblood and Peter Kenez have argued, the war film proved to be an exceptionally important genre in Soviet cinema, for films made about military conflicts frequently provided a highly contested space for challenging Soviet versions of history.[5] War provided the anchors upon which the Soviet system moored itself—born in World War I, tempered in the Civil War, recast in World War II, and undermined by the Afghan War, the USSR's history was intimately connected to warfare. Soviet officials frequently employed the rhetoric of armed conflict to describe their attempts to build a new socialist society, a tactic also used by cultural figures.[6] Every state tells its history through the prism of war, but few nations have used war as a defining feature of life and as a means to identify what it meant to be "one of ours" as Soviet leaders, writers, artists, filmmakers, and citizens did.

Post-Soviet Russia has also been shaped by war. The bloody conflict with Chechnya has defined Russian politics and culture since it began in 1994. For President Vladimir Putin and other Russian politicians, the conflict has provided a mission, one connected to the "war on terrorism." Putin's phenomenal success at the polls has rested in part on his ability to persuade Russians that he can supply a sense of stability through a defeat of Russia's enemies. Opponents of Putin's, on the other hand, often use the brutal means employed in the Caucasus as proof of renewed authoritarianism. In the eyes of many Russians (and Western observers), Putin's Chechen War is a reminder of his KGB past and thus Soviet imperialism, while others view the war as a revival of Russia's pre-Soviet attempts to build an empire in the south.

Cinema, as Oleg Sulkin reminds us, has played a vital role in how many Russians have viewed the war—Sergei Bodrov's *Prisoner of the Mountains* (*Kavkazskii plennik*, 1996) appeared at the beginning of the conflict and reminded audiences of nineteenth-century Russian imperialism, while Aleksei Balabanov's *War* (*Voina*, 2002), reflected the ways in which the ongoing Chechen conflict had hardened each side's view of one another. In short, films of the Chechen War have continued the tendency of Soviet filmmakers to use the genre of war film as a way of challenging official versions of armed conflict, while others have used film to support the ongoing conflict.

Surprisingly, one important event that had not received much attention in post-Soviet Russian cinema before the Putin era was World War II. Known as the Great Patriotic War in Russia, the fight against Hitler and the Nazi armies became the most important myth of Soviet life from 1945 until the late 1980s. Although the regime's uses of the conflict as a sustaining myth waxed and waned, the experience of the Great Patriotic War, as Amir Weiner has argued, "became a yardstick by which identity, meritocracy, and status were measured throughout the Soviet polity."[7] While the victory over the Nazi invaders continues to serve as an important holiday in Russia, the memory of the war had remained largely uncontested in post-Soviet life before 2002. The "cult of World War II in Russia" may have waned by the Gorbachev era,[8] but certain versions of the Soviet myth survived. The new Museum of the Great Patriotic War in Moscow, for example, serves as a very visible reminder of the Soviet suffering endured during the period 1941–1945, ensuring that Russians remember the war as one during which they endured incredible hardships but ultimately triumphed because of their collective spirit. The addition of an Orthodox chapel on the site of the museum may reflect certain changes in post-Soviet conceptions about the war, but the decision to place a Holocaust memorial around the back of the main building attests to the tenacity of Soviet versions of the war.[9]

Given the willingness of Russian directors to question the Chechen War, the fact that no post-Soviet film before 2002 reexamined World War II seems surprising. Some of the best Soviet films dealt with World War II and its ramifications and helped to construct a multifaceted memory of that conflict.[10] At the same time, Soviet films of the Great Patriotic War did not challenge certain aspects of the fight against the fascists. Every Soviet film about the war stressed the suffering of the Soviet people on some level, even while many films from the Thaw focused on how the war affected ordinary men and women in making difficult decisions. Thus, Soviet war films in part confirmed the necessity of the fight against Hitler's forces.[11] Everyone, even children such as Tarkovskii's Ivan, became an insider to the war and how it shaped Soviet experience.

Two films that appeared in 2002 challenged traditions of the Russian war film as a genre by focusing on outsiders. Aleksandr Rogozhkin's *The Cuckoo* and Andrei Konchalovskii's *House of Fools* depict events during World War II and the Chechen War, respectively. Both use outsiders as a means of exploring these conflicts and articulating pacifist messages. Both attempt to reexamine the past in an effort to create a post-Soviet culture, and both received considerable critical attention as a result. While Russian critics overwhelmingly preferred Rogozhkin's film over Konchalovskii's, the reaction to the films demonstrated how outsiders became insiders in the search for a usable past.

Cuckoos in War

Aleksandr Rogozhkin has become one of the most popular and critically acclaimed Russian directors. Since 1991, his films have consistently explored Russian history, captured the realities of post-Soviet anxieties, and presented characters that embody Russian traits. *The Chekist*, Rogozhkin's 1991 controversial film, explored the role of violence in the Bolshevik project through the life of a member of the first Soviet political police. Beginning with 1995's breakthrough hit *The Peculiarities of the National Hunt* (*Osobennosti natsional'noi okhoty*), Rogozhkin made comedies with the same characters that explored life after the Soviet Union and the attempts to preserve Russian national traits (the others were 1998's *The Peculiarities of the National Fishing* [*Osobennosti natsional'noi rybalki*] and 2000's *The Peculiarities of the National Hunt in Winter* [*Osobennosti natsional'noi okhoty v zimnii period*]).[12] Rogozhkin expanded on his interests in Russian comedy and war with his 1996 semi-sequel to *Peculiarities*, *Operation "Happy New Year"* (*Operatsiia 'S novym godom'*) and his 1998 metaphoric view of the Chechen War in *Checkpoint* (*Blokpost*).[13] Rogozhkin, in other words, represents the rare filmmaker who tackles various subjects, genres, and cinematic forms that find both critical and commercial success.

The Cuckoo tells the story of three outsiders and their wartime experiences. Set in September 1944, the entire film takes place in one of the most remote theaters of the war—the Lapland regions of Finland, near

Figure 9.1. Anni's Nest: The Three Outsiders.
From Aleksandr Rogozhkin's *The Cuckoo* (2002).

the Soviet border. The setting immediately establishes a difference from other Russian depictions of World War II—Moscow does not appear at all, nor does the Nazi invasion of the USSR factor into the action. Instead, the film concentrates on an area that adds to its focus on outsiders. It begins with a Finnish sniper named Veikko (played by Ville Haapasalo, a regular in Rogozhkin's films) being chained to a rock by Nazi soldiers. Veikko is a pacifist who has been conscripted into the Nazi army. Because of his views, he has been punished—left with only a few supplies and bullets for his sniper's rifle, Veikko has been cast away from the conflict. When one of the Nazi officers tears away his dog tags, Veikko is marked as an outsider.

The second scene of the film introduces the second outsider, a Soviet Captain who has been arrested for "anti-Soviet activities" and is being taken to a court-martial. The Captain (played by Viktor Bychkov, Kuz'mich in Rogozhkin's national comedies) sits in the back of a jeep while a fellow officer tells him, "I believe you're innocent. You're a good man and an honest officer." With his character established, the Captain rides off into the border region, passing by Veikko (although the Soviet officers do not see him). As the jeep pauses for a break, Soviet planes strafe the area and kill all the soldiers except for the Captain, who sustains a concussion. Veikko watches through the scope of his rifle in between attempts to free himself from the rock.

The third outsider then appears, a Saami woman named Anni (played by Anni-Kristiina Juuso). Anni lives in a traditional Saami hut near the region where both Veikko and the Captain have been abandoned, and she stumbles upon the bodies of the Soviet soldiers on a periodic trip to get water. Anni is the ultimate outsider of the threesome—she attempts to live according to her traditional customs, but the war and the worlds of Veikko and the Captain have invaded hers. She starts to bury the Russian dead, but as she throws sand on the Captain's face, he stirs. She drags him back to her hut to treat his wounds as Veikko again watches. Once the two have left, Veikko renews his efforts to free himself. Through a mixture of cleverness and strength, he eventually succeeds and wanders toward Anni's home. The first third of the film ends when all three outsiders encounter each other—up until that point, minimal dialogue, long shots of the remoteness of the region, and clues into why these three have been emotionally wounded by the war set the stage for the remainder of the picture.

The rest of the film explores how the three outsiders react to each other and how the war has shaped each of their perceptions of the other (see fig. 9.1). The main tension of the story is the relationship between Veikko and the Captain, while Anni provides the only source of understanding. Both combatants respond to her beauty and the fact that the war has intruded upon her life. Anni's husband, we learn, has been gone for four years, conscripted to fight the Soviet Army in the Winter War between Finland and the USSR. Each of the three characters speaks only in their native tongues. Because of their failure to understand each other's statements (a lack of communication between "enemies" that has parallels to Julian Graffy's discussion of *Tommi* earlier in this volume), the ways in which the war has conditioned both Veikko and the Captain determine how each responds to the other's actions.

Veikko immediately announces that the war is over for him—condemned to die but now free, his earlier pacifist leanings have found confirmation. The Soviet Captain cannot understand Veikko's pronouncements and instead sees only his Nazi uniform. Because Veikko's clothing bears Nazi insignias, the Captain sees only "them" and not one of "us." As a result, the Captain calls him "Fritz" and labels him a "fascist." The wounded officer also introduces the first meaning of the title when he calls Veikko a "cuckoo," the name Russian troops gave to Finnish snipers. The term refers to a Russian folkloric belief about the birds—if someone hears a cuckoo in the forest, he asks the bird how many years he has left to live, then counts the bird's cries to get an answer.

Cuckoos appear as a theme in two famous Soviet World War II films.

Sergei Bondarchuk's *Fate of a Man* (*Sud'ba cheloveka*, 1959) follows the story of a single Russian soldier, Andrei Sokolov, and his wartime journey. Sokolov (played by Bondarchuk) survives battle, imprisonment, a concentration camp, and a death sentence over the course of the film. After a daring escape, Sokolov returns to the Soviet front lines. As he walks through a trench, a cuckoo calls out three times. Soon after hearing its call, Sokolov finds out that his wife and two daughters died during the Nazi invasion.

Similarly, Andrei Tarkovskii's *Ivan's Childhood* (*Ivanovo detstvo*, 1962) also traces the wartime fate of a single Russian, the title character. The film opens with Ivan playing outside near his home. When he hears a cuckoo, the young boy runs up to his mother and speaks the first words of the film: "Momma, a cuckoo's there (*Mama, tam kukushka*)." Ivan's mother smiles as the noise of a bombardment breaks the idyllic scene. Ivan, a hardened veteran of war even as a child, wakes from his dream of his former childhood. Tarkovskii uses this element of Russian folklore to foreshadow the tragedy that befalls Ivan. His dream sequences portray Ivan's childhood as it should have been, but from the very beginning the cuckoo calls for him.

In Rogozhkin's film, by contrast, the first use of the term "cuckoo" is ironic and serves as a means of understanding the cultural divide that separates Veikko and the Captain. The Soviet officer sees the Finn solely as a sniper who desires his death, while Veikko insists in Finnish that he no longer wants to be a part of the war. Rogozhkin also uses this failure to understand each other humorously. When Veikko attempts to learn everyone's name, he points to himself and says, "Veikko." Anni understands and gives her name, but when the Soviet Captain is asked his name, he replies "Poshel ty (get lost)." For the remainder of the film, both Veikko and Anni refer to him as "Psholty."

The film alternates between humorous exchanges, Psholty's distrust of Veikko, and Anni's attempts to understand what both have brought into her life. Although none of the characters learn to understand each other, the viewer learns that all have been emotionally scarred by the war. Anni has lost her husband and must try to live off the land alone, Veikko has had his student days interrupted and been forced to fight in a war that repels him, while even Psholty admits that his "soul has been emptied by the war."

Although Anni nurses both men, in the end, Psholty's inability to come to terms with Veikko's character nearly produces tragic results. When a Soviet plane crashes near Anni's hut, the war intrudes again. Both Veikko and Psholty rush to see the plane. Veikko immediately spots the cargo—fliers that announce Finland's exit from the war. Psholty ignores the fliers, which are printed in both Russian and Finnish, and sees only the two dead female pilots, "ours." For him, this sight is confirmation of his hatred toward "them," namely the Germans, embodied by Veikko. Psholty takes a pistol from the plane and shoots the "fascist." As Veikko gasps for his life, he forces a flier into Psholty's hand and states: "I surrendered a long time ago."

Only at that moment does Psholty read the flier and understand what Veikko has been saying all along. Conditioned by Soviet calls for revenge, he has refused to recognize Veikko as a human being. Once he reads the flier, however, Psholty carries Veikko back to Anni's hut, where the Saami woman performs a ritual designed to bring Veikko back from the land of the dead. After an all-night vigil, Veikko survives. Anni does not know that the Captain shot the Finn, and asks the Russian to sleep with her. Before they do so, she tells Psholty in her native language that her name is not Anni, but "Cuckoo" (we later learn that Psholty's name is Ivan). Thus Anni/Cuckoo becomes a woman who enables two men to regain a sense of humanity in the midst of war. She is, in Rogozhkin's words, "a cuckoo who raises two nestlings."[14] The film provides further irony to the use of the term "cuckoo," for many cuckoos do not raise their young. Scientists have discovered that species of "parasitic cuckoos" use "mafia-style tactics" in parental care, preferring to lay their eggs in the nests of other birds and "persuade" them to accept their eggs and raise their chicks.[15] By contrast, Anni accepts the nestlings rejected by the Nazi and Soviet regimes, raising them and the children she later bears from them.

Rogozhkin's film uses outsiders embodied in the cuckoo metaphor to advance ideas not usually present in previous Russian films about the Great Patriotic War. *The Cuckoo* contains very little about the war, how it began, and the struggle of the Soviet people under German occupation. Instead, Rogozhkin focuses on a remote slice of life and how war—any war—affects individuals. Each of the three protagonists has experienced deprivations and their wartime experience has left them emotionally shattered. Ivan in particular has lived through the Stalinist era and the early stages of the war and thus has been shaped by attempts to define who belongs and who does not, who is *svoi* and who is *chuzhoi* (as Josephine Woll discusses in this volume). The conclusion of the film explicitly blurs these distinctions— Anni sits on a hillside telling her twin sons (who could be either Veikko's or Ivan's) about their "fathers." (See fig. 9.2.) Rogozhkin, who stated that "war is a dirty and clumsy business" as a reason why he did not include much combat in his film, produced a vision that runs counter to the dominant myths and memories of the Great Patriotic War. His outsiders have become insiders in their attempts to articulate a challenging vision of the war and how it can be understood in post-Soviet Russia.

Figure 9.2. The Cuckoo's Nest.
From Aleksandr Rogozhkin's *The Cuckoo* (2002).

Russian film critics praised Rogozhkin's film and the way it tackled such a complex subject as World War II. Tat'iana Iensen wrote that Rogozhkin created a story of three "exiles/outsiders" (*izgoi*), one that offered "an unprecedented interaction between reality and the screen" because of the way in which it presented the ambiguities of the wartime experience. All three characters have become outsiders in different ways, but the meeting between the three, a meeting that only could have taken place in such a war, produces a new myth about the conflict, one that simply tells the story of "one Finn and one Russian soldier." Although neither fully understands the other by the end, for Iensen, the barriers that existed between the two have opened enough—the boundaries between "us" and "them" have been transgressed. This "strict, verified, and ascetic" film, she concludes, has become part of that era of history.[16] *The Cuckoo*'s achievement, in other words, is to add more layers of meanings and interpretations to the memory of the Great Patriotic War.

Rogozhkin's film enjoyed a great deal of critical success because of the reception it received from critics such as Iensen. The film opened the Russian program of the 24th Moscow Film Festival in 2002. After its release, headlines announced the "triumphant flight of *The Cuckoo*" and predicted it would captivate audiences and critics alike.[17] Because of the success of his earlier films, Rogozhkin's account of the war did well at the box office. *The Cuckoo* also captured the 2003 Nika Award (Russia's top honor) for Best Film, Best Director, and Best Actress; the 2003 Golden Eagle Award for Best Film, Director, and Actor (Viktor Bychkov); and the 2002 Best Film and Director prizes at the European Film Festival in Italy. Rogozhkin's use of outsiders in war set off a cinematic explosion—between 2002 and 2006, Russian directors have produced sixteen feature-length films about the war and eight television serials that explore Soviet experiences in the conflict.[18] Rogozhkin himself returned to the theme of outsiders in war with his next film, 2006's *Transit (Peregon)*, which focuses upon the interactions between Soviet and American soldiers in the far north.

Fools and Chechens

By contrast, Andrei Konchalovskii's *House of Fools* polarized critics for its use of outsiders to tell a story of the ongoing Chechen War. Konchalovskii's film takes as its inspiration an actual event from the First Chechen War. In 1996, a mental institution near the Chechen-Ingushetia border found itself in the midst of the action. The hospital staff fled the building, leaving the patients literally running the asylum. Amazingly, they managed to survive as battle raged around them. The story of sane inmates in the middle of an insane war proved irresistible to Konchalovskii. *House of Fools* uses this factual basis as a starting-off point to focus upon these true outsiders to war.

The main character of the film is Zhanna (played by Julia Vysotskaia, who spent two months with mental patients to prepare for the role). Zhanna serves as an emotional anchor for the rest of the patients, who represent an assortment of mental handicaps and nationalities. As a way of adding a touch of realism to his film, Konchalovskii uses actual mental patients for many of his roles—the actors blend in with physically and mentally handicapped people. Zhanna believes that she is engaged to Bryan Adams, the Canadian pop star (who appears throughout the film). Dreamlike sequences featuring Adams romancing Zhanna contrast with scenes of the squalid conditions one expects to see in a former Soviet mental institution. For the patients in this "house of fools," the major conflicts concern bathroom privileges and the quality of the food.

The war soon changes this situation. One day the doctor finds the phone dead and, after a troop transport glides by, concludes that he must evacuate the patients. As he prepares to leave, his staff announces that they will not spend the night in the asylum. When morning dawns the inmates find themselves alone. While they celebrate their "freedom," the patients soon learn how it was obtained—explosions rock the hospital and a portrait of Boris Yeltsin falls from the wall while a television plays images of a Russian general smugly talking about the war. A group of Chechen soldiers enters the hospital, quickly realizes that it is full of mental patients, and promises not to hurt anyone. As they set up camp inside, a Chechen paints, in enormous black letters on the side of the building, "SICK PEOPLE (*bol'nye liudi*)."

The film then focuses on the interactions between Chechens and patients, particularly on Zhanna's relationship with a single Chechen soldier named Ahmed. Zhanna discovers Ahmed and some of his fellow soldiers playing her accordion, and agrees to sing and dance for them. As a joke, Ahmed asks Zhanna to marry him, a proposal she takes seriously. She leaves the Chechens assuming that if she agrees to marry Ahmed, she should turn up that evening for a wedding. Although a "sick person," Zhanna's human emotions contrast with the cynicism of the Chechen troops.

After apologizing to Bryan Adams, Zhanna is convinced by her roommate's argument that she should marry Ahmed because she should "not give up a chance to be happy." She makes her decision, and the rest of the patients help her prepare for her wedding—one of the inmates, Vika, gives Zhanna a white hat and tells her that "it is a powerful symbol. As the world ignores this tragedy, you are marrying a man who is fighting against Russian imperialism. It's an act of international significance. The media should know about it."

Zhanna bids farewell to her friends and goes to Ahmed. When his fellow soldiers make fun of him and his Captain bellows at him for making such a promise, Ahmed announces that he intends to keep his word of honor. Zhanna and the Chechen soldiers dance, drink, and sing. Eventually, however, she tells Ahmed she cannot marry him because her love for Bryan Adams is too strong. As the two sit outside, Zhanna informs Ahmed: "We are alive because someone somewhere loves us. They pray for us and give us strength." Faced with this observation from a "sick person," Ahmed confesses that he never intended to marry her and asks for forgiveness. He also tells Zhanna that he never intended to fight in a war, but when his brothers were killed and his father's house was destroyed, he asked for a gun. Like the understanding reached between Ivan and Veikko, this agreement marks a similar transgressing of the boundaries between "us" and "them": Russians and Chechens, in this vision of war, share more similarities than differences.

As the Chechen and patient reach this understanding, the war intrudes again. Russian shells strike the building and Ahmed's unit prepares to attack

Figure 9.3. Imperial to National Identities.
From Andrei Konchalovskii's *House of Fools* (2002).

Russians who are in a nearby market. Zhanna, still clad in her wedding attire and holding her accordion, attempts to play songs that will drive the madness of war away. As she appeals to Ahmed for help, he tells her to get back to where she belongs. Stung, Zhanna stumbles around the hospital courtyard as Vika, who has grabbed a machine gun, shoots at the Russians yelling, "down with Russian chauvinism." In the defining scene of the film, a downed Russian helicopter crashes near Zhanna and the resulting explosion blows her hat off of her head. The war has made Zhanna truly mad.

The Chechens do not return to the hospital; instead, the doctor reappears and recounts how he attempted to get a bus for the patients but was captured. Soon Russian troops enter the hospital and immediately act more suspicious and brutal than the Chechens who had previously brought "freedom." This characterization of Russian troops had been established earlier in the film, when a brief ceasefire brought the two sides together. The Chechen soldiers wanted to retrieve the body of a fallen comrade and offered money for his return while Russian soldiers only wanted marijuana and traded ammunition for it. At the same time, the Russian officer recognizes a tattoo on the Chechen leader's arm and realizes that it is the tattoo of a Soviet unit that saved his life in Afghanistan. The commanders of both sides reminisce about Afghanistan, a time when they had both been "one of ours," connected by an imperial identity. When a Russian soldier who had already smoked a joint accidentally fires his rifle, it reminds everyone

Figure 9.4. He's One of Us.
From Andrei Konchalovskii's *House of Fools* (2002).

that the definitions of "ours" and "theirs" have changed—the Chechen
commander and Russian commander are now separated by ethnic and
national differences. (See fig. 9.3.) The episode, the only time when Russian
troops appeared before the final ten minutes of the film, also established the
soldiers along certain stereotypes—uncaring, uneducated, unpatriotic, and
consumed with the desire to get out of Chechnya any way possible.

When the Russian troops enter the hospital, the earlier characterization is fleshed out. All the troops fear that the Chechens booby-trapped
the building. One soldier sits in a state of shock and cannot move. When
the Russian commander (a cameo by Evgenii Mironov) comes to check
on him, he breaks down before the doctor, declaring: "It's crazy out there."
For good measure, the Russian quotes Tolstoy and offers a conclusion for
the film—"Why is man happy when he kills another? What's there to be
happy about?"

The Russian troops capture the few remaining "bandits" except for
one—Ahmed. The film closes with Ahmed appearing in line for food at the
hospital. When the doctor demands to know who he is, Ahmed answers: "I
am sick. I need to be treated." The patients concur: "He's one of us [*eto zhe
nash bol'noi*]. He's Ahmed." (See fig. 9.4.) Both Russians and Chechens at
the end realize that the outsiders, the "sick people," understand life better
than they do, and that ultimately "they" are "ours."

The War over Outsiders

Russian critics by and large blasted Konchalovskii's film. In part their anger stemmed from the fact that the Russian Oscar Committee, led by Koncha-lovskii's brother, Nikita Mikhalkov, selected *House of Fools* as Russia's official entry for the Academy Award over *The Cuckoo*. Articles in the Russian press had a field day with Konchalovskii, Mikhalkov, and the film, prompting an unusual discussion about the merits of these two war films and the themes they featured. The public debate provides a rare opportunity to examine how films represent history, their implications in present-day Russia, and how both films led to discussions about Russian national identity.

When the "Oscar" decision appeared, initially a number of journalists cried foul and relished using the title of Konchalovskii's film. "A Foolish Choice," "Taken by Fools," and other headlines blared across various news-papers the day after the selection was announced.[19] For many film critics and journalists, the decision appeared rigged because Mikhalkov led the committee that awarded the Oscar (the fact that Mikhalkov and his brother do not get along and that Mikhalkov voted for Valery Todorovskii's film *The Lover* seemed not to have mattered).[20] Even other Russian directors weighed in on the controversy—Ivan Dykhovichnyi, the director of *Music for December*, *Moscow Parade*, and 2002's *The Kopeck*, gave an interview where he argued that Konchalovskii had become a victim of his brother's intrigues. For Dykhovichnyi, Mikhalkov's decision to vote for another film was only part of his devious plan to *prevent* his brother or any other Russian director from equaling his Oscar (Mikhalkov won in 1994 for *Burnt by the Sun*). In this view, Mikhalkov tapped a weaker film (in Dykhovichnyi's words, *"The Lover* is clearly a hundred times weaker than *Dom durakov,"* proof that Mikhalkov intended for Konchalovskii's film to receive the Oscar nomination). The real "victim" in Mikhalkov's megalomania was Aleksandr Rogozhkin, whose film many believed actually could win the Oscar.

Part of the controversy stemmed from the fact that very few people, including critics, had actually seen *House of Fools* when it received the surprise elevation. Konchalovskii's film had captured the Grand Jury Prize at the Venice Film Festival, had been snapped up by Paramount for a U.S. release, but had not appeared widely on Russian screens. By contrast, *The Cuckoo* had premiered both in Russia and abroad and had received nearly universal acclaim from Russian critics. When Rogozhkin's film debuted at the Moscow Film Festival in July 2002, the Moscow paper *Nezavisimaia gazeta* declared: "Tolstoy has provided us with brothers" and praised *The*

Cuckoo as "the doubtless leader of the festival."[21] Just as importantly, Rogozhkin's film had not captured any awards at the major European festivals where it appeared. For some Russian journalists, this "snub" confirmed a belief that the West did not understand Russian art, while an "outsider" such as Konchalovskii pandered to Hollywood conventions and won awards outside of Russia. In the eyes of many critics and viewers, *House of Fools* was not "ours," while *The Cuckoo* was. When Konchalovskii's film debuted in Russia, the battle lines had been drawn—many critics went to the film angered over the "Oscar Affair" and savaged *House of Fools*.

Gleb Sitkovskii, writing in *Iskusstvo kino*, stated in the first paragraph of his review: "Andrei Konchalovskii has released a bad and thoroughly false film." Among other criticisms, Sitkovskii labels *House of Fools* "Western political correctness," a thinly veiled attack on Konchalovskii's life in the West (he resides in Los Angeles and London).[22] For Sitkovskii and other critics, Konchalovskii's film panders to the West in its attempt to send an "obviously didactic" message of "good Russians, bad Chechens." Comparing the film to Aleksei Balabanov's controversial film, *War*, Sitkovskii finds Konchalovskii's depiction lacking—Balabanov depicted the Chechens as too bad, while Konchalovskii reversed this characterization. "In general, add Konchalovskii onto Balabanov and you will get *War and Peace*," he wrote.[23] Other critics decried Konchalovskii's supposed influences and blasted *House of Fools* as completely derivative. Reviewers labeled the film a copy of *One Flew Over the Cuckoo's Nest*, reminiscent of *Volga-Volga*,[24] and even, in Sitkovskii's imaginative criticism, a rip-off of Lars Von Trier's *Dancer in the Dark* and Hieronymus Bosch's 1490–1500 painting *The Ship of Fools* (complete with Bryan Adams as the Christ figure).[25]

The perceived slight that *The Cuckoo* received at the hands of Russia's official cinema figures colored many of the reviews for *House of Fools*. After the initial onslaught of negativity, many Russian critics began to re-examine Konchalovskii's film and its themes. One writer for *Iskusstvo kino*, Dmitrii Bykov, centered his article about the film on the controversy and the resulting reaction to it. Bykov stated that he could, like everyone else, "review the film badly," but then noted that most reviewers tend to comment on how the film "meanly bypassed *The Cuckoo* for an Oscar."[26] With this in mind, Bykov sets out to view the film more favorably. He compares the acting, pacifist message, and the way in which the realities of war are presented in both *The Cuckoo* and *House of Fools* and concludes that the former contains nothing better than the latter, and perhaps even "strongly concedes to it." Ultimately, he concludes that "Konchalovskii's film seems to me not pacifist at all," but provides a more complex message where "the irrational inevitability of war is shown with frightening detail." Bykov sees the film as one where all kinds of people caught in the "rage, dullness, and ugliness" of war remain human, people for whom the viewer can feel pity while also remember vividly.[27]

Elena Plakhova, writing in *Moskovskie novosti*, compared the virtues of both films in her article "'Fools' + 'Cuckoo' = 'Oscar'?" Plakhova calls *House of Fools* "a candid and fair film" that represents a sort of "anti-*War*" free from one of "Balabanov's interpretations." In Konchalovskii's vision, the Chechens "are not shown as degenerate murderers, but as beautiful, noble people placed in a monstrous situation." At the same time, Plakhova praises Rogozhkin's vision of war and its outsiders, branding it "a poetic fairytale/ballad capable of touching even the hardest heart." Taken together, Plakhova muses, the two films' depictions of two very different wars are worthy of the Academy Award.[28]

After the initial furor had begun to subside, other writers began to situate Konchalovskii's depiction of the Chechen War in the context of the times. Aleksei Balabanov's film *War*, which appeared earlier in 2002, contained characterizations of heroic Russian soldiers combating villainous Chechens. By comparison, according to Valerii Kichin (writing in *Rossisskaia gazeta*), Konchalovskii has created "humane and noble" characters suffering because of war. Kichin states that the film "has now left the screen and will work on the public consciousness of the masses," a process that he hopes will allow Russians "to forget about Volgodonsk, the Moscow explosions, 'Nord-Ost,' and, possibly, a destroyed Manhattan." Instead of the "generic images of bearded villains with automatic weapons," Konchalovskii uses "loonies" to remind the viewer that the Chechens remain people too.[29] Because of the general tenor of Russian culture in 2002 regarding the ongoing war, Konchalovskii, as something of an outsider himself, has produced a significant achievement, if not a work of real art.[30]

Conclusions

The protracted, public debate over *The Cuckoo* and *House of Fools* reveals a great deal about post-Soviet culture just as it obscured much about the two films and their role in adding to the historical memories of the Great Patriotic War and the Chechen War. Both of these films contained important ideas about war and its importance in Russian history and both created striking visual scenes that add to previous cinematic explorations of Russia's wars. The controversy over the Oscar Committee tended to preclude any discussions about how Rogozhkin and Konchalovskii wrestled with the myths and memories of the wars they depicted.

Jay Winter has warned against reading any film "directly and in an unmediated way as a text to be incorporated within discursive fields of different origins and character."[31] In the case of Russian critics who wrote about the "Oscar Affair" and both films involved, most tended to view the works of Konchalovskii and Rogozhkin through one lens—Konchalovskii's "didactic film" and Rogozhkin's "poetic film." "Film," as Winter persuasively argues, "does not instruct or indicate or preach. It ministers, it challenges conventional categories of thought, it moves the viewer." Ultimately, "no film is strictly didactic, since images have a power to convey messages of many kinds, some intentional, some not."[32]

How then do the films of Konchalovskii and Rogozhkin minister and challenge? Both offer important ways to think about the memories of war in post-Soviet culture and national identity. Both continue the tradition of the war film as an important, highly contested space for challenging versions of history. Both contain images of war and characterizations of outsiders that leave any viewer with much to consider. Often lost in the hullabaloo over which film should be the official Russian selection for the Academy Award was any discussion about how Rogozhkin's film represented the most important cinematic vision of the Great Fatherland War since Elem Klimov's *Come and See. The Cuckoo* is populated by three true outsiders of the war, and created new opportunities for discussions about the war and its myths in Russian memory. In fact, *The Cuckoo* helped to open up new spaces in which the war could be discussed through visual means—since its release in 2002 Russian cinema has been dominated by new visions of the war.[33]

Only a few writers placed *House of Fools* in the context of most discussions of the Chechen War taking place in 2002. Alongside films such as Balabanov's *War* and in the midst of fears resonating as a result of recent Moscow bombing attacks, Konchalovskii's use of outsiders to convey humanistic themes about war and its culture represented a much more complex message about post-Soviet life and the increasing tendency to view all Chechens as "them."

At the very least, these two films released in the same year attest to the multiple ways Russian filmmakers approached and appropriated the past, a point made by Diliara Tasbulatova in an optimistic article published at the end of 2002. Pessimistic pronouncements from the mid-1990s about the impending destruction of Russian cinema at the hands of Hollywood imports did not prove correct, for "2002 was extremely fruitful for Russian cinema." Nearly seventy films appeared, audiences increased, and directors released films about war (including Rogozhkin, Konchalovskii, and Balabanov, but also Nikolai Lebedev's *The Star*), post-Soviet crime (*Anti-Killer*, made by Konchalovskii's son Egor), the imperial past (Sokurov's *Russian Ark*), literary classics (Kira Muratova's *Chekhovian Motifs*), and social life (Irina Evteeva's *The Clown* and Todorovsky's *The Lover* were two of the most critically acclaimed in this genre). Overall, Tasbulatova concludes, "Russian cinema displayed films across all genres, except the boring ones."[34] The Oscar affair helped to overshadow the fact that Russian films won prizes at festivals across Europe and North America. The arguments over which vision of war should be considered the best Russian film of the year provided a fascinating paper trail to read, yet it also attests to the various attempts cinema endeavored to represent Russia's past, present, and future.

Both *The Cuckoo* and *House of Fools* present intricate details of war in general and Russia's wars in particular. Rogozhkin claimed that he is "a historian" who finds "much in domestic war films that irritates" him. Even in the Great Patriotic War, for the director "war all the same remains war — there is nothing more foul or mean."[35] His film thus undermines many of the ways war films presented conflict in the Soviet period and offers a much more complex view about how "normal people are forced to become enemies in wartime."[36] Konchalovskii's film also presents war's impact on its participants as well as people who cannot fathom why people fight. His version of events in Chechnya adds to previous antiwar films such as *Prisoner of the Mountains* (Sergei Bodrov, 1996), among others. War films, in Russia and elsewhere, frequently portray victims and innocents to tell their stories, but rarely do outsiders to war figure so prominently and contest versions of warfare as significantly as do these two films.

House of Fools is set within a madhouse, which, as Angela Brintlinger has recently argued, represents one of the most important sites for artists attempting to confront the Russian past and post-Soviet present.[37] Novelists such as Viktor Pelevin and Vladimir Makanin have set their works and their "outsider heroes" in the madhouse as a means to examine the relationship between self and society. In doing so, both "sift through the debris of Russian history, searching for what they can use to better understand their present moment."[38] The same could be said of the use of the madhouse in *House of Fools* and Anni's nest in *The Cuckoo*. Both places allow for viewers to see how attempts to define clearly who is "ours" and who is "theirs" break down. Fools and cuckoos, it seems, say a great deal about Russian memory, history, and nationhood in the post-Soviet era.

NOTES

1. Julian Graffy, "Brother," *Sight and Sound* 10, no. 5 (May 2000): 44.

2. See all of Balabanov's films, particularly *Of Freaks and Men*, and the films of Pavel Lungin for other particularly important examples of outsiders in post-Soviet Russia. Anthony Anemone's essay in this volume explores Balabanov's use of the vigilante hero as an outsider. For another time and place where "outsiders" held such appeal in the cultural sphere, see Peter Gay's classic work (the inspiration for this article in many respects): *Weimar Culture: The Outsider as Insider* (New York: W. W. Norton, 1968).

3. See Kathleen Smith, *Mythmaking in the New Russia: Politics and Memory during the Yeltsin Era* (Ithaca, N.Y.: Cornell University Press, 2002); and Robert Service, *Russia: Experiment with a People* (Cambridge, Mass.: Harvard University Press, 2003). On the subject of Russian cinema, see Yana Hashamova, "Two Versions of a Usable Past in (Op)position to the West: Mikhalkov's *The Barber of Siberia* and Sokurov's *Russian Ark*," *Russian Review* 65, no. 2 (2006): 250–66.

4. Susan Larsen explores the search for a usable past in post-Soviet blockbusters in her article "National Identity, Cultural Authority, and the Post-Soviet Blockbuster: Nikita Mikhalkov and Aleksei Balabanov," *Slavic Review* 62, no. 3 (Fall 2003): 491–511.

5. Denise Youngblood, *Russian War Films: On the Cinema Front* (Lawrence: University Press of Kansas, 2006). See also Birgit Beumers, "Myth-making and Myth-taking: Lost Ideals and the War in Contemporary Russian Cinema," *Canadian Slavonic Papers* 42, nos. 1–2 (March–June 2000): 171–89.

6. Youngblood, *Russian War Films.*

7. Amir Weiner, "The Making of a Dominant Myth: The Second World War and the Construction of Political Identities within the Soviet Polity," *Russian Review* 55, no. 4 (October 1996): 638. See also Weiner's monograph, *Making Sense of War: The Second World War and the Fate of the Bolshevik Revolution* (Princeton, N.J.: Princeton University Press, 2000).

8. See Nina Tumarkin's *The Living and the Dead: The Rise and Fall of the Cult of World War II in Russia* (New York: Basic Books, 1994).

9. Nurit Schleifman, "Moscow's Victory Park: A Monumental Change," *History and Memory* 13, no. 2 (Fall 2001): 5–34.

10. For more on the revival of the war in Russian cinema since 2002, see my article, "Guiding Stars: The Comet-Like Rise of the War Film in Putin's Russia: Recent World War II Films and Historical Memories," *Studies in Russian and Soviet Cinema* 2, no. 1 (February 2007): 163–89.

11. See Beumers, "Myth-making and Myth-taking." As Beumers notes, "The [cinematic] soldiers in the Great Patriotic War—from Alesha Skvortsov of *Ballada o soldate* (Ballad of a Soldier, Chukhrai, 1959) to Nadezhda Petrukhina of *Kryl'ia* (Wings, Shpeitko, 1966)—put their task over personal ambitions" (171).

12. For one reading of the 1995 film, see Susan Larsen, "In Search of an Audience: The New Russian Cinema of Reconciliation," in Adele Marie Barker, ed., *Consuming Russia: Popular Culture, Sex, and Society since Gorbachev* (Durham, N.C.: Duke University Press, 1999): 200–204. Larsen also discusses Vladimir Khotinenko's 1995 film

The Muslim (*Musul'manin*) and discusses how this film and Rogozhkin's comedies use "outsiders" as a means to articulate Russian national identity.

13. See Beumers, "Myth-making and Myth-taking," 186–89; and Andrew Horton, "Boredom and Oppression: Alexander Rogozhkin's *Blokpost*," *Central European Review* 1, no. 6 (August 2, 1999); online at http://www.ce-review.org/99/6/kinoeye6_horton2 .html for more on this film (accessed July 26, 2007).

14. Interview with Alexander Rogozhkin by Petr Shepotinnik, "Chelovek—eto zvuchit," *Iskusstvo kino*, November 2002. Available online at http://www.kinoart.ru/ magazine/11–2002/repertoire/Cookoo2/ (accessed July 26, 2007).

15. See Arie J. van Noordwijk, "The Tale of the Parasitic Cuckoos," *Nature* 416 (April 18, 2002): 687–90. The term "mafia-style tactics" comes from Andy Coghan, "Raise My Chick or Your Eggs Get It," *New Scientist* 193, no. 2594 (March 10, 2007): 42.

16. Tat'iana Iensen, "Nezlye nadezhdy," *Iskusstvo kino* 11 (2002). Available online at: http://www.kinoart.ru/magazine/11–2002/repertoire/Cookoo/ (accessed July 26, 2007).

17. Valerii Kichin, "Triumfal'nyi polet 'Kukushki,'" *Rossiiskaia gazeta*. Available online at http://www.film.ru/article.asp?ID=3612 (accessed July 26, 2007).

18. Norris, "Guiding Stars."

19. Diliara Tasbulatova, "Snimaetsia kino," *Itogi* 52 (December 30, 2002). Available online at http://www.itogi.ru/paper2002.nsf/Article/Itogi_2002_12_30_14_3018 .html (accessed July 26, 2007).

20. For the relationship between the two brothers, see Denise Youngblood, "The Cosmopolitan and the Patriot: The Brothers Mikhalkov-Konchalovskii and Russian Cinema," *Historical Journal of Film, Radio, and Television* 23, no. 1 (March 2003): 27–41; for Mikhalkov's vote, see Ekaterina Barabash, "Postuchit li 'Oskar' v 'Dom Durakov'?" *Nezavisimaia gazeta*. Available online at http://www.film.ru/article.asp?ID=3497 (accessed July 26, 2007).

21. Ekaterina Sal'nikova, "Tolstoi obzavelsia Bratiami a Rogozhkin pobratal russkikh s finnami," *Nezavisimaia gazeta*, July 2, 2002. Available online at http://www .ng.ru/kino/2002–07–02/9_mmkf.html (accessed July 26, 2007).

22. Gleb Sitkovskii, "Tridtsat' shest' s polovinoi," *Iskusstvo kino* 2 (2003). Available online at http://www.kinoart.ru/magazine/02–2003/Repertoire/Fools/ (accessed July 26, 2007).

23. Ibid.

24. See Valerii Kichin, "Liubite vragov vashikh . . . ," *Rossiiskaia gazeta*. Available online at http://www.film.ru/article.asp?ID=3525 (accessed July 26, 2007).

25. Sitkovskii, "Tridtsat'shest' s polovinoi."

26. Dmitrii Bykov, "Oksiumoron, ili s nami Bog," *Iskusstvo kino* 2 (2003). Available online at http://www.kinoart.ru/magazine/02–2003/Repertoire/Bykov/ (accessed July 26, 2007).

27. Ibid.

28. Elena Plakhova, "'Duraki' + 'Kukushka' = 'Oskar'?" *Moskovskie novosti* 2002. Available online at http://www.mn.ru/issue.php?2002-41-44 (accessed July 26, 2007).

29. Kichin, "Liubite vragov vashikh . . ."

30. Ekaterina Barabash eventually reached similar conclusions in a later article she wrote for *Nezavismaia gazeta*. Barabash compared the critical reaction of Konchalovskii's film to the heavy criticism of Nikita Mikhalkov's *The Barber of Siberia* in 1999. In both

cases, Barabash argues, critics went to the film already armed with "biases" and "venomous reproaches." Barabash does not consider *House of Fools* to be a masterpiece, but also contrasts its representations of Chechens with the "dangerous influence" of Balabanov's depiction of noble Russians and hateful Chechens. See Barabash, "Kak Konchalovskii-kon"iunkturshchik s"el Konchalovskii-khudozhnika ?)," *Nezavismaia gazeta*. Available online at http://www.film.ru/article.asp?ID=3519 (accessed July 26, 2007). For more on the reception to Mikhalkov's film, see Stephen M. Norris, "Tsarist Russia, *Lubok*-Style: Nikita Mikhalkov's *Barber of Siberia* (1999) and Post-Soviet National Identity," *Historical Journal of Film, Radio, and Television* 25, no. 1 (March 2005): 99–116.

31. Jay Winter, "Film and the Matrix of Memory," *American Historical Review* 106, no. 3 (June 2001): 857.

32. Ibid., 857–58.

33. See Norris, "Guiding Stars."

34. Diliara Tasbulatova, "Snimaetsia kino." For another interesting view of the revival of Russian cinema by 2002, see Tat'iana Moskvina, "'Papino kino' i otechestvennaia kul'tura," *Iskusstvo kino* 2 (2003). Available online at http://www.kinoart.ru/magazine/02-2003/Here%20and%20Now/moscvina/ (accessed July 26, 2007).

35. Interview with Alexander Rogozhkin by Petr Shepotinnik, "Chelovek—eto zvuchit," *Iskusstvo kino*," November 2002. Available online at http://www.kinoart.ru/magazine/11–2002/repertoire/Cookoo2/ (accessed July 26, 2007).

36. Ibid.

37. Angela Brintlinger, "The Hero in the Madhouse: The Post-Soviet Novel Confronts the Soviet Past," *Slavic Review* 63, no. 1 (Spring 2004): 43–65.

38. Ibid.

Contributors

ANTHONY ANEMONE is Associate Professor of History in the Department of Modern Languages at the College of William and Mary. In addition to numerous articles on Russian literature (for example, on Konstantin Vaginov, Mikhail Bakhtin, Daniil Kharms, Boris Poplavsky, Vladimir Nabokov, Leo Tolstoy) and culture (The Kunstkamera of Peter the Great), he has written on the films of Balabanov, Sokurov, and Aleksei German.

JULIAN GRAFFY is Professor of Russian Literature and Cinema at the School of Slavonic Studies, University College, London. He is the author, editor, or translator of numerous works on Russian cinema, most recently *Bed and Sofa: The Film Companion* and *Lines of Resistance: Dziga Vertov and the Twenties* (edited and with an introduction by Yuri Tsivian, Russian texts translated by Julian Graffy).

PETER KENEZ is Professor of History at the University of California at Santa Cruz. He is the author of seven books, most recently *Hungary from the Nazis to the Soviets: The Establishment of the Communist Regime in Hungary, 1944–1948* and *Cinema and Soviet Society from the Revolution to the Death of Stalin.*

JOAN NEUBERGER is Professor of History at the University of Texas. She is the author of *Hooliganism: Crime, Culture and Power in St. Petersburg, 1900–1914* and *Ivan the Terrible: The Film Companion.* She produced the special-feature documentary, "The Politics and History of Ivan," for the Criterion Collection DVD, *Eisenstein: The Sound Years.*

STEPHEN M. NORRIS is Associate Professor of History at Miami University, Oxford, Ohio. He is author of *A War of Images: Russian Popular Prints, Wartime Culture, and National Identity, 1812–1945* and coeditor (with Helena Goscilo) of *Preserving Petersburg: History, Memory, Nostalgia* (Indiana University Press, 2008). He has published articles on post-Soviet film in *The Historical Journal of Film, Radio, and Television; Studies in Russian and Soviet Cinema; KinoKultura;* and *The Russian Review.*

OLEG SULKIN is a film critic and journalist at *Novoye Russkoye Slovo,* a Russian American daily newspaper published in New York. Before moving to the United States in 1995, he worked at Novosti Press Agency, *Sovetskii Ekran* magazine, and was an editor-in-chief of the *Sovetskii Film* monthly magazine. He is the author of hundreds of articles, essays, and reviews on film, arts, and culture.

YURI TSIVIAN is William Colvin Professor, Departments of Art History, Slavic Languages and Literatures, and Comparative Literature at the University of Chicago. His books include: *Silent Witnesses: Russian Films, 1908–1919; Early Cinema in Russia and Its Cultural Reception; Ivan the Terrible;* and *Lines of Resistance: Dziga Vertov and the Twenties.*

EMMA WIDDIS is University Senior Lecturer in the Department of Slavonic Studies at Trinity College, University of Cambridge. She is the author of *Visions of a New Land: Soviet Cinema from the Revolution to the Second World War* and *Alexander Medvedkin: The Filmmaker's Companion.* She is editor, with Simon Franklin, of *National Identity in Russian Culture: An Introduction.*

JOSEPHINE WOLL is Professor of Modern Languages and Literatures at Howard University. She is the author of numerous books and articles on Russian cinema, among them *Real Images: Soviet Cinema and the Thaw* and the I. B. Tauris Film Companions to *The Cranes Are Flying* and *Repentance* (with Denise Youngblood).

Volume Editors

STEPHEN M. NORRIS is Associate Professor of History at Miami University, Oxford, Ohio. He is author of *A War of Images: Russian Popular Prints, Wartime Culture, and National Identity, 1812–1945* and coeditor (with Helena Goscilo) of *Preserving Petersburg: History, Memory, Nostalgia* (Indiana University Press, 2008). He has published articles on post-Soviet film in *The Historical Journal of Film, Radio, and Television; Studies in Russian and Soviet Cinema; KinoKultura;* and *The Russian Review.*

ZARA M. TORLONE is Assistant Professor of Classics at Miami University, Oxford, Ohio. Her publications include articles on Vergil's Eclogues, the Roman Love Elegy, Petronius's *Satyricon,* and the reception of antiquity in Russian poetry. Her book *Russia and the Classics: Poetry's Foreign Muse* will appear in 2009.

Index

Page numbers in italics indicate illustrations.

Lightning Source UK Ltd.
Milton Keynes UK
UKHW021842170123
415517UK00008B/1028